A Practical
Guide
to
Bible Translation Projects

Book II:
Bible Translating Series

A Practical Guide to Bible Translation Projects

Book II:
Bible Translating Series

By
Dr. Steve Combs

ISBN 979-8-9866583-8-4

Published in the USA by
The Old Paths Publications
www.theoldpathspublications.com

The Author may be contacted by writing:
bpsg.scombs@gmail.com

The Bible Translation used in this book is the King James Bible. Illustrations of translation methods and techniques are taken from the King James Bible and the Greek Textus Receptus, Global Edition, 2019. Other versions occasionally for illustration purposes only.

ISBN 979-8-9866583-8-4

Published in the USA
byThe Old Paths Publications
www.theoldpathspublications.com

Dedication

This book is dedicated to my wife, Suzanne, who has loved me and put up with me and helped me for over forty years.

Other Books by the Author

Election and Predestination?
The Fellowship of the Mystery – The Book of Ephesians
The Power of the Gospel – The Book of Romans
Every Word for Every People
The Translator's Grammar of the Textus Receptus
The LSB and Other Unusual Bible Questions
A Practical Theology of Bible Translating

Books Edited by the Author

The Greek New Testament
Parallel Greek TR – English KJV New Testament

Contents

Table of Contents

9

Table of Contents

Introduction

Several years ago, I was struggling to put together what I envisioned as a large anthology on the subject of Bible translating. It was simply not coming together. There were several major difficulties. It was then I realized that I needed to go back to the old paths. So, I laid aside the anthology and embarked on a study of the theology of Bible translating. I had never seen anything published on this subject, and it is not taught as a doctrine in college theology classes nor in theology books. At one time, Dr. H.D. Williams wanted to publish a book on that subject, but he had never done so because other projects interfered and took his time. Nevertheless, it was through him that I got the idea. Surely, I thought, God has something to say about Bible translating in His Word. The result was *A Practical Theology of Bible Translating*, published in 2019. I was never to return to the anthology (at least, not to date).

Then, in 2020, as I was reviewing and updating our web site (www.bpsglobal.org), I noticed the numerous articles we had scattered around the site explaining various aspects of Bible translation projects. I further called to mind how we write a short guide to starting translation projects for each new translation project. We call it "an assessment." I realized that we already had nearly all the material we needed for a practical project guide. We just needed to bring it all together and flesh it out. The result is the book you hold in your hands.

Therefore, this is the second book written in a series on Bible translating. The first was *A Practical Theology of Bible Translating,* which should be *studied **first***. This second book adds to the theology, but focuses more on the practical aspects of starting, conducting, and finishing a translation project. Some material in the first book is summarized in this book so that the reader will have full continuity in the thoughts presented.

A book like this is extremely important. We live in an age when the old paths have been all but forgotten when it comes to Bible translating.   Many have forgotten the importance of the actual words God inspired. They think the only thing that matters is to carry the meaning or message into the translation. The words are flexible. I agree that meaning is important, but I argue that the meaning is imbedded in the inspired words, and that it is those words with the proper meaning that are to be translated. I believe the Bible makes that case. That is why we subscribe to a formal equivalent translation method. In the following pages we make the meaning of that method crystal clear.

Translation projects and local situations differ greatly. So, there is no one standard plan or pattern that fits all projects. A lot will depend on the local situation and current schedules of the people included on the translation team. The translators will need to make decisions about how they will apply these guidelines.

There are six categories in this plan for translation. *You must read these categories in the order they are presented to get the most from the guide.* For example, you should not begin the process of organizing the team until you have read the foundational convictions and principles. We suggest that the entire team read the guide at the same time and periodically gather to discuss it. Also, if you are reading this book with a goal to translate the Bible into a specific language, please contact us using the email address on the copyright page, through our website, or on the Facebook page for Global Bible Translators. We would be glad to answer questions and walk through this process with you.   There are also other translation ministries, committed to the Received Text, that can help, also.

The first category of the book is about **convictions** that are absolutely necessary to be a good translator. These include believing in your heart that each and every word of the Bible was inspired by God when it was given. You must be convicted deep in your heart that God has preserved every one of these words. You need to know that they are available now and that you can have them in your possession. You need to know where to find them. Without these convictions, how can you be sure that you are truly translating the Word of God? How can you be certain that you are using the correct source texts?

The second includes **information on several practical subjects** that are not absolutes but are still foundational. They are time tested and practical. The translators must agree on the principles they will follow. If all the translators follow the same rules, it will result in a more accurate and consistent translation.

Category three is about **organizing and operating** the translation team. These are a list of ideas that work well in various translation projects. It includes types of team organizations and a list of the different jobs that need to be accomplished by the translation team. Some of these ideas may work well for you, while others may not.

The fourth category is about the **theology and practice** of the actual work of translation. These include issues you will see in the Biblical text that can present difficulties for translators. It includes issues that can be challenging, to say the least, such as, figures of speech, whether to use italics, choosing a name for God, and being careful to avoid adding to or taking from the Word of God.

The fifth category helps you implement **some techniques to check and test** the translation for accuracy and clarity. There are several techniques accepted and practiced by various translation ministries and professional translation services. We include some of them. The general rule is simple: the more checking and testing there is, the greater will be the accuracy of the translation.

In the last category, we give guidance on **printing and distributing** your translation.

It is our prayer that this guide will result in many new translation projects and further spread the preaching of the precious Word of God.

For we preach not ourselves, but Christ Jesus the Lord; and ourselves your servants for Jesus' sake. (2 Corinthians 4:5)

1 Who's Carrying the Ark?

This chapter was based on an outline and ideas from Dr. Steve Zeinner, Director of Global Bible Translators/Bearing Precious Seed Global

---

2 Samuel 6:1-4, 6-7 Again, David gathered together all the chosen men of Israel, thirty thousand.
2 And David arose, and went with all the people that were with him from Baale of Judah, to bring up from thence the ark of God, whose name is called by the name of the LORD of hosts that dwelleth between the cherubims.
3 And they set the ark of God upon a new cart, and brought it out of the house of Abinadab that was in Gibeah: and Uzzah and Ahio, the sons of Abinadab, drave the new cart.
4 And they brought it out of the house of Abinadab which was at Gibeah, accompanying the ark of God: and Ahio went before the ark.
6 And when they came to Nachon's threshingfloor, Uzzah put forth his hand to the ark of God, and took hold of it; for the oxen shook it.
7 And the anger of the LORD was kindled against Uzzah; and God smote him there for his error; and there he died by the ark of God.

Exodus 25:10-14 And they shall make an ark of shittim wood: two cubits and a half shall be the length thereof, and a cubit and a half the breadth thereof, and a cubit and a half the height thereof.
14 And thou shalt put the staves into the rings by the sides of the ark, that the ark may be borne with them.

Numbers 4:15 And when Aaron and his sons have made an end of covering the sanctuary, and all the vessels of the sanctuary, as the camp is to set forward; after that, the sons of Kohath shall come to bear it: but they shall not touch any holy thing, lest they die. These things are the burden of the sons of Kohath in the tabernacle of the congregation.

During the last days of the judges, the Ark of God was taken by the Philistines. After God punished the Philistines severely, they sent it away back to Israel in a cart (I Sam. 5, 6). The Ark ended up in the town of Kirjathjearim for twenty years. 2 Samuel 6 tells the story of how King David attempted to bring the Ark into Jerusalem. They put it on a cart and started the journey to Jerusalem, rejoicing as they went. On the way the cart became unstable and Uzziah put his hand on the Ark to steady it in violation of Numbers 4:15. He died.

David had made two mistakes. He was using the wrong methods to transport the Ark and he used the wrong people. Under Moses' leadership, God had the artisans of Israel put golden rings on each side of the Ark and staves to put in the rings. The purpose of the staves was for carrying the Ark. David should have had the Ark carried by people holding the staves and walking with it. Only the Levites of the family of Kohath were allowed to do this. The work of God in these New Testament times, including Bible translation work, also requires the right methods performed by the right people.

What is the passion and purpose of God? "Go ye into all the world, and preach the gospel to every creature" (Mark 16:15). G. Campbell Morgan said, "If the church is to be missionary it must be spiritual and if the church is spiritual, it will be missionary." Going into all the world to preach the gospel means to carry the Truth into all the world. The One who is called the Word and the Truth said, "Man shall not live by bread alone, but by every word that proceedeth out of the mouth of God" (Mt. 4:4). The Word of God is Vital. Satan will do all he can to discredit it or destroy it if possible. It is the only thing that totally proves him wrong. And the Word of God is all about the Lord Jesus Christ.

> **Colossians 1:26-29** *Even the mystery which hath been hid from ages and from generations, but now is made manifest to his saints:*
> *27 To whom God would make known what is the riches of the glory of this mystery among the Gentiles; which is Christ in you, the hope of glory:*
> *28 Whom we preach, warning every man, and teaching every man in all wisdom; that we may present every man perfect in Christ Jesus:*
> *29 Whereunto I also labour, striving according to his working, which worketh in me mightily.*

We must preach the gospel in all the world among all nations. We must warn everyone and teach them in all wisdom that they may stand perfect before God. The only way to accomplish this is to give everyone the pure, accurate, and complete Word of God in their language.

Must we once again lay the foundation of God's purpose? I think not! Surely, we have passed this point. What must be laid is the reason, purpose, and commandment of God that we take care of His Word and see that it goes forth into all the world. Consider the day and time in which we live. Computers, mobile phones, the internet, presses, bindery lines, transportation (containers and shipping), and even Coca Cola have gone into all the world. Yet, when it comes to the translation and distribution of the Word of God, we are falling short!   According to Wycliffe, there are 7,378 languages on earth. Out of these languages, only about 717 have the whole Bible, 1,582 have only the New Testament, and 1,196 have less than a New Testament. That leaves 3,883 languages with no published Scripture at all!

> **Psalms 138:2** *I will worship toward thy holy temple, and praise thy name for thy lovingkindness and for thy truth: for thou hast magnified thy word above all thy name.*

It has been said:
1/3 of the world professes to be Christian
1/3 of the world professes they don't want to be Christian.
1/3 of the world says what is a Christian?

Who is Carrying the Ark?

In Deuteronomy 31:24-26, Moses turned the law over to the Levites and Priests to protect and preserve, which was a responsibility they extended to the rest of the Old Testament. The priests were commanded to read the law before the people every seven years (Deut. 31:11-13). Kings were commanded to make a copy for themselves and read it all the days of their lives (Deut. 17:18-20). During the times of the Kings, the priests and Levites neglected their God given responsibility. This neglect contributed to the failures and darkness of that time and helped lead to the exile of God's people. After the exile, the priest, Ezra, joined God's people who had returned to Jerusalem. Ezra was a ready scribe, who *"had prepared his heart to seek the law of the LORD, and to do it, and to teach in Israel statutes and judgments"* (Ezra 7:10). Under his leadership and that of others the Levitical priesthood experienced a revival of their responsibility to guard and preserve the Old Testament. Jewish scribes continued to preserve it until the Protestant Reformation.

In New Testament times, the Scribes and the priests had added Jewish tradition to the Law. Jesus' reaction to this was, "Full well ye reject the commandment of God, that ye may keep your own tradition" (Mk 7:9) and, "Why do ye also transgress the commandment of God by your tradition" (Mt. 15:3)? By Jesus' day, most of the national leadership had turned from the truth to lies.

The surrender of the Truth does not come all at once. It is a subtle process. It is not planned or premeditated. It happens by underestimating the enemy (1 Chron. 13:2, 4). It is a slow process that little by little erodes and destroys the very foundation of faith. "If the foundations be destroyed, what can the righteous do" (Psa. 11:3)? We know the destructive force of eroding the foundations and this is where we are now with the very Words of God.

Bible translation work has been left in the wrong hands for far too long.   There is an organization in England called the United Bible Societies (UBS). It is a Bible distribution and translation organization that has about 155 member societies around the world. Each society is usually named for the country in which they are located, for example the British and Foreign Bible Society, the American Bible Society, the Scottish Bible Society, the Kenya Bible Society, and the Uganda Bible Society. The United Bible Societies has become one of two premier Bible translation organizations in the world, along with Wycliffe Bible Translators. The UBS has edited and printed their own New Testament Greek text, which is used by most other Bible translation ministries, including Wycliffe Bible Translators. Unfortunately, the United Bible Society Greek text was edited by religious liberals and Catholics such as Kurt Aland, Bruce Metzger, Carlo Martini (a Roman Catholic Cardinal), and others. The UBS text has over 8000 differences in words as compared to the Textus Receptus, the Greek text on which the King James Bible was based. *This is the wrong group attempting to carry the wrong Ark.*

Eugene Nida (1914-2011) worked for the American Bible Society (ABS) and was associated with the United Bible Societies (of which the ABS was a member). He promoted a theory of the method of Bible translating he called "Dynamic Equivalence." This is the theory that meaning is paramount in Bible translating and the words, themselves, are of little importance. It promotes translating meaning-for-meaning or sense-for-sense from one language to another. The goal is to get people today to react to the Word the same way the people reacted when the Word of God was first written. Words other than the original words may be used if they have the same meaning and produce the same results. Of course, it is the translator who makes the decisions about meaning and effect. It is easy for his prejudices and preferences to enter the process. Dynamic Equivalence and similar theories are the cart now being used to carry the Word of God to other languages. *They are the cart, the wrong method.*

Who *Should* be Carrying the Ark?

If the Jewish priests of the Old Testament protected and preserved the Scriptures, how were they preserved in New Testament times? The answer to that is simple, but it needs an explanation. The preservation of the Scriptures is now in the hands of the New Testament priesthood. All believers are "built up a spiritual house, **an holy priesthood**, to offer up spiritual sacrifices, acceptable to God by Jesus Christ" (1 Peter 2:5). God has made believing Jews and Gentiles "one new man, so making peace; And that he might reconcile both unto God in one body by the cross, having slain the enmity thereby: ... And are built upon the foundation of the apostles and prophets, Jesus Christ himself being the chief corner stone; In whom all the building fitly framed together groweth unto an holy temple in the Lord: ... In whom ye also are builded together for an habitation of God through the Spirit" (Eph. 2:15-16, 20-22). Together, we are one body, one new man, one building, one temple, and one habitation of God. And, we are one holy priesthood, which includes all believers. This priesthood of believers is manifest in local churches. The churches are charged with the responsibility to translate the Word of God.

Before Jesus ascended to heaven, He gave the Great Commission. "All power is given unto me in heaven and in earth. Go ye therefore, and teach all nations, baptizing them in the name of the Father, and of the Son, and of the Holy Ghost: Teaching them to observe all things whatsoever I have commanded you: and, lo, I am with you alway, even unto the end of the world" (Mt. 28:18-20). Now the churches have their marching orders, to go into all the world, among all the languages and all the peoples of the earth. The church is commanded to teach all nations. How will we do that without the Word of God in their language? God did not preserve His Words through the many Greek scholars of that day. He had chosen holy men separated unto himself and empowered them to accomplish this great task. He chose Holy men just like He chose holy men through whom to inspire His word, "holy men of God spake as they were moved by the Holy Ghost" (2 Peter 1:21).

The great commission requires that we put the Word of God into the language of the people. If we do not, we cannot teach them. When Paul spoke to the elders of the Ephesian church for the last time, he said, "And now, brethren, I commend you to God, and *to the word of his grace*, which is able to build you up, and to give you an inheritance among all them which are sanctified" (Acts 20:32).   How can a missionary commend people to the Word of God's grace if they do not have that word in their language? How can they live "by every word that proceedeth out of the mouth of God" (Mt 4:4), if they do not have the Word of God in their language? Bible translating is required to meet this need. If God chose Holy men to inspire His Word and to preserve His Word, then it stands to reason that He wants Holy men and women to translate His Word.

The Bible does not have a place that says "these are the qualifications of a translator," like it lists the qualifications of a Bishop and Deacon (1 Timothy 3).   However, it does give basic qualifications that a translator must be seeking to fulfill. No one is perfect, but there are standards. These are listed below.

> 1. A translator must be a saved person. That means he must believe the gospel with his heart (1 Cor. 15:1-5). Translating takes spiritual discernment and an unsaved person has none (1 Cor. 2:14).
>
> 2. A translator must be taking steps to separate from sin in his life. (1 Pet. 1:14-15). When he falls, he confesses his sin to God, gets up, and goes on (1 John 1:9; Prov. 24:16).
>
> 3. A translator must also separate from associations and relationships that hinder the work of God (2 Tim. 2:19-20; 2 Cor. 6:14-18).
>
> 4. A translator must believe that all Scripture in inspired by God (2 Tim. 3:16).

5. A translator must believe that the individual words of Scripture are inspired and not just the message (Ps. 12:6-7).

6. A translator must believe that every word has been providentially preserved by God (Mark 24:35). A translator must be sure that the text he is translating is the true Word of God.

7. A translator must know where he can get a copy of God's Word. It is not enough to say I have a Greek or Hebrew text. There is more than one. Which one is right? The same is true with different Bible versions. The next chapter helps answer this question.

8. A translator must know both the *source language* (the language *from which* you are translating) and the *target language* (the language *into which* you are translating).

9. A translator must be educated in the Bible and theology. The Bible is where you get to know God and understand His will (Eph. 5:17). You must get to know Him (Phil 3:10; John 5:39). This is a requirement for every Christian, but especially for translators.

10. A translator must reject the concept of ownership. The translator will never own his translation. It belongs to God.

11. Finally, a translator must be committed to the Biblical method of Bible translating, formal equivalence.

12. A translator must have absolute conviction that God has called him to the task, and he must have total commitment to seeing it through to the end and beyond. He must have the approval of his church to be a translator.

This is the kind of person needed for Bible translation work. This is the kind of person who needs to be carrying that Ark. According to Acts 13, that kind of person is called by God and sent from their local church, not hired by Bible societies or other parachurch organizations. A translator who does the job merely because he is hired to do it is nothing more than a hireling, a rented worker.

Who is the Biblical custodian of the Word of God? Are Bible societies the custodians of the Word of God? Are non-church mission boards the custodians of the Word of God? Is any individual the custodian of God's Word? Are bookstores, large box stores, online stores, or publishers the custodians of the Word of God? No! The church is the custodian of the Word of God. Spurgeon said that he thanked God for the Bible societies, and that during his time they were doing a good job, but it is the church's responsibility to take care of God's Word. We thank God for all those who stand for the true Word of God, but we recognize it is the responsibility of the churches to take care of God's Word and the translating of it for all nations.

Regaining the Truth

How did David follow up on his failure with the Ark? He had left the Ark in the house of Obededom and when he saw that God blessed Obededom, he knew it was time to bring the Ark into Jerusalem.   In regard to Bible translating, regaining the truth will come from within the churches.

> **1 Chronicles 15:2-4** *Then David said, None ought to carry the ark of God but the Levites: for them hath the LORD chosen to carry the ark of God, and to minister unto him for ever.*
> *3 And David gathered all Israel together to Jerusalem, to bring up the ark of the LORD unto his place, which he had prepared for it.*
> *4 And David assembled the children of Aaron, and the Levites:*

The first step is to acknowledge that a mistake had been made (v. 2). David realized that he had done something wrong when Uzziah died, but he didn't give up the idea. He sought to learn from God what he had done wrong and how to correct it. He learned that it was the responsibility of the Levites to carry the Ark into Jerusalem, the place God had chosen to put His name. This first step came from the top leader. Each pastor should recognize that the care, preservation, and propagation of the Word of God is his church's responsibility and that part of the propagation of the Word is Bible translation work. Every church should be involved in translation work. A local church mission program is not complete unless it includes Bible translation work.

The second thing David did was to gather Israel to Jerusalem to accomplish the task of bringing in the Ark (vv. 3-4). Then he gathered the Levites. David realized 1) he, himself, was not called to carry the ark, because he was not a Levite, 2) he could not do the job himself, because he was responsible for all the needs of all Israel, but he could lead and see that the care of the Ark gets done. The Pastor has many jobs, so he cannot accomplish the job of Bible translating himself. However, he can see to it that the church is involved in this necessary work in a strategic way. His first job is to pray for and teach the church, so that they will know that God wants the church involved.

> **1 Chronicles 15:11-16** *And David called for Zadok and Abiathar the priests, and for the Levites, for Uriel, Asaiah, and Joel, Shemaiah, and Eliel, and Amminadab,*
> *12 And said unto them, Ye are the chief of the fathers of the Levites: sanctify yourselves, both ye and your brethren, that ye may bring up the ark of the LORD God of Israel unto the place that I have prepared for it.*
> *13 For because ye did it not at the first, the LORD our God made a breach upon us, for that we sought him not after the due order.*
> *14 So the priests and the Levites sanctified themselves to bring up the ark of the LORD God of Israel.*

The third thing David did was to appoint leadership for the work (v. 11). How can a pastor do this? The leadership is composed of those God raises up in the church to commit themselves to direct involvement in Bible translation. It is also composed of others who will never be translators but are nevertheless burdened for that work. These leaders will promote the work of Bible translation within the church and even to other churches. The first thing a pastor must do is pray. Jesus said, "The harvest truly is great, but the labourers are few: pray ye therefore the Lord of the harvest, that he would send forth labourers into his harvest" (Lk. 10:2). The pastor also must be committed to continuing in prayer for this and to recruit others to join him, although he may pray for a long time before the answer comes.

In the current day, many churches and many pastors lack a vision for Bible translating. They are strong in their vision for church planting, as they should be. Yet, the success of church planting is completely dependent on having a Bible translation that is translated accurately from the right source language texts. Some pastors feel that if they are supporting one missionary translator or one translating organization, they have their bases covered. But, is this so? If they supported only one church planting missionary or mission agency, would that be sufficient? Churches support several church planting mission agencies. Church planters work on different fields. The same is true of translators. They work on different fields. Why should your vision be limited to translating a Bible into only one language? The author is aware of four mission organizations devoted to Bible translating and also committed to the Greek and Hebrew Received texts and the King James Bible. They are Global Bible Translators (also called Bearing Precious Seed Global), World View, First Bible, and the Trinitarian Bible Society. They are all translating in different languages with only a small amount of overlap.

The fourth thing David did was to make sure the Levites were prepared (vv. 12-14). It may be that the only thing a lot of churches will do for the Bible translating ministry is to pray and give. If the church is helping support a translator, then they should also pray for him. The Pastor is the leader to make that happen.

Bible translators need abundant prayer. They cannot do the work without it. On the other hand, if God calls someone to the Bible translating ministry from within his church, the pastor should see to it that he is prepared. The prospective translator will need guidance and advice. He will need encouragement. If the pastor does not know how to advise him, he should bring in someone who can, such as the leaders of one of the ministries listed above. Also, any missionary that God calls should be given great honor by his church. They need to know that the church is for them and standing behind them. They need to know that the *church* is their *partner* in the ministry.

> **1 Chronicles 15:15** *And the children of the Levites bare the ark of God upon their shoulders with the staves thereon, as Moses commanded according to the word of the LORD.*

Finally, after taking responsibility to do the work in God's way with God's chosen people, appointing leadership, and helping to prepare the leadership and workers, they moved ahead with the work. They did not wait. They were convinced what God wanted them to do, so they moved ahead. Nothing stopped them from fulfilling the will of God.

> **1 Chronicles 15:16, 25-26** *And David spake to the chief of the Levites to appoint their brethren to be the singers*

with instruments of musick, psalteries and harps and cymbals, sounding, by lifting up the voice with joy.
25 So David, and the elders of Israel, and the captains over thousands, went to bring up the ark of the covenant of the LORD out of the house of Obededom with joy.
26 And it came to pass, when God helped the Levites that bare the ark of the covenant of the LORD, that they offered seven bullocks and seven rams.

When we obey the Lord to do His work His way, it is more than God's personal calling on our lives that gets fulfilled. There is also a great effect on others. It causes widespread joy and worship that is not confined to just one congregation. It is more than worship and joy that spreads. When David took the lead, the elders and the captains got involved. The work itself spreads to other churches and more leaders are raised up. The work multiplies. More fields and more languages are reached with gospel preaching and Bible translations into those languages are increased.

Who is carrying the Ark? Who is the caretaker, guardian, and steward of the Word of God? The New Testament does not place that responsibility in the hands of extra-church organizations, such as Bible Societies. History tells us that some of these organizations have done a good job at times, but today Bible translating is in the hands of religious liberals and Catholics, for the most part. However, most of these organizations have not been created under the authority of a local church and they do not answer to the church. The responsibility to keep the Word of God, to propagate the word of God throughout the world, and to translate the Word of God into all languages lies squarely on the local churches. It lies on those in the local churches whom God has called to this work. It lies on you.

2 Basic Beliefs Every Christian Needs

All scripture is given by inspiration of God, and is profitable for doctrine, for reproof, for correction, for instruction in righteousness: (2 Tim. 3:16)
For the prophecy came not in old time by the will of man: but holy men of God spake as they were moved by he Holy Ghost. (2 Pet. 1:21)
Man shall not live by bread alone, but by every word that proceedeth out of the mouth of God. (Mat. 4:4)

Presuppositions are beliefs you hold that you do not need to be proven. A person cannot be a Christian unless certain facts are accepted by faith. "Believe on the Lord Jesus Christ and thou shalt be saved" (Acts 16:31). Facts that are proven do not require faith. Presuppositions do require faith. Faith must be placed in the gospel, the death and resurrection of the Lord Jesus Christ. Faith may not require proof, but faith has a basis. "So then faith cometh by hearing, and hearing by the word of God" (Rom. 10:17). Faith requires confidence in the Bible and that requires that you believe the Bible to be the Word of God.

1 Thessalonians 2:13 *For this cause also thank we God without ceasing, because, when ye received the word of God which ye heard of us, ye received it not as the word of men, but **as it is in truth, the word of God**, which effectually worketh also in you that believe.*

So, the Bible, the Scriptures, comes to us from God. He has also declared that He will preserve it word-perfect; therefore, the Bible carries the authority of God, and we can read it today. This truth was expressed many years ago in the 1689 Baptist Confession of Faith and in the 1646 Westminster Confession of Faith.

The Old Testament in Hebrew (which was the native language of the people of God of old), and the New Testament in Greek (which at the time of the writing of it was most generally known to the nations), being immediately inspired by God, and by His singular care and providence kept pure in all ages, are therefore authentic; so as in all controversies of religion, the church is finally to appeal to them. [1]

A firm faith in the Word of God is extremely important to a translator. In regard to the Bible, three things are absolutely required for a translator, if he wishes to do a complete and thoroughly accurate job: 1) A belief that the Bible is verbally and plenarily inspired by God, 2) A belief that the Word of God has been verbally and plenarily preserved by God, and 3) the knowledge of where he can get a copy of the Word of God.

> The very foundation of Bible translating is a firm Biblical conviction about the nature of the Bible itself. God has an extremely high view of His Word. Every translator must have the exalted view of Scripture that God Himself has. Everything depends on this. The accuracy and clarity of a translation depends on it. [2]

The Inspiration of the Bible

2 Timothy 3:16,17 *All scripture is given by inspiration of God, and is profitable for doctrine, for reproof, for correction, for instruction in righteousness:*
17 That the man of God may be perfect, throughly furnished unto all good works.

2 Timothy 3:16 is the basic doctrinal verse explaining the truth of the inspiration of Scripture. The word *inspiration* comes from a Greek word that means *breathed out by God*. It is clearly expressed by Matthew 4:4, "Man shall not live by bread alone, but every word that proceedeth out of the mouth of God." Theology books tell us that the Bible was *plenarily* and *verbally* inspired. These two verses also tell us what these words mean. Plenarily means that "all Scripture" is inspired and verbally means that "every word" is inspired. God is the author of every word in all of Scripture. He used men as His instruments to write the words down, but the words were all from His heart and mind. It has been stated this way: "The perfect author of the perfect Bible is God." [3]

The words of God were inspired when they were *"given"* (2 Tim. 3:16). Inspiration points to the time when God first gave them to mankind in Hebrew, Aramaic, and Greek. The term does not belong to any time or period of time afterward. It does not refer to the making of copies and it does not refer to translations. Copies and translations have to do with the *transmission* of Scripture *through* history. Inspiration pertains to the *entrance* of Scripture *into* history.

I do not want anyone to misunderstand me here. When people talk about the inspiration of a translation, they are usually referring to the King James Bible. I believe the KJB is the Word of God without error. Some, who think they are disagreeing with me, prefer to say that the King James is an *accurate* translation but not without error. Indeed, it is accurate. But what does that mean? The word accurate is defined as "free from error especially as the result of care." [4] If the KJB is an *accurate* translation (and it is), then, by definition, it is *without error*. However, it is not the accurate Word of God by *inspiration*. It is the accurate Word of God by *providentially guided translation* of the words that had already been given by inspiration and then preserved. For a full explanation refer to my book, *A Practical Theology of Translating,* the first volume in this series.

How did God give Scripture and how did He use men to do it? God gave the Scriptures through men using various methods. The Scriptures themselves give us several examples of how God did this. Foremost among them is 2 Peter 1:16-21.

> **2 Peter 1:16-21** *For we have not followed cunningly devised fables, when we made known unto you the power and coming of our Lord Jesus Christ, but were eyewitnesses of his majesty.*
> *17 For he received from God the Father honour and glory, when there came such a voice to him from the excellent glory, This is my beloved Son, in whom I am well pleased.*
> *18 And this voice which came from heaven we heard, when we were with him in the holy mount.*
> *19 We have also a more sure word of prophecy; whereunto ye do well that ye take heed, as unto a light that shineth in a dark place, until the day dawn, and the day star arise in your hearts:*

20 Knowing this first, that no prophecy of the scripture is of any private interpretation.
21 For the prophecy came not in old time by the will of man: but holy men of God spake as they were moved by the Holy Ghost.

God started with holy men. The Spirit of God "moved" these men to speak words that He chose. These words were written down by an assistant who was listening. Other examples of this are Jeremiah (Jer. 36:1-4) and Paul (Rom. 16:22). God also used several other methods including the following.

1. Writing the material themselves (1 Cor. 16:1; Gal. 6:11)
2. Speaking the Word and then writing it (Deut. 31:9)
3. God dictated a portion of Scripture and wrote it Himself (Exodus 34:1)
4. God dictated a portion of Scripture and commanded that it be written down (Ex. 17:14; 24:4; 34:27; Num. 5:23; and much of the prophets).
5. God put words into the heart and they were written down (Num. 33:2).

In whatever way God gave the word, it was given by the miracle of inspiration. The Words were given by God. In whatever way the prophets and Apostles were *"moved"* (2 Peter 2:21), it was the Holy Spirit who moved them. They were led by the Spirit. *"The Spirit of the LORD spake by me, and his word was in my tongue"* (2 Sam. 23:2). Because of this, we must conclude that it is not just the meaning of the words that matter, it is the words themselves. When one is translating the Bible, he must be concerned about the meaning of the text and about the meaning of each word. *God cares about each of His words*.

Psalms 12:6 The words of the Lord are **pure words**

Psalms 119:103 How sweet are **thy words** unto my taste! yea, sweeter than honey to my mouth!

Psalms 119:130 The entrance of **thy words** giveth light; it giveth understanding unto the simple.

Psalms 138:4 All the kings of the earth shall praise thee, O LORD, when they hear the **words of thy mouth.**

Deuteronomy 4:2 Ye shall not add unto **the word** which I command you, neither shall ye diminish ought from it, that ye may keep **the commandments** of the LORD your God which I command you.

Proverbs 30:6 Add thou not unto **his words**, lest he reprove thee, and thou be found a liar.

John 3:34 For he whom God hath sent speaketh the **words of God:** for God giveth not the Spirit by measure unto him.

Revelation 17:17 For God hath put in their hearts to fulfil his will, and to agree, and give their kingdom unto the beast, until the **words of God** shall be fulfilled.

Revelation 22:19 And if any man shall take away from the **words of the book** of this prophecy, God shall take away his part out of the book of life, and out of the holy city, and from the things which are written in this book.

"Inspiration" refers to the words of Scripture that were given by God to man and through man and for the benefit of man. The words are the very words of God and yet given through the use of human instruments in a way that made use of their personalities and did not override their will. Inspiration does not refer to the pen and ink and paper on which the words were originally written, that is, the original autographs. It refers to the "words." Notice that the term "scripture" is applied to the spoken words given by God to Abraham hundreds of years before Moses wrote them down. "And the scripture, **foreseeing** that God would justify the heathen through faith, **preached** before the gospel unto Abraham, **saying**, In thee shall all nations be blessed" (Gal 3:8). The words were spoken in Genesis 15, many years before being written.

The Divine Preservation of the Scriptures

The inspiration of the Scriptures would mean nothing, and it would be impossible for mankind to live by the Words of God, if God did not *preserve* His words. This should be self-evident, but many miss it. Nevertheless, the Scriptures make it clear that God has preserved His words.

> *But continue thou in the things which thou hast learned and hast been assured of, knowing of whom thou hast learned them; And that from a child thou hast known the holy scriptures, which are able to make thee wise unto salvation through faith which is in Christ Jesus.*(2 Tim. 3:15-16)

Timothy had the Scriptures, but the copies he had were not the original writings. The original pen, paper, and ink had long since perished. Contrary to what some have said, there is no evidence Timothy was using a Greek Old Testament translation (the Septuagint designated LXX). Timothy had copies of the Hebrew Old Testament. Paul called these copies "holy scriptures" indicating that they had been copied accurately. God had preserved His word.

The Fact of Providential Preservation

Many have long denied that the Bible teaches the providential preservation of Scripture. Nowadays, some have adapted their teaching to include preservation. I suspect this is because of all the Bible believing voices that have been raised in its favor. However, many have limited preservation to the "message" of Scripture and have not applied it to the "words." Following are a few of the verses that teach the Biblical doctrine of the providential preservation of the Word of God.

> **1 Peter 1:23** Being born again, not of corruptible seed, but of incorruptible, by the Word of God which liveth and abideth forever.

> **Psalm 12:6-7** The words of the Lord are pure words: as silver tried in a furnace of earth, purified seven times.

Thou shalt keep them, O Lord, thou shalt preserve them from this generation forever.

Ps. 111:7-8 The works of his hands are verity and judgment; all his commandments are sure. They stand fast for ever and ever, and are done in truth and uprightness.

Is. 40:8 The grass withereth, the flower fadeth: but the word of our God shall stand for ever.

Ps. 117:2 ... the truth of the Lord endureth for ever. Praise ye the Lord.

Ps. 119:152 Concerning thy testimonies, I have known of old that thou hast founded them for ever.

Ps 119:160 Thy word is true from the beginning: and every one of thy righteous judgments endureth for ever.

Matthew 24:35 Heaven and earth shall pass away, but my words shall not pass away.

Psalm 33:11 The counsel of the Lord standeth forever, the thoughts of his heart to all generations.

Psalm 100:5 For the Lord is good; his mercy is everlasting; and his truth endureth to all generations.

Ps 119:89-90 For ever, O LORD, thy word is settled in heaven. Thy faithfulness is unto all generations: thou hast established the earth, and it abideth.

Psalms 119:160 Thy word is true from the beginning: and every one of thy righteous judgments endureth for ever.

Matthew 5:18 For verily I say unto you, Till heaven and earth pass, one jot or one tittle shall in no wise pass from the law, till all be fulfilled.

Isaiah 59:21 As for me this is my covenant with them, saith the Lord; My spirit that is upon thee, and my words which I have put in thy mouth, shall not pass out of the thy mouth, nor out of the mouth of thy seed, nor out of the mouth of thy seed's seed saith the Lord, from henceforth and forever.

These are just a few verses that prove providential preservation is a fact. What do we learn from these verses? We learn His Word is kept for all generations (Psalm 33:11; Psalm 100:5; Ps 119:89-90). His Word has been kept for *us*, for our good (Is. 59:21). The preservation of the Word of God is a series of supernatural acts by the Lord Himself (Ps. 12:6-7). The Word is alive, with the life of God, which is forever (1 Peter 1:23; Heb. 4:12). Perhaps it would be more easily understood if we viewed it in graphical form. Below is a chart that presents the doctrinal foundation of providential preservation in just such a manner.

References	What will be preserved?	How long?
1 Peter 1:23; Is. 40:8 Ps. 119:89, 90, 160	The Word of God	Forever
Mt. 24:35	Christ's Words	Never pass away
Ps. 12:6-7; Is. 59:21	God's Words	Forever
Ps. 111:7-8	His Commandments	Forever and ever
Ps. 119:152	His Testimonies	Forever
Ps. 33:11	His Counsel	Forever
Ps. 33:11	His Thoughts	To all generations
Ps. 100:5	His Truth	To all generations
Ps.119:160	His Judgments	Forever
Mt. 5:18	Every Jot and Tittle	Till all be fulfilled
Ps. 119:89-90	His Faithfulness	To all generations

Finally, some point to Psalms 119:89, *"For ever, O LORD, thy word is settled in heaven,"* and say that preservation is only in Heaven. However, Isaiah 59:21 counters that idea by explaining *"my words which I have put in thy mouth, **shall not pass out of the thy mouth, nor out of the mouth of thy seed,** nor **out of the mouth of thy seed's seed** saith the*

Lord, <u>from henceforth and forever</u>." God's Words will not only be in Heaven, but they will be *in the mouth of people* forever. The Words of God are for us to live by. "*And **these words**, which I command thee this day, **shall be in thine heart***" (Deut. 6:6).

The Definition of Providential Preservation

Providential Preservation is a Biblical doctrine, and it is proved by the Scriptures I have listed, along with many others. The Doctrine of Providential Preservation states:

> God has *promised* to *miraculously preserve forever* all of His Word, His individual words, and all His teachings with the words in which they are expressed. He has further promised to make them available to mankind for our good and for our lives. He has determined to do this in His own way depending on Himself alone.

We may not understand how God has done this. We may be confused by all the unbelieving statements made by modern textual critics. Nevertheless, our responsibility is to "*Trust in the LORD with all thine heart; and lean not unto thine own understanding*" (Prov. 3:3). We may not be able to see how God has preserved each of His Words, but we can rest assured that He has done so, based on His own statements and promises.

Just as the Bible teaches verbal plenary inspiration, these verses teach *verbal plenary preservation*. Each individual word is preserved and the entire body of the 66 books of Scripture is preserved.

Take special note of *what words* have been preserved. The words that were inspired were Hebrew, Aramaic, and Greek words. They were not English, German, Spanish, or any other language. When God made the promises of preservation, the words He promised to preserve were Hebrew, Aramaic, and Greek words. He did not promise to preserve English, Spanish, German, or any other language words. This is evident by the Scriptures themselves: "*Till heaven and earth pass, **one jot or one tittle** shall in no wise pass from the law, till all be fulfilled*" (Mt 5:18). The jot (yod) is the smallest *Hebrew* letter and the tittle is a small part a *Hebrew* letter. The promise in Matthew 5:18 is to preserve words of Scripture in the Hebrew language. Clearly the Lord's promise is to preserve the Hebrew, Greek, and Aramaic words he inspired.

> Jesus taught that the same Divine providence which had preserved the Old Testament would preserve the New Testament … The Holy Spirit providentially guided churches to preserve His Words during the manuscript period. **First,** faithful scribes produced many trustworthy copies of the original New Testament manuscripts. **Second,** these trustworthy copies were read and recopied by true believers down through the centuries. **Third,** untrustworthy copies were not so generally read or so frequently recopied. Although they enjoyed some popularity for a time, yet in the long run they were laid aside and consigned to oblivion. Thus, as a result of this special providential guidance, the true text won out in the end, and today the believer may be sure that the text found in the vast majority of the Greek New Testament manuscripts, preserved by the God-guided usage of the Greek churches, is a trustworthy reproduction of the Divinely inspired original. Some have called it the Byzantine text, thereby acknowledging that it was the text in use in the Greek churches during the greater part of the Byzantine period (452-1453). It is much better, however, to call this text the Traditional Text because this text, which is found in the great majority of Greek New Testament manuscripts, has been handed down … to the present day.[5]

The All Sufficiency of the Word of God

The Word of God came from God. It had its origin in Him. Therefore, it was perfect when it was inspired, because God is perfect and makes no mistakes. Finally, God has preserved it, and because He never fails, it has been preserved perfect. Notice how God exalts the Word.

> **Psalms 138:2** I will worship toward thy holy temple, and praise thy name for thy loving kindness and for thy

truth: for thou hast magnified thy word above all thy name.

Psalms 8:1 O LORD our Lord, how excellent is thy name in all the earth! who hast set thy glory above the heavens.

If God has exalted His Word above His name, then His view of the Word is so high it's immeasurable. The glory of His name is very important to God, but His Word is in a higher place. Consider that. His glory is above the Heavens! His Word is higher! How much must we exalt His Word and hold it precious? How much ought we to support efforts to translate His Word into every language?

Consider this. There was a time in history when people held their reputation to be of highest importance. When they gave their word, they kept their word. If they broke their word, their reputation would be lost. "A good name is rather to be chosen than great riches" (Proverbs22:1).

Consider this. The glory of God's name depends on Him keeping His Word. Consider, the nature of God's Word.

Gal.3:8 And the scripture, foreseeing that God would justify the heathen through faith, preached before the gospel unto Abraham, saying, In thee shall all nations be blessed.

Romans 9:17 For the scripture saith unto Pharaoh, Even for this same purpose have I raised thee up, that I might shew my power in thee, and that my name might be declared throughout all the earth.

Heb. 4:12 For the Word of God is quick, and powerful

There was no written Scripture when God gave the message in Galatians 3 and Romans 9 to Abraham and Pharaoh. The Scriptures had not been written, except possibly the Book of Job. Yet, Paul said it was the Scriptures which spoke. It was God who spoke. The word *Scriptures* was substituted for the word God. This clearly indicates that whenever God speaks to men in words that will eventually be written, His voice and words are Scripture. They proceed out of His mouth. They are God-breathed. The Scriptures are part of God. Therefore, the Scriptures are as true as God is, and the Scriptures are as authoritative and sufficient as the "King of kings and Lord of lords."

The Attack on Authority and Sufficiency

The authority and sufficiency of God's Word is no longer believed in America and Europe like it once was. We can debate the reasons for this, but I believe it is because the *accuracy* of Scripture has been attacked for over one hundred years. Well over a hundred new English versions have been published since 1881 and many of them have been translated into other languages. Bible publishing is very big business producing a great deal of money. Every time a new version is published it uses different words than the others. It must do this, or it cannot get a copyright. The constant barrage of new versions worded differently produces doubt in the minds of believers and unbelievers. I have been in Bible studies where several versions were used and much of the discussion was about which version is preferred, "I like the way this version says it." All the while, it was obvious that the different versions said something different in the same verses and I doubt anyone learned much.

As far as society at large is concerned, the Bible is almost totally ignored, and it seems many Christian follow along. Occasionally it is mentioned (often in a bad light), but it is never consulted for answers or guidance. In his book, *God's Wisdom in Proverbs*, Dan Phillips said, "Modern Christian thought often drinks long and deep at the trough of sociology and psychology, adds a sprinkling of pixie-dust, and merely closes in prayer." [6] The world is filled with self-help books and programs fed on by Christians. Various *experts* have *different* opinions on how you ought to live and handle the issues of your life. Many churches are more like entertainment centers, some are even like a night club environment. Professing Christians can be found on both sides of the abortion issue. Confusion and deception abound in the world and in Christian circles.

Colossians 2:8 *Beware lest any man spoil you through philosophy and vain deceit, after the tradition of men, after the rudiments of the world, and not after Christ.*

There has been a distinct rise of Christian mysticism. I've personally heard, "Doctrine is passé." Another Christian lady, years later, told me she did not see the need to read the Bible. When Christians reject the Bible, the only things left are worldly philosophy, psychology, science, sociology, and the opinions of others; in other words, the opinions of man. Beyond that one must depend on feelings and inner impressions ("I *feel led* to divorce my husband"), which can easily be from the devil.

What matters is not my opinion, my experience, my feelings, or my desires. What matters is what God says about it in His Word.

If you don't accept the authority of the Bible, you will be open to every wind of false doctrine that blows your way (Eph. 4:13-14).

The Fact of Scripture's Sufficiency

The ultimate goal of Christian growth is to be conformed to the image of Christ (Rom. 8:28-29). How does that happen? The Scriptures are the key to this growth. The mechanism that accomplishes this is explained in 2 Cor 3.

> **2 Corinthians 3:18** *But we all, with open face beholding as in a glass the glory of the Lord, are changed into the same image from glory to glory, even as by the Spirit of the Lord.*

This verse speaks of someone who is looking in a glass (a mirror), they see an image, and they are changed into that image one step at a time (from glory to glory). Normally, when one looks in a mirror, he sees himself. But, when one looks into *this* mirror, he sees the "glory of God." Gazing at this image changes the beholder into the same image, the glory of the Lord. This is quite a different mirror! We need to know what the mirror is and what the glory of God is.

> **James 1:23, 24** *For if any be a hearer of the word, and not a doer, he is like unto a man beholding his natural face in a glass:*
> *24 For he beholdeth himself, and goeth his way, and straightway forgetteth what manner of man he was.*

These verses identify the mirror. The man looking into the Word of God is like a man looking into a mirror. The mirror is the Word of God. But, in 2 Cor. 3:18, he is not seeing his own reflection. He is seeing the glory of God. What is that?

> **2 Corinthians 4:6** *For God, who commanded the light to shine out of darkness, hath shined in our hearts, to give the light of the knowledge of the* **glory of God** *in the* **face of Jesus Christ.**

The "glory of God" is seen in the face of Jesus Christ. So, when we look into the Word of God, we see Jesus Christ. As we continually look into His Word, we will begin to be changed into the image of what we see, Jesus Christ. This will happen from "glory to glory" or step by step becoming more and more like Jesus Christ. This transformation is produced by the Word of God.

> **2 Peter 1:3** *According as his divine power hath given unto us* **all things** *that pertain unto life and godliness,* **through the knowledge** *of him that hath called us to glory and virtue:*
> 4 *Whereby are given unto us* **exceeding great and precious promises***: that by these ye might be partakers of the divine nature, having escaped the corruption that is in the world through lust.*

After Peter said "all things," he listed several: partaker of the divine nature, virtue, knowledge, temperance, patience, godliness, brotherly kindness, and charity. These things come through knowledge and God's promises. Where do we get this knowledge and learn these promises? The Word of God of course. The following benefits also come from the Word of God.

1. We are cleansed by the word (Ps 119:9, 11)
2. We become disciples by keeping the word (John 8:31-32)
3. The Scriptures teach us how to live (Mt. 4:4; 2 Tim. 3:16)
4. The Scriptures equip us for service (2 Tim. 3:17)
5. The Scriptures strengthen us (build us up) (Acts 20:32)
6. The Scriptures give an inheritance (Acts 20:32)

The Absolute Infallible Guide to Life

Ps. 19 shows us some further benefits of the Word of God. In verses 7-14, there are Six lines of thought with three elements each: a title or effect of the Word, a Characteristic of the Word, and a benefit of the Word (except the last one).

> **Ps. 19:7-9** *The law of the LORD is perfect, converting the soul: the testimony of the LORD is sure, making wise the simple.*
> *8 The statutes of the LORD are right, rejoicing the heart: the commandment of the LORD is pure, enlightening the eyes.*
> *9 The fear of the LORD is clean, enduring for ever: the judgments of the LORD are true and righteous altogether.*

The Scriptures: The Word of God is law, testimony, statutes, commandment, judgements, and produces the fear of the Lord.

Characteristics of the Word: perfect, sure, right, pure, clean, true and righteous altogether.

Benefits of the Word: converts the soul, makes wise the simple, rejoices the heart, enlightens the eyes, and endures forever.

The Greatest Source of Life's Benefits

> **PSALMS 19:10-14** *More to be desired are they than gold, yea, than much fine gold: sweeter also than honey and the honeycomb.*
> *11 Moreover by them is thy servant warned: and in keeping of them there is great reward.*
> *12 Who can understand his errors? cleanse thou me from secret faults.*
> *13 Keep back thy servant also from presumptuous sins; let them not have dominion over me: then shall I be upright, and I shall be innocent from the great transgression.*

14 Let the words of my mouth, and the meditation my heart, be acceptable in thy sight, O LORD, my strength, and my redeemer.

The Word of God is:
1. The Greatest source of wealth (v. 10), a wealth greater than silver and gold.
2. The Greatest source of pleasures (v. 10), beyond the physical and emotional.
3. The Greatest source of protection (v. 11), warning us of danger and error.
4. The Greatest source of profits (v. 11). It provides rewards beyond any earthly rewards.
5. The Greatest source of purification (vv. 12-13), deliverance from presumptuous and addictive sins, making us upright and innocent, and giving us a great desire for our whole life to be acceptable to Him.

3 The Source Texts with Recommended Resources

Isaiah 34:16 Seek ye out of the book of the LORD, and read: no one of these shall fail, none shall want her mate: for my mouth it hath commanded, and his spirit it hath gathered them.

Organizing a new translation project involves answering a series of questions. The first of those questions is *what will be the source languages and the source texts*. Every translation project must have a final authority. This chapter will point the translator in the right direction.

Before answering that question, it is important for the reader to understand the terms "source language"/"source text" and "target language"/ "target text."

> **Source Text:** The Bible text *from which* we are translating.

> **Source Language:** The language of the text *from which* we are translating.

> **Target Language:** The language *into which* we are translating.

> **Target Text:** The Bible text in the target language that will be created when the translation is finished.

The New Testament was inspired in Greek and the Old Testament was inspired in Hebrew with a little Aramaic. *The ideal situation is to translate from the Greek and Hebrew texts.* Not everyone can do that. We will discuss what to do in that case, later. These are the guidelines about the source text from the translation principles of Global Bible Translators.

The source text for the New Testament will be the Greek Textus Receptus as found in the edition by Scrivener ... The source text of the Old Testament will be the Ginsberg edition of the Ben Chayim Hebrew Masoretic Text published by the Trinitarian Bible Society.

When the Greek and Hebrew Texts are the primary source texts, the King James Bible will be used as translation guide. Difficult and uncertain word choices will be guided by the word choices of the KJB. Where the KJB translated the same Greek or Hebrew word by the same English word, due consideration will be given to doing the same in the translation to maintain proper cross-references.

In cases where the translator is not familiar with the Greek and Hebrew source texts, but he speaks and reads English, the translator may use the King James Bible as the source text. The translation advisors can help by using the Greek/Hebrew text.

Other target language translations may be consulted for help. [7]

The Greek and Hebrew Source Texts

The normal translating procedure is to translate from the original languages. This means the translator should be trained in Greek and Hebrew and familiar with the Greek New Testament and the Hebrew Old Testament. This is the *ideal* situation and has been accepted practice for centuries. However, translation situations are rarely ideal, as we will discuss later.

There is a great argument over which Greek text is the right one. There are two major texts and several minor ones. The two major competing texts are the *Textus Receptus (TR)*, first printed in 1516, and the *United Bible Societies Greek Text (UBS)*, whose forerunner, the Westcott and Hort Text, dates to 1881. We also call the UBS text the *Critical text.* These two texts differ from one another in over 8000 words. The third, more minor text, is called *Majority Text,* which is actually published in two different editions and differs from the Textus Receptus about 1000-1500 times. There are others that are very similar to the UBS text. We believe the right Greek New Testament is the Textus Receptus. Some of the reasons for this below are summarized below. If you want in-depth detail and information, we encourage you to consult the first book in this series on Bible translating, *A Practical Theology of Bible Translating*. You will find there several chapters explaining this matter, including an appendix on the history of modernism and unbelief that is the foundation of the UBS text and its sisters, the SBL text, the Tyndale, and the Nestle-Aland text. You should also read the book, *In Defense of the Textus Receptus,* by Dr. Jim Taylor.

There have been several editions of the Textus Receptus printed between 1516 and 1881. The recommended edition was published by Frederick H.A. Scrivener, in 1881. A new edition of Scrivener's Textus Receptus was published in 2020 by Global Bible Translators and called "The Global Edition." The Global edition differs from the words of the 1881 TR in *one word*. In Ephesians 6:24, this text adds the word ἀμήν (amen). The word was included in the Beza 1598 edition of the TR and several other TR editions and in the KJB but was overlooked by Scrivener in the 1881 edition.

Before summarizing our reasons for believing that the Textus Receptus is the preserved Word of God in Greek, it would be worthy to note that the UBS text and its sisters (Nestle, SBL, Tyndale, etc.) is the basis for all the popular modern English versions. Of course, the New King James professes to be based on the TR, but it translates some things like the other modern versions, and it has footnotes that refer to UBS text readings. The only popular version that is *fully* based on the TR is the King James Version.

The following summary is given with full knowledge that it does not present proof or corroborating evidence. Therefore, it is not meant to be an apologetic for the identity of the New Testament Text. That evidence and apologetic is presented in the above two books and in many others which can be found at www.theoldpathspublications.com. This information is presented to show reasons why this author is committed to the Greek Textus Receptus and the Hebrew Masoretic Text and the King James Version, personally and for translation work.

1.   Two lines of ancient manuscripts: God inspired the New Testament between about 29 AD to 100 AD. Two things happened during that time. First, many copies were made and distributed wherever there were churches: Asia minor, Egypt, Palestine, Rome, etc. The copies were all handwritten until the invention of the moveable-type printing press by Johannes Gutenberg about 1440 AD. The second occurrence was that many people tried to introduce corruptions into the Scriptures. This happened while Paul was still writing his letters, "For we are not as many, which corrupt the word of God: but as of sincerity, but as of God, in the sight of God speak we in Christ" (2 Cor. 2:17). There were numerous false teachings, which were eventually put into the Scriptures by those championing the heresies. These corrupt copies were recopied and further spread around the Roman world.

During the Manuscript Period of textual history (about 100-1500 AD), two categories of manuscripts developed. They are clearly demonstrated by the body of ancient manuscripts that are available today. There are over 5,800 Greek manuscripts and fragments available dating from about 50 AD to 1600 AD, ranging from a few fragments to nearly complete New Testaments, lectionaries (church service guides), and quotes by ancient church writers. In addition, there are ancient translations. All of these can all be divided into two great categories. The first category is called by several names (Traditional, Byzantine, Majority, Syrian). We will call it the *Traditional* text. The Textus Receptus is the printed form of the Traditional text. The Traditional text contains about 93 percent of all the manuscripts, because they are basically in agreement with one another. The second category includes the other 7 percent, which does not agree with the majority in a great many places, and which do not agree among themselves. Scholars have further divided the manuscripts into smaller categories, because of their disagreements. The largest of these smaller categories is called the Alexandrian text, but the manuscripts of this category also do not agree among themselves. About 4 percent of the manuscripts support the Alexandrian text. Dr. Jim Taylor says, "In actuality, there are only two families of manuscripts – the right ones, and the wrong ones!" [8]

2. The Alexandrian Manuscripts: Out of this small group of manuscripts, the Scholars love two Alexandrian manuscripts the most:

Vaticanus (dated about 350 A.D.), which is reposing in the Vatican Library, and Sinaiticus (dated about 350 A.D.), which was found by Constantin Tischendorf in the monastery at the traditional Mt. Sinai. Here are some characteristics of the Alexandrian text.

Number: The Alexandrian text only exists in about 4 % of manuscripts.

Age: The oldest papyrus fragments assigned to this category are given dates of the second century. The oldest Uncial (capital letter) manuscripts are dated 350 A.D.

Agreement: There is great disagreement among the Alexandrian manuscripts. Vaticanus and Sinaiticus differ from one another over 3,000 times in the gospels alone. The Chester Beatty group of papyri (AD 250) and the Bodmer group of Papyri (AD 200) are considered to be Alexandrian. The Chester Beatty papyri (shares 78 verses with the Bodmer Papyri. Out of these 78 verses, the two disagree in over 70 places! The text of Sinaiticus has been repeatedly altered by at least 9 correctors from the 4th to the 12th centuries. Some of the variant readings in Sinaiticus are unmatched by any other document. By one count, Sinaiticus has a total of 23,000 alterations. Compare this disagreement with the agreement of the Traditional text below.

Influence on printed Greek Texts: The Alexandrian text is the basis for the Westcott and Hort text (1881), the Nestle-Aland text (*"Novum Testamentum Graece"* NA1-first published in 1898, 28th edition, NA28, 2012), the United Bible Societies Greek text (UBS first publish in 1966, now in 5th edition as of 2014), the SBL Greek New Testament (2010), and the Tyndale House Greek New Testament (2017). The UBS-5 and NA28 share an identical Greek text. Collectively, we call these the "Critical Text," especially the UBS, which is most often used for translations.

Influence on modern English translations: The Alexandrian text is the basis of all but two of the popular modern versions. The two which profess to be from the Textus Receptus are the New King James Version and the Modern English Version. However, both exhibit translations that show the influence of Modern textual criticism, which favors the Alexandrian text (e.g., 2 Cor. 2:17). The NKJV has footnotes which favor the Critical Text. Therefore, these two are, at best, mixed translations. Remember, "A little leaven leaveneth the whole lump" (Galatians 5:9).

Differences from the Textus Receptus: The UBS text differs from the Textus Receptus in over 8000 words and leaves out 17 whole verse that are in the TR. Hundreds of the words left out of the UBS include the names of God and the Lord Jesus. It leaves out or changes doctrinal passages such as omitting the great trinitarian passage in 1 John 5:7 and changing the proof text that Jesus is God in 1 Timothy 3:16, so that the Deity of Christ is removed.

3. The Traditional Text:

Majority: There are more than 5800 ancient manuscripts. The Traditional text manuscripts are the great majority of these, representing about 93% of all them. Scholars of all opinions agree with this.

Age: Traditional text manuscripts and early translations from it date back to the mid-second century, about 150 A.D. and possibly as far back as 50-60 A.D. If one looks up "Byzantine text-type" in Wikipedia, he will find that they admit that the Traditional text is the majority of all manuscripts. However, he will also find a short list of Traditional text manuscripts and their dates. The earliest date is the fifth century. Only one papyrus (P73) is listed and it is 7th century. A spot check of the rest does not reveal anything before the 5th century. However, there is manuscript evidence that Wikipedia does not show and that many proponents of the Alexandrian text will not admit.

1. In my personal examination of P52 (100-175 A.D.) and P32 (200 A.D.) I found that the words match the TR.

2.   P66 is a mixed text that has distinctive Traditional text readings and is dated 125 A.D. by many. [9]

3. I also compared P64, a fragment of Mat. 26, with the TR and found that the clear words in it match the TR. P64 was dated 180-200 A.D., but Carsten Peter Thiede, a qualified papyrologist, made a compelling argument for dating it at about 60 AD!

4. Many of the so-called church fathers and ancient writings quote the Traditional text, e.g., the Didache (50-100 AD). In fact, the Traditional text was consistently the predominate text quoted in the first to the fourth centuries.

5. Since many of these "fathers" also quoted something other than the Traditional text, it is also evident that the corruptions in the text originated very early in church history. Furthermore, it shows that the corruption of the text was worse in Alexandria, Egypt, where the Alexandrian text manuscripts were primarily found.

7. An early date for the Traditional Text is supported by the ancient translations. A list of some of these is below.

> The Old Latin 120-150 A.D.
> The Old Syriac 150-160 A.D.
> The Syriac Peshitta 150 A.D.
> Tatian's Diatessaron (Syriac) 150-160 A.D.
> Ethiopic 300 A.D.
> Gothic 350 A.D.

6. The evidence places the Traditional text at least as far back as the Alexandrian text (or any other text). If P64 is indeed dated at 50-70 A.D., the Traditional text is older than the Alexandrian, according to physical evidence.

The Continuity of the Traditional Text: The manuscript evidence shows that the Traditional text was not only *present* but was also consistently *used* from at least 100 A.D. to the present time. There is a brief gap in the manuscript evidence for the Traditional text in the first half of the fourth century. This is probably due to the tenth Roman persecution of the churches, which took place around 300 AD. It mainly took place in the eastern part of the Roman Empire, where most of the traditional text manuscripts were. One of the greatest characteristics of the tenth persecution was the destruction of many Bible manuscripts. Hundreds, perhaps thousands, were destroyed. The Alexandrian text may have been dominate in the early fourth century due to this, but the traditional text was dominate by the fifth century and thereafter.

In 395 A.D., the Roman Empire divided into a Western Empire, ruled form Rome, and an Eastern Empire, ruled from Constantinople. The Christianity of the Western Empire fell under the control of the Roman Church. The Eastern Empire became Eastern Orthodox. The language of speech and of the New Testament of the west was Latin. The Roman Catholic Church adopted Jerome's Latin translation as its official text and the Greek text ceased to be used. The Alexandrian text continued to be used in the Latin Vulgate. The language of the east was Greek, and they continued to use a Greek New Testament. What kind of New Testament was it in the east, Alexandrian or Traditional? Subsequent history gives the answer.

In a reaction to the promotion of the Alexandrian text in the 18th and 19th centuries, the Patriarch of Constantinople appointed a commission in 1899 to examine the textual tradition of the Eastern Orthodox Church. They gathered manuscripts from the monastery at Mt. Athos (Greece), from Constantinople, from Athens, and from Jerusalem. They made a goal to create a standard New Testament text from the manuscript evidence. The resulting text was published in 1904. It is clearly a Traditional type of text. For example, it contains Acts 8:37 and 1 John 5:7, which all the Critical Greek texts listed above omit. The 1904 New Testament also has the correct reading in 1 Timothy 3:16. It is clear to me that the Eastern Orthodox Church has maintained the textual tradition they inherited from before the Eastern Roman Empire existed, a text that was used long before the division of the empire, the Traditional text.

Agreement: There are thousands of disagreements between the manuscript witnesses of the Alexandrian text. This is not so with the Traditional text. There is over 99% agreement between the manuscripts of the Traditional text. The agreement actually goes beyond that. The manuscripts come from such diverse locations as to make it impossible for many of them to copy from one another. For those that did copy, many of their exemplars (the one they copied from) are perfectly identical! An example of this agreement was discovered by Wilbur Pickering when he compared the readings of the various manuscripts of Family 35 of the Traditional text.

> Notice that of twenty-one MSS, eleven of their exemplars (over half) were 'perfect', and another five were off by only one variant (the worst was only off by six, for two books) … I conclude that all twenty-one MSS were independent in their generation, and I see no evidence to indicate a different conclusion for their exemplars … I now invite attention to location and date. The MSS come from all over the Mediterranean world. The six Mt. Athos MSS were certainly produced in their respective monasteries … Ecclesiastical politics

tending to be what it tends to be, there is little likelihood that there would be collusion between the monasteries on the transmission of the NT writings—I regard the six as representing independent lines of transmission (five of the exemplars were not identical). MSS from Trikala, Patmos, Jerusalem and Sinai were presumably produced there; 18 was certainly produced in Constantinople; 35 was acquired in the Aegean area. The MSS at the Vatican and Grottaferrata may very well have been produced there … The implications of finding a perfect representative of any archetypal text are rather powerful. All the 'canons' of textual criticism become irrelevant to any point subsequent to the creation of that text (they could still come into play when studying the creation of the text). For MS 18 to be perfect, all the generations in between had to be perfect as well. Now I call this incredibly careful transmission. Nothing that I was taught in Seminary about New Testament textual criticism prepared me for this discovery! Nor anything that I had read, for that matter. But MS 18 is not an isolated case; all the twenty-one MSS in the chart above reflect an incredibly careful transmission—even the worst of the lot, minuscule 201 with its 6 variants [the 'singulars' in 1893 and 1248 are careless mistakes (unhappy monks), is really quite good, considering all the intervening generations. (Author's emphasis) [10]

When considering all of the points above, it is just a matter of adding 2 plus 2 to conclude that the Traditional text is the correct text descending from the original New Testament. After the moveable-type printing press was invented, it was only a short time until the traditional text was published. This happened first in 1516 with a text that came to be called the Textus Receptus or the Received Text.

The Textus Receptus

The Textus Receptus Greek New Testament was first published by Desiderius Erasmus in 1516. This first printing was not perfect. it had numerous errors by Erasmus and numerous printing errors. Erasmus published additional editions to correct printing errors and his own in 1519, 1522, 1527, and 1535.

Other editors came after Erasmus. The following are all the editions.

1. Erasmus, five editions in 1516, 1519, 1522, 1527, and 1535.
2. Simon Colinaeus, one edition in 1534.
3. Robert Stephens, four editions in 1546, 1549, 1550, and 1551.
4. Theodore Beza, ten editions in 1560, 1565, 1567, 1580, 1582, 1588/89, 1590, 1598, 1604, and 1611.
5. The King James Bible, 1611. (Regarding why this is included, see below under "The King James Bible.")
6. Abraham and Bonaventure Elziver, published three editions in 1624, 1633, and 1641.
7. Frederick H. A. Scrivener, one edition in 1881, also printed in 1894. In 2020, the Scrivener edition was printed by Global Bible Translators and called "The Global Edition."

While Erasmus was working in central Europe, in Spain another group was preparing an edition of the whole Bible in Greek, Latin, Aramaic, and Hebrew. The effort was led by Cardinal Francisco Jiménez de Cisneros (1436–1517), sometimes called Cardinal Ximenes. It was called the *Complutensian Polyglot*. The work went on from 1502 to 1517. The Greek New Testament was printed in 1514, but not issued. However, Erasmus' Greek New Testament was published and issued first. This was not part of the Textus Receptus tradition. It was a Catholic approved effort even though Cisneros apparently had a number of Traditional text manuscripts to work from.

1516-1611 was a period of purifying the printed Greek text. This was not for the purpose of purifying God's words, because the Bible says, "The words of the Lord are pure words …" (Ps. 12:6). However, a printed text was something that had never existed before. The manuscript letters were without spaces and without punctuation, so careful prayerful effort was needed to get it right. Here is an example of what Erasmus may have seen from James 5:12.

ΑΛΛΟΤΙΝΑΟΡΚΟΝΗΤΩΔΕΥΜΩΝΤΟΝΑΙΝΑΙΚΑΙΤΟΟΥΟΥ
ΙΝΑΜΗΥΠΟΚΡΙΣΙΠΕΣΗΤΕ

If this was in one's mother tongue, he might be able to understand it. Greek was not the mother tongue of Erasmus or any of the other editors, but they were thoroughly learned in Greek. An editor must separate the words. In this passage, "ΥΠΟΚΡΙΣΙ" means "hypocrisy." However, if you separate the words into "ΥΠΟ ΚΡΙΣΙ" it means "into condemnation." So, which is it? Erasmus had to make a decision. He opted for the first. So, it became "hypocrisy" through the editions of Stephens. But, when Theodore Beza published his editions, he found further reasons that caused him to choose the second option, no doubt by the leading of the Holy Spirit. The KJB is primarily based on the 1598 edition of Beza, so the KJB reads "into condemnation." Coming to this point was a process of purification of the Textus Receptus. There was never any more than about 250 differences between editions of the TR and most of these were small matters of spelling, accent marks, breathing marks, word order, and other minor differences. When compared to the thousands of differences between manuscripts of the Alexandrian text and the more than 8,000 differences between the UBS text and the Textus Receptus, the differences between editions of the TR are small indeed. However, when the Scrivener text was printed, the editing of the TR ceased (except for a single word I will explain later). So, the Scrivener text was the last and final edition of the Textus Receptus. How did it come about? That is where the King James Bible comes into the TR history.

The King James Bible

The KJB was translated from 1604 to 1611 by 47 of the most eminent Greek and Hebrew scholars in England. The title page of every KJB says, "Translated out of the original tongues with the former translations diligently compared and revised." The King James Bible was the culmination of about a century of English Bible translating, starting with William Tyndale who published a complete New Testament in 1526. He also translated some of the Old Testament but did not finish it. The Old Testament was completed by Myles Coverdale and the entire Bible was published as The Coverdale Bible in 1535. Then, the Matthew Bible was published by John Rodgers in 1537. This was followed by The Taverner's Bible by Richard Taverner in 1539. Myles Coverdale also published the Great Bible in 1539. The Geneva Bible was published in 1560 and the Bishops Bible in 1568. Finally, the King James Bible was published in 1611. The entire century was another period of purification; this time of the English Bible. However, when the King James Bible was translated and published, all English Bible translating ceased. It was as if God had reached His goal.

The title page of a KJB points out that it was "translated out of the original tongues …" The original tongues were Hebrew and Greek and a small amount of Aramaic. What text did they use for the New Testament? Dr. Scrivener determined that the primary Greek text the KJB translators used was the 1598 edition of Beza's Textus Receptus. However, they did not use that alone.

In 1603, the Received text was still developing, so the translators were open to the possibility that the text may yet need to be edited. How did the KJB translators decide what edits to make to the TR? They certainly arrived at their conclusions by divine guidance. They started with Beza 1598, but they also used the other editions of the TR, the Complutensian Polyglot, and other language translations, such as Martin Luther's German, the Reina-Valera Spanish, and the Erasmus and Beza Latin translations. Nevertheless, the adjustments they made were *the pinnacle of the edits made to the TR text*. However, the edits of the KJB translators to the Received Text of Beza were made in English, not Greek. Their edits to the Received Text of Beza were incorporated into the Greek Text by Scrivener. The KJB translation and its suggested changes to Beza's 1598 text was an important step toward a completely pure Greek text. Due to the editing work of the KJB translators, it was Dr. Edward Hills' opinion that "the King James Version ought to be regarded not merely as a translation of the Textus Receptus but also as an independent variety of the Textus Receptus." [11]

The Scrivener Text

Frederick H. A. Scrivener (1813-1891) issued an edition of the Received Text in 1881, which is usually ignored by liberal and liberal leaning scholars. Even some KJB Bible believers ignore it. However, it is a valid edition of the text and a further purification. It is entirely based on the Beza 1598 edition with the edits made by the King James translators. When it was published in 1881, it was said to be "According to the text followed in the Authorized Version." Scrivener used a process to find and adjust the differences between Beza's text and the KJB.

> 1) First , Scrivener compared each verse of the KJB New Testament with Beza 1598 to see if they matched.
> 2) He found about 190 places where they were different.
> 3) For each difference, he looked for the Greek manuscript evidence or Greek text that had the necessary reading. He would not make a change in Beza without Greek authority.
> 4) He made changes in the 190 places based on what he found in the Greek evidence.
> 5) He corrected printer errors in the Beza text.
> 6) He corrected Beza for inconsistent and incorrect Greek spelling.
> 7) He adjusted the paragraphs and punctuation.

The KJB translators helped to make an excellent text better, by choosing alternative readings that already existed in the historic Traditional Greek Text that the Biblical church had used since the first century. God has preserved all His inspired Greek words. They were already pure (Prov. 30:5) and were available.

So, on the one hand, the men of the KJB translated God's Words that had been in existence since the days of the Apostles. On the other hand, the King James translators were also editors of the Received Text. Their edits were made in English, rather than Greek. It was Dr. Scrivener, who placed those edits into the Greek Received Text after searching for the Greek source of the edits. Then, he produced the "Greek text that underlay the KJB." It should be noted that the edits in the Received Text made by the translators of the King James Bible **_were the final edits made to the Received Text._** The Elzevir bothers' edits did not flow into the Scrivener text. The KJB translators' edits did. God, who is sovereign in history, did not make a mistake here. The God of history led the work that was done on the TR by Dr. Scrivener. His edition was the final edition of the TR.

Frederick Scrivener's TR with notes was published in *Scrivener's Annotated Greek New Testament*, by the Dean Burgon Society in 1999. The appendix of this book contains two lists by Dr.

Scrivener. The first is a list of items in the Beza 1598 text that he changed to match the readings of the King James Version. The second list is said to be a list of readings in Beza that were different from the KJB readings, but that Scrivener *did not change*. The first list is quite impressive. It covers variances in 166 verses and 13 New Testament book titles. All of them represent actual changes Scrivener made to the Beza text.

The second list is of variances Scrivener did not change, according to his own statements. The reason for this is that he could not find Greek evidence for the reading chosen by the KJB translators. It appeared to him that the KJB readings came from the Latin Vulgate. However, I have compared each of these KJB readings with Scrivener's TR. I found a total of 58 items. They are listed in a table on the website, www.bpsglobal.org. The interesting thing I found is that 57 are not variances at all, but the Scrivener TR text and the KJB match. Eight of these are apparent differences, but in my opinion these differences between the Greek text and the KJB are not textual differences. They are not because of a faulty Greek text or a variance between that text and the KJB. Rather, they are apparent differences because of translation choices made by the KJB translators. This in no way indicates there are errors in the KJB. It indicates there are differences between Greek, as a language, and English. For example, several times the KJB did not translate a conjunction, no doubt, because they believed the verse was more correct in English without it. Sometimes small words like that work well in Greek, but not in English. It is simply the nature of languages. There are two times the KJB added words, but they are not in italics. Scrivener pointed out that the KJB was inconsistent in its use of italics (or, perhaps, the printers were inconsistent).

There are two issues among these 58 items that give true challenges. The first is in Acts 19:20 which says, "So mightily grew the word of God and prevailed." The Greek word translated "God" here is the word *Kurios*. The usual translation of Kurios, when it is applied to God and the Lord Jesus Christ, is "Lord." The normal Greek word for God is *Theos*. The KJB translators translated Kurios as "God" here, even though in every other use of the word it was translated "Lord." This is not a textual problem. No Greek text, to my knowledge, has Theos in this verse. However, I encourage the reader to read the article "God or Lord?" on the website mentioned above, where I argue that Kurios can *legitimately* be translated "God." The KJB made no mistake here.

The final issue in Scrivener's second list comes from Ephesians 6:24. This issue involves a single word, and it is a true issue. In the KJB, the verse ends with the word "amen." Scrivener stated that *amen* is not in any Greek text and the KJB seemed to get it from the Latin Vulgate. How he came to this conclusion is a mystery. The word *amen* is in several Greek texts. I have found it in Beza 1598 (which means there was never a difference with this word between Beza 1598 and the KJB), Stephens 1550, Erasmus 1522, and Elzevir 1633. So, the word *amen* is a legitimate part of the New Testament and should be in Scrivener's text, but it is not. This single omission is the only variance between the KJB and Scrivener that I have found. I disagree with anyone who says this is a minor issue. "Amen" is one of God's words. The Scripture says that "every word of God is pure" (Prov. 30:5), and Psalm 12:6-7 says they will *all* be preserved. Every word of God is important. Therefore, Scrivener's New Testament appears to be entirely correct except for this one word. The *Global Edition* of Scrivener's TR text includes this word at the end of Ephesians 6:24.

As I have said, the ideal situation is to translate the New Testament from the Greek Text. The correct Greek text is the Textus Receptus Scrivener Edition. Specifically, the best representative of the Scrivener text that we know of is the Global Edition published by The Old Paths Publications. The Global edition also comes in a parallel version. The Greek Text is in the left-hand column and the KJB is in the right-hand column.

The Hebrew Text

The Masoretic Hebrew text is the traditional Hebrew text of the Old Testament. When the KJB translators started translating in 1604, the current Masoretic text of the Hebrew Old Testament was the Second Rabbinic Bible edited by Jacob Ben Chayim. This was the source text for the KJB Old Testament translation. Where did this Hebrew OT come from? Can it be relied on as the preserved Word of God in the Old Testament?

The Old Testament was inspired between 1491 B.C. and 400 B.C. (with the possible exception of Job, which may have been written earlier).

During the history of Israel and Judah, the Israelites often deviated from God's book. Several times revival took place. One such revival occurred during the reign of Josiah, just a few years before the Babylonian captivity. It was brought about by the discovery of the Book of the Law in the temple.

> **2 Kings 22:8, 10-11** *And Hilkiah the high priest said unto Shaphan the scribe, I have found the book of the law in the house of the LORD. And Hilkiah gave the book to Shaphan, and he read it.*
> *10 And Shaphan the scribe shewed the king, saying, Hilkiah the priest hath delivered me a book. And Shaphan read it before the king.*
> *11 ¶And it came to pass, when the king had heard the words of the book of the law, that he rent his clothes.*

From that time to the time of Jesus, a standard copy of the Scriptures was kept in the temple. So, what condition was the Old Testament in during Jesus' time?

I believe the Lord Jesus Christ is a good and reliable witness about these matters, don't you? After all, He is the Word (John 1:1) and He is God (1 Tim. 3:16). From a study of the Gospels, it is evident that the Lord Jesus knew the Hebrew text of the Old Testament. He quoted from it and clearly approved of it. From Him, we can establish that the Hebrew text in use in His time was an accurate and faithful copy of the originals. Several times, He commented on the Hebrew text that was current in His day.

> **Mt. 5:17-18** *Think not that I am come to destroy the law, or the prophets: I am not come to destroy, but to fulfil.*
> *18 For verily I say unto you, Till heaven and earth pass, one jot or one tittle shall in no wise pass from the law, till all be fulfilled.*

The "jot" and the "tittle" refer to Hebrew letters. Therefore, Jesus was clearly referring to the Hebrew Old Testament that was readily available in His time. The Lord mentions the Law and the prophets specifically here, and if He was concerned about the preservation and fulfillment of the Law (verse 18), certainly He was just as concerned about the preservation and fulfillment of the rest of the Old Testament. Verse seventeen is proof of that. The mention of the Law and the Prophets is proof that the Lord Jesus was referring to the Hebrew text of His day, not the so-called Greek "Septuagint." The Hebrew Old Testament was and is divided into three parts: The Law, the prophets, and the Writings. The "Septuagint" is not divided that way. According to this statement, the copy of the Hebrew OT in circulation at that time was a perfectly preserved copy of the original words, even to the "jot" and "title."

The Lord Jesus Christ had complete confidence in the perfect preservation of every word in the Hebrew Old Testament.

> **Lk. 24:27** *And beginning at **Moses** and all the **prophets**, He expounded unto them the things concerning Himself.*
> **Lk. 24:44** *And He said unto them, These are the words which I spake unto you, while I was yet with you, that all things must be fulfilled, which were written in the **law of Moses**, and in **the prophets**, and in **the Psalms**, concerning Me.*

Again, the Lord Jesus is quoting and teaching from the Hebrew Bible. He mentioned all three divisions of the Hebrew Old Testament in these verses: Law, Prophets, and Writings (the Psalms were part of the Writings). The Lord Jesus affirms the accuracy of the then current Hebrew OT by these comments.

Therefore, we have established that during the life of the Lord Jesus Christ there was an exact copy of God's original Hebrew and Aramaic words in circulation. So, this accurate Hebrew Old Testament had been preserved word-perfect from the time that Moses started writing the Law in about 1490 BC. If God preserved His Hebrew Old Testament Words that long, about 1500 years, why couldn't He preserve them another 2000 years? Did He suddenly lose His mind? Did He lose His power? What happened to the Word of God after the death and resurrection of the Lord Jesus Christ?

According to the Talmud, there was a standard copy of the Hebrew OT kept in the temple at Jerusalem for copyists to use. After the period of the gospels the Rabbis helped to preserve the text.

However, in 70 AD, the Roman General, Titus, crushed a rebellion of the Jews, destroyed the temple, and destroyed Jerusalem. Many Scripture manuscripts perished in the violence. This loss increased Jewish urgency to accurately preserve the text. It must be understood that from the time of the return from Babylonian exile to the time of Jesus Christ, the Old Testament had been thoroughly taught to the people. By the Lord's time on earth, the Hebrew text was firmly established in the Jewish heart and mind. After the 70 AD destruction, the urgency to preserve the text was very strong.

So, after the temple was destroyed, the Hebrew text was preserved by groups of Jewish scribes. The first of these, *the Tannaim* in the Holy Land, kept the text until about 250 AD. The second group was called the *Amoraim.* and they copied the text, carrying on the written text and the oral tradition of the pronunciation until about 500 AD. They were concentrated in the land of Israel and in Babylonia.

The Amoraim were followed in the 500's AD by the *Masoretes*, Jewish scholars located mainly in Tiberias, Jerusalem, and Babylonia. The text preserved by the Masoretes became known as the *Masoretic Text*. They preserved the Old Testament through extremely careful copying throughout the Middle Ages. Finally, the Hebrew Old Testament was printed on the newly invented moveable type printing press in 1488. Since then, preserving the Masoretic text has been easier. The Ben Chayim edition was printed by Daniel Bomberg in Venice in 1524-25. This edition, in effect, became the Received text of the Hebrew Old Testament.

The Ben Chayim Masoretic text was the standard text. In fact, it was the only text in use for over 400 years. As such, it bears the stamp of approval from God's people and is obviously the text which God preserved. This text follows the vast majority of the Hebrew manuscripts which have been discovered.

Another Hebrew text, the Kittel text, is commonly called the Ben Asher text. This text was based on a different Hebrew manuscript called the Leningrad manuscript. The Kittel text was published in 1937 and contains what is estimated to be about 20,000 changes from the Ben Chayim Masoretic text. Many of the differences between the two Hebrew texts are based upon vowel points. The vowel points were inserted into the Hebrew manuscripts by the Masoretes around the eighth century A.D. Admittedly, most of these changes from Ben Chayim are minor, but some of them are not. Since we stand on the verbal plenary inspiration of the Scriptures, even the minor changes should not have been done.

One example where your choice of Hebrew manuscripts will affect your translation comes from Joshua 21:36-37 ... The New Jewish Publication Society and other modern Hebrew Bibles do not contain these two verses. There are a few other places where the differences between the two manuscripts will affect the translation. Thus, the two Hebrew texts are similar but not quite the same. Obviously, this will affect your translation work. If your goal is to produce a translation that is as good as the King James Bible, then you must use the same Hebrew text that the King James translators used. And the King James translators used the Ben Chayim text. [12]

David Christian Ginsberg published an edition of the Ben Chayim text in 1894. That edition is now the standard text issued by the Trinitarian Bible Society. The greatly touted Dead Sea Scrolls, found in the Qumran caves, support our Masoretic text. God has preserved the Old Testament in the Masoretic Hebrew Text of the Ben Chayim tradition and the Ginsberg edition. God has preserved the Old Testament in the Hebrew Text that underlies the King James Bible.

Use of the King James Bible in Translating

We always recommend that the KJB is given a priority spot in Bible translating. We approach this subject in two ways.

First is the case of translators who can translate from Greek and Hebrew. To them, we recommend that they translate from the Greek and Hebrew texts as their primary source texts. However, they should be careful to use the KJB as a translation guide and give priority to the words used by the KJB. This should not be a slavish following of the KJB. The KJB has older English, and some words are no longer used or do not mean the same thing they did in 1611. An appropriate dictionary, like the 1828 edition of the Webster dictionary, should be used. Also, since the KJB is English, it has English idioms that may not work in other languages. Languages vary in how they use such things as prepositions, participles, and adjectives, and even nouns. These differences are also found between Hebrew and Greek and other languages. For example, Hebrew is a verbal type of language, and many things are spoken of in terms of action. English differs from Hebrew in this. Greek also has differences that will be looked at later.

Regardless of these differences, the meaning of words, grammar, and idioms transferred from the source text to the target text must be exactly the same.

The second approach to using the KJB in translating is in the case of translators who do not know Greek and Hebrew. I recommend that they do not delay translating until they have learned Greek and Hebrew. They may proceed to translate using the KJB as the source text, observing the same carefulness described in the previous paragraph. Also, there are Greek and Hebrew tools that can allow the translator to gain many of the benefits in knowing these languages. These tools should be used to supplement the KJB while translating.

Situations differ the world over and these situations affect what and how resources are used. A translator cannot have too many resources at his disposal, although there may be a limit due to cost. However, many resources are free, but most of them are in English. We recommend that the translators do the following two things. First, the translator should have a good dictionary that explains KJB words. We recommend several dictionaries that we have listed in the resources below. Second, learn to use the Greek and Hebrew tools in free Bible programs, such as E-sword.

Recommended Resources

Software:

1. **E-Sword (www.e-sword.net)**
   KJB
   KJB with Strong's numbers
   Greek TR with Strong's Numbers
   Hebrew Text with Strong's Numbers
   King James concordance
   Albert Barnes Notes
   Jamieson, Faussett and Brown Commentary
   John Gill's Synopsis
   John Wesley's Notes on the Bible
   Matthew Henry's Commentary
   Brown-Driver-Briggs Hebrew Definitions
   Scofield Reference Notes
   Easton's Bible Dictionary

Fausset's Bible Dictionary
International Bible Encyclopedia
Robinson's Morphological Analysis Codes
Webster's Dictionary of the English Language 1828
Vine's Expository Dictionary of New Testament Words (Not free, but important)
Vine's Expository Dictionary of Old Testament Words (Not free, but important)

2. E-sword is available free for I-phones and I-pads. it is also available for android phones, but it is this author's opinion that, as of this writing, my-sword (see below) is better for android phones.

3. My Sword: A free software similar to e-sword for android mobile phones. Download from the internet, https://www.mysword.info/

4. Sword Searcher: https://www.swordsearcher.com for $69.99. It contains the Hebrew text and is well worth it.

5. 1828 Webster dictionary is available free for computer at https://webstersdictionary1828.com and for android phones on Google Play.

6. Modern English dictionaries are available online at https://www.thefreedictionary.com and on Google Play and Apple store.

7. Archaic and Unfamiliar Words in the KJB https://www.northsidebaptistchurch.org.au/wp-content/uploads/Archaic-and-Unfamiliar-Words-in-the-KJB.pdf

Books:

1. Greek New Testament, Global Edition, (www.oldpathspublications.com)
2. Parallel KJB-TR New Testament, (www.oldpathspublications.com)

3. Hebrew Bible (Basis of the KJB) (Trinitarian Bible Society (www.tbs-sales.org)
4. A Practical Theology of Bible Translating, (www.oldpathspublications.com)
5. In Defense of the Textus Receptus, (www.amazon.com)
6. Issues in Missiology Volume III, Thoughts about Translation, Dr. Robert Patton, free pdf (www.theoldpathspublications.com) download
7. Analytical Greek Lexicon Revised (www.amazon.com)
8. Biblical Bible Translating, Charles Turner (www.amazon.com)
9. Vine's Expository Dictionary of Old and New Testament Words (www.amazon.com)
10. Brown, Driver and Briggs Hebrew Lexicon (www.amazon.com)
11. Word for Word Translating of the Received Texts (www.theoldpathspublications.com)
12. Strong's Exhaustive Concordance (www.amazon.com) Available in e-sword
13. Wilson's Old Testament Word Studies (http://www.christianbook.com)
14. Ancient Hebrew Lexicon of the Bible by Jeff Brenner (www.amazon.com)

4 The Formal Equivalent Method

Mark 7:34 *And looking up to heaven, he sighed, and saith unto him, Ephphatha, that is, Be opened.*

The Bible is not silent on the subject of Bible translating and it reveals the proper method of Bible translating. The method that seems to be most often used these days is called "Dynamic Equivalence." It boils down to slightly paraphrasing the Biblical text based on what the translator *thinks* it means. The words of the Bible mean little, but *meaning* is all important. However, God perspective is quite different. Both words and meaning are important to Him. The meaning is carried in the words, so different words can easily change the meaning. Once again, this chapter is a summary of information in the first book, *A Practical Theology of Bible Translating*.

> **Exodus 24:4** *And Moses wrote all the words of the LORD …*
> **Joshua 3:9** *Come hither, and hear the words of the LORD your God.*
> **1 Samuel 8:10** *And Samuel told all the words of the LORD unto the people …*
> **2 Chronicles 11:4** *And they obeyed the words of the LORD …*
> **Psalms 12:6** *The words of the LORD are pure words:*

John 1:42 says, "And he brought him to Jesus. And when Jesus beheld him, he said, Thou art Simon the son of Jona: thou shalt be called Cephas, which is by interpretation, A stone." The word *interpretation* means to *translate*. The Bible mentions translation in several other places. Each of those places and some similar places are listed below.

> **Mark 7:34** *And looking up to heaven, he sighed, and saith unto him, Ephphatha, that is, Be opened.*

John 1:38 *Then Jesus turned, and saw them following, and saith unto them, What seek ye? They said unto him, Rabbi, (which is to say, being interpreted, Master,) where dwellest thou?*
John 1:41 *He first findeth his own brother Simon, and saith unto him, We have found the Messias, which is, being interpreted, the Christ.*
John 9:7 *And said unto him, Go, wash in the pool of Siloam, (which is by interpretation, Sent.) He went his way therefore, and washed, and came seeing.*
Acts 4:36 *And Joses, who by the apostles was surnamed Barnabas, (which is, being interpreted, The son of consolation,) a Levite, and of the country of Cyprus,*
Acts 9:36 *Now there was at Joppa a certain disciple named Tabitha, which by interpretation is called Dorcas: this woman was full of good works and almsdeeds which she did.*
Acts 13:8 *But Elymas the sorcerer (for so is his name by interpretation) withstood them, seeking to turn away the deputy from the faith.*
Hebrews 7:1-2 *For this Melchisedec, king of Salem, priest of the most high God, who met Abraham returning from the slaughter of the kings, and blessed him; To whom also Abraham gave a tenth part of all; first being by interpretation King of righteousness, and after that also King of Salem, which is, King of peace;*
2 Peter 1:20 *Knowing this first, that no prophecy of the scripture is of any private interpretation.*

In each of the examples, the subject word is translated into a word in another language that has the same meaning. For example, in Hebrews 7:1-2, the name Melchisedec is interpreted. Melchisedec consists of two Hebrew words, *Melek* and *Tsedek*. Melek translates into *King* in English. Tsedek translates into *righteousness*. Since Melchisedec was a king, he was the king of Salem. *Salem* is a Hebrew word that translates to *peace*. Therefore, Melchisedec was the King of Peace and Righteousness. These translations are exactly correlated meanings of words between languages. Melchisedec was not a president or a governor. He was a Melek, a king. He was royal. That is what the word melek means and that is how it should be translated.

Melchisedek was not a king of calm and good. He was King of peace and righteousness. The source words are words with specific meanings, so the target words must be specific words with matching meanings.

This type of translating is called *formal equivalent translating*. Sometimes, it is also called *word-for-word translating.* This kind of translating refers to a translation approach which attempts to retain the language words and forms of the original as much as possible in the translation. The Bible translation text must accurately translate all of the words of the source text into words of equivalent meaning in the clearest manner according to the grammar of the target language, and at the same time read and flow naturally as in the standard spoken target language. To accomplish this, the translator translates each **word** in the source language into a **word** with the **nearest equivalent** meaning in the target languages. **Grammar** in the source language should be translated into **grammar** with the **nearest equivalent** meaning in the target language. Finally, **idioms** in the source language should be translated into **idioms** with the **nearest equivalent** meaning in the target language or be translated literally.

Word to the nearest Equivalent Word

Every word is important to God. Therefore, every word should be retained as much as possible, while also producing a target language translation that is grammatically accurate and has the same meaning. The usage and syntax of the target language must prevail. The target language translation must read clearly, smoothly, and naturally. When literal translating works well in the target language, it should be used.

Example: John 1:1

<u>**Literal Translation from the Greek:**</u> In beginning was the word and the word was with the God and God was the word.
<u>**KJB John 1:1**</u>: In the beginning was the Word, and the Word was with God, and the Word was God.

The English and Greek are almost exact word-for-word translations. Notice that a definite article was inserted between "in" and "beginning" (εν αρχη). Notice also that a definite article was left out before the last "word" (λογος). These actions were necessary because of English grammar. Finally, word order was reversed in the last phrase.   The final phrase contains a predicate nominative. The subject of the phrase has the article; therefore, it was placed first in the English translation.

Grammar to the Nearest Equivalent Grammar

A grammatical structure in one language may require a different grammatical structure in another language to have the same meaning. Sometimes the same grammatical structure used in two languages causes a different meaning or creates an unnatural construction.

Example 1: John 1:1

The grammar in John 1:1 is the same in Greek and English with the differences in the articles mentioned above.

Example 2: Matthew 2:8

Matt. 2:8 Literal Translation from Greek: And **having sent** them to Bethlehem, he said, **When you have gone**, diligently search for the young child. And when you have found, bring word to me, that I also, **having come**, may worship him.
Matt. 2:8 KJB: And **he sent** them to Bethlehem, and said, **Go** and search diligently for the young child; and when ye have found him, bring me word again, **that I may come** and worship him also.

The Greek verse has three participles. To translate these with the same grammar in English is awkward, not good English. To produce a clear natural translation in English requires that the participles not be translated as participles. The first is translated as an English active verb, the second as an imperative, and the third was translated as an English subjunctive. The words used have the same meanings and the meaning of the verse is the same in Greek and English. This kind of thing happens frequently in the New Testament. See the information in chapter Thirteen on how the KJB handled the Greek perfect tense, and review the discussion in chapter Fifteen on the historical present.

Idiom to the Nearest Equivalent Idiom

Idioms are expressions that are of two types. The first type is how a language expresses ordinary everyday meaning or figurative language. For example, we may say, "What is your name?" Germans may say it differently, "How are you called?" The second type of idiom is such that the words used bear little relationship to the real meaning. For example, the meaning of *the cat is out of the bag* has nothing to do with cats or bags. It means *the secret is revealed.* Sometimes an idiom cannot be translated literally and retain its meaning. The goal should be to translate it in a way that makes it accurate and sound natural in the target language. The following are some general guidelines for translating idioms.

1) Sometimes an Idiom is Translated by Modifying the Words or Grammar of the Source Language.

Biblical Example: Matthew 1:23

Literal Translation of the Greek: Behold, the virgin in stomach shall have and shall bring forth a son...
KJB Mat 1:23: Behold, a virgin shall be with child, and shall bring forth a son...

The Greek idiom "in stomach" is translated in the KJB as "be with child." Both expressions mean "to be pregnant."

Biblical Example: Romans 3:4

Rom 3:3-4 KJB For what if some did not believe? shall their unbelief make the faith of God without effect? **God forbid**
Literal Translation from Greek: May it not be! (the Greek does not use the word God. The KJB used an English idiom to translate the Greek idiom. The English idiom means the same as the Greek idiom.)
Meaning of English Expression: May it not be!

The German Luther translation has it *Das sei ferne! Far be it!* Each expression was an idiom with the same meaning in each language.

2) An idiom may be translated literally if the translator does not know the meaning of a particular idiom or when the literal translation is not seriously difficult to understand.

Biblical Example from the KJB: John 10:35

John 10:35 If he called them gods, unto whom the word of God came, and the scripture **cannot be broken ...**

"Cannot be broken" is a Jewish idiom that means "cannot be refuted." The phrase was often used by Jewish debaters to refer to any argument they believed to be irrefutable.

3) An idiom may be translated literally if it is explained in the Greater Context

Biblical Example: Philemon 1:7

Philemon 1:7 For we have great joy and consolation in thy love, because the **bowels** of the saints are refreshed by thee, brother.

The term "bowels" refers to the seat of the emotions and attitudes of a person. It is used in the sense we may use the word "heart." However, that is not clear from this verse.

It is clear, however, from Colossians 3:12

Colossians 3:12 Put on therefore, as the elect of God, holy and beloved, **bowels of** mercies, kindness, humbleness of mind, meekness, longsuffering;

4) An idiom may be translated literally by adding an explanation (even if that explanation is in the greater context)

Once again, the example is from Philemon 1:7

Philemon 1:7 For we have great joy and consolation in thy love, because the **bowels** of the saints are refreshed by thee, brother.

The added explanation is found in 1 John 3:17

1 John 3:17 But whoso hath this world's good, and seeth his brother have need, and shutteth up his **bowels *of compassion*** from him, how dwelleth the love of God in him?

The words "of compassion" are in italics in the KJB showing that they are not in the Greek text but were added by the translators to increase understanding. Adding words can be helpful to readers.

5) Idioms are difficult.

Sometimes, it is especially difficult to translate idioms. Normally, an idiom has a specific and clear meaning. Sometimes they can have more than one meaning. It can be difficult to determine whether to translate an idiom literally or according to its meaning. Translate idioms with much prayer and study.

6) A Warning!

Idiomatic translating can become a trap. Some translators use an idiomatic translating style in all or most of the Scriptures. The meaning of any phrase, sentence, or verse becomes dependent on the understanding and, sometimes, the bias of the translator. This is the condition of the translation method known as *Dynamic Equivalence*. It leads toward paraphrase, that is the Scriptures are translated into the words of the translator. The verse "I charge you by the Lord that this epistle be read unto all the holy brethren" (KJB-1 Thess. 5:27) is translated in the *Message* as "And make sure this letter gets read to all the brothers and sisters. Don't leave anyone out" (The Message-1 Th. 5:27). *This is NOT acceptable translating!*

The meaning of Scripture is set in the mind of God. The words God chose matter, and the translator must be faithful to render those words as closely and accurately as possible into the target language. True idioms normally have a *specific meaning*, not in any way dependent on the imagination of a translator. Idiomatic translating should be done *rarely*. The words of Scripture should only be translated idiomatically when it is *necessary* and when the translator *knows* the specific meaning of the idiom. God has called you to translate what is in the text, not your personal interpretation of what is in the text (2 Peter 1:20).

We do not have God's permission to take away from His Words or to add to them or to change them. God's Words are perfect. God knows every culture throughout history, and He has chosen words that will communicate to all of them. We do not do any of the cultures of earth a favor by changing the words God inspired. The meaning that God wishes to communicate to the world is intrinsic in the words themselves. The words ARE the meaning. Thought and meaning do not exist in a vacuum by themselves. Thought and meaning are carried by words. God's Words carry the meaning he wants the world to know. To change the words is to change the meaning.

5 Does Your Language Need a Translation?

So, you're a missionary or a minister. You have fulfilled your God given dream. After many years of preparation, you are now ready to go. You are ministering among the people. That was when you made a *startling* discovery. The Bible you have in their language is far from a good one. When you preach, you find yourself having to correct verses, because they were incorrectly translated. You may find that verses are missing in various places. It makes teaching difficult. *You may not realize this, but when you correct the current Bible in their language, you have become a Bible translator.*

On the other hand, you may be among a people group who does not have any Bible at all. Every time you tell them what God has said, you have to put the Bible's words into their language. When you do that, you have become a translator by necessity. The people cannot get God's words in their language unless you give the words to them. To do *that* you must *translate*.

In either case, you are faced with the reality that there is a need for translation work. In the first case, the current Bible needs to be updated and corrected to true accuracy or there may be a need for a new translation. In the second case, there is no choice. An entire Bible must be translated. You are face to face with the stark reality that, in both cases, the people need a true and accurate and faithful translation of God's word. You see the need and you are concerned.

Then you have another heart shaking revelation. It is YOU who sees the need. As far as you know, there is *no one else* who sees the need like *you* do. So suddenly, you *know* that God wants *you* to do *something* about it! But, what can you do? You're not a translator, right? You've not been trained, have you? You don't have the time, do you? You have to pray, plan, study, preach, teach, evangelize, and train.

Yes, you are busy. And, no, you are not trained in Bible translation. However, if you are a missionary, it is highly likely you are in one of the two circumstances described above. If so, you cannot avoid becoming a translator on some level. Those who have a poorly translated Bible need to know *what God has really said.* You may only tell them in teaching, but to do that you have to translate portions of the true word of God into their language. If you are ministering to a people who does not have a Bible at all, *everything* you tell them from God's mouth must be translated.

So, you need to do something to make the situation better. How are you to go about it? What steps do you need to take? Which step is first? In this article, we hope to answer these questions and to give you encouragement and direction.

Step One: Assess the Need

The first thing you must know is the need. You may have already seen some problems with the translation you have been using, but you need to know how extensive the problem is. You should find out about all the translations available in the national language and assess their quality.

Make a list of all the available translations in your ministry language. A good place to learn what translations are available is the internet. A simple search for "Bible translations in the ---- language" could reveal much. Another place to look is the *Ethnologue* at www.ethnologue.com. The Ethnologue is the most complete source of information available about the world's languages. Another source of information is the Bible Society of the country where you are. Many countries have a Bible Society that is a member of the United Bible Societies headquartered in England. Although the United Bible Societies is the organization that issues the Critical Greek New Testament, it is still a good source of information on available Bible translations. Also, do not overlook the local library if any are available on your field. Other pastors can also show you the translations with which they are familiar.

Research the origin, history, and availability of these translations. Who published the translation? When was it published? Who were the translators? Is there any connection between the translators and the United Bible Societies? Were the translators connected with any heretical group? Are the translations in print? Are any of them in digital format? If you can get copies of the translations, the introduction or preface will often give you all the information you need on their history and origin. You may be able to get this information from the internet or the local Bible Society.

Were the New Testaments of these translations from the Critical Greek Text or the Textus Receptus? Check the translations to determine their faithfulness and accuracy to the Hebrew Masoretic OT Text and Received Greek Text of the NT. This can easily be done by comparing the translations with the King James Version, which is the best representative of the Hebrew and Greek texts. Most Bible translations being done these days around the world are based on the United Bible Societies' Critical Greek Text or the Nestle-Aland Text (which is currently identical). Therefore, there are similar errors made in nearly all the translations.   A large fairly complete check-list is available on the Global Bible Translators' web site at: *https://www.bpsglobal.org/information-for-translators.html*

If you find a translation that was based on the Textus Receptus, you will have to evaluate its worth. Simply because a translation was based on the Textus Receptus does not automatically make it a good translation. The translation may have many translation errors. It may be so old and the national language has changed so much that the translation can no longer be used effectively. Changes in English would have made the 1611 King James Bible unusable if it had not gone through a revision in 1769 to extensively update the spelling. In China, one team made the determination not to revise the Peking Version (which was largely based on the TR). They determined that that translation had so many problems it would be easier to make a new translation.

List any other difficulties you have with your national translation. There may be problems in the translation you are using that are not related to the Critical Text. In China, the translators considered the style of writing in the Peking Version to be out of sync with how the public uses their language. In Togo the current version in the Ewe language uses a word for *baptism* that specifically means *sprinkling*. That makes it hard for a Baptist to use it.   After you have researched these things, you will have an answer for anyone who asks why a new translation is needed. You will be the resident expert on such matters.

Step Two: Prayer and Commitment

Every spiritual accomplishment begins with prayer. This circumstance is no exception. Jesus said, "The harvest truly is great, but the labourers are few: pray ye therefore the Lord of the harvest, that he would send forth labourers into his harvest" (Luke 10:2). You should pray that God would raise up translators. Ask God to raise up nationals from among those to whom you are ministering to be translators. We have seen this happen around the world: in Asia, in Africa, and in South America. God has been preparing and using nationals all over the world for many years. God is able to do the same where you are.

However, your prayers should not only center on asking God to raise up *someone else* to do the job. You need to ask God what He wants *you* to do. God has called you to be a missionary in this place. That obviously means you must give them "all the counsel of God" (Acts 20:27). How can you do that when they do not have a Bible, or they have an inadequate Bible? Someday in the future you will have to leave them and they will never see you again.   If you have not provided a true and accurate Bible to the people, how can you follow Paul's example in Acts 20:32, "And now, brethren, I commend you to God, and to the word of his grace?" As a missionary, you look at your field and think about what you must do to fulfill the ministry there. When you do that, remember "to him that knoweth to do good, and doeth it not, to him it is sin" (James 4:17).

Nevertheless, you're already busy enough, right? Besides, you haven't been trained in translation techniques. **Very few missionaries have had formal training in translation work.** Maybe you haven't thought about it, but when you studied the national language, you started by learning how the words of your mother tongue translate into that language. So, could it be that you *have* had *some* training in translation work? You speak at least two languages now. So, you are familiar with the differences between languages. Therefore, you have already learned a lot of what you need to know.

There are many ways to be involved in a translation project. Very possibly, you will be the leader of such a project, but you do not necessarily have to be a translator. The leader of the Chinese team was not very involved in actual translating. He provided the meeting schedule, the place to meet, translation advice, theological advice, and discussed special translation problems with the team. On the other hand, the team leader in Togo, West Africa, is one of the chief translators. The beginning team leader in Paraguay spoke Spanish, but he was not yet fully fluent in the tribal target language of the translation, Guarani. He motivated and guided the team. He made the Bible translation project a part of his Bible Institute program. So even if you are not a translator there are ways to lead a team. Here are some ways you can lead a team.

1. You can train your people on issues about the Bible text.
2. You can initiate the project
3. You can guide the project and keep it on track
4. You can recruit translators
5. You can organize the team
6. You can work with an international Translation organization to get the team motivated and trained, and to check their accuracy.
7. You can help the translators with resources they need.

It may be, as you pray for laborers and for guidance, that God will lay it on your heart to be directly involved in starting and leading the necessary translation project. You may have no idea what the next step is or how to recruit a team or how to organize them or anything about how to precede. At this point, that doesn't matter. Trust God. ***What is important, at this stage of the game, is that you fully commit yourself to the task as a calling from God.*** The task of translating the Bible will take years to finish. You must have a conviction in your heart that God wants you to help make it happen and be fully committed to the task. This is necessary if you are to remain faithful and finish it. However, you do not have to do it alone. God will raise up the translators. "He that handleth a matter wisely shall find good: and whoso trusteth in the LORD, happy is he" (Prov. 16:20).

Step Three: Survey the Situation

The very next thing you must do is gather some vital information. You need to look at the situation around you and determine what resources and difficulties are there. Gain a thorough understanding of your circumstances as they relate to a possible new Bible translation project.

First, look closely at the surrounding church situation. The first church to examine is your own. You, of course, are very familiar with the size and membership of your church. Are there members of your church who are concerned about problems they see in the Bible they use? Are there members who are familiar with the issues between the Critical Text and the Textus Receptus? Are there members of your church who you feel would be capable of translating the Bible? Have you started a Bible school with students who are capable?

Are there other churches of like faith and practice within driving distance? Are any of these churches and their pastors concerned with the condition of the local language Bible? The ideal situation for a translation project is to have multiple churches involved. The more churches involved, the more likely the nationals will accept the new translation. However, this is not always possible. Sometimes the project must begin small and grow slowly. If this is the case, do not let it discourage you from starting and continuing a new project.

Are there other missionaries in the country who share your concerns? Do these missionaries also share your conviction that the Textus Receptus is the correct New Testament Greek text? The knowledge gained in this survey will be part of the foundation of your efforts to build a support base for the translation project. Do not limit yourself to listing churches or missionaries of your own denomination only. There may be some of other denominations who will agree with your goals and be in favor of a translation project. The primary agreement needs to be on the textual foundation of the translation, the Textus Receptus and the KJB. You may not feel people from those churches should be part of the translation team, but they can be used to check the translation and, hopefully, they will be users of the translation after it is finished.

Step Four: Build a foundation

Begin by educating your church about the need. Teach them about the issues of the Bible text. If you have a Bible institute, this is especially important knowledge for Bible students to have. Teach your people what your concerns about the Bible translation are and tell them you believe God wants you to help fix these problems. Look closely at your people. Are any of them concerned about the national Bible translation? Are any of them capable of helping with a translation project?

When educating your people, especially in a Bible institute, it may be helpful to get *A Practical Theology of Bible Translating.* It teaches the doctrine of the inspiration and preservation and authority of the Bible, the Biblical basis for Bible translating, basic Biblical principles of translating, how those principles apply to the practice of translating and the history of the correct Bible text and gives answers to many of the textual issues that trouble Bible students.

Continue by approaching the Pastors and missionaries you identified in step three. Ask them about their thoughts concerning the local language Bible. Share with them your concerns and why you have them. Ask them if they would be supportive of a Bible translation project. You are not trying to raise financial support with this. You are seeking for moral and prayer support. You want the pastors and missionaries to get behind a translation project, as much as possible. Ask if they would be willing to attend a Bible translation training conference.

It is possible that you will gain little support from other churches and missionaries. You must be ready for this. It is an intimidating and scary prospect, but you may have to proceed without their help. This will be a time when your commitment and certainty that God has called you to translation work will be severely tested. I trust that, as a missionary, you are committed to doing God's will no matter who helps you and who rejects you. As a missionary you are willing to carry on God's work in spite of no help, recognition, or thanks. You know that you labor only for the glory of God and expect a rich reward from Him, who is the great Physician, the great Encourager, the great Healer, and the Giver of great power, strength, and success. If this is the circumstance you find yourself in, *do not give up*. Martin Luther began his great German translation alone. Later, God gave him the help of others. Adoniram Judson labored in translation work alone for many years. Many others have done so. Do not give up. Choose two to six translation helpers from your church and proceed.

Step Five: Begin to Identify a Potential Team

Start making a list of potential translation team members. Look for individuals who love God and are seeking to live an obedient Christian life. This is very important. Look for those who are fluent in the target language, preferably those who speak it as their mother tongue. Seek individuals who are proficient in the spelling and grammar of that language. Find people who have knowledge and experience reading various types of literature in the target language. In addition to this, look for those individuals who are proficient in Greek and/or in a major language that has a good Textus Receptus based translation, such as English, Spanish, or French. This is a tall order, but God is a great God who provides. Keep these people in mind and invite them later when you have a Bible translation training conference.

Translation teams do not have to be large. The King James Version translation committee consisted of forty-seven individuals, but historically it seems that few projects have had a team that large. Teams around the world are not usually large. One team in Chinese started with six individuals and have added three or four more over time. A team in Togo had fifteen workers. A team in Paraguay had more, but they made the project a part of their Bible institute. A team that translated the first Isan New Testament for the Isan people of Northeast Thailand had two and sometimes a third person, consisting of the missionary and one or two translation helpers. However, the more you have, the better the translation can be.

Finally, call on an international translating ministry to help you train the translators.

Conclusion

Your Bible situation and problem is one of several thousand just like it. There are about 7,000 languages on earth. Over 3,000 languages do not have any published Scripture. Many hundreds, even thousands have inadequate or poorly translated Bibles. Our God is a wise and mighty God, and He is using many of these translations in spite of their short comings. Nevertheless, the Lord Jesus Christ has declared, "It is written, Man shall not live by bread alone, but by every word that proceedeth out of the mouth of God" (Mt. 4:4). It is God's will that His people have all of His words. It is imperative that every missionary be sensitive to this need. Bible translating is a greatly neglected mission ministry, especially among Bible-believing fundamental missionaries. When it comes time for you to leave your mission field, will you be able to confidently say with Paul, "And now, brethren, I commend you **to God**, and **to the word of his grace**, which is able to build you up, and to give you an inheritance among all them which are sanctified" (Acts 20:31)?

6 General Rules of Translating

In 1604, King James issued fifteen rules for the translation of the King James Bible. General rules are important to help keep a translation project on track working toward its goal of a true, trustworthy, accurate, faithful, and complete translation. These general rules will help to accomplish that task.

1. Every Bible translation project must be preceded by, continued with, and closed in much prayer for His guidance, wisdom, assistance, and grace for the needs of each person, family, and church involved.

2. All translators and other helpers with the translation, including checkers and testers and other assistants, must be born again by faith in the Lord Jesus Christ. They must be baptized members of a Bible believing, Gospel preaching local church. They must be in good standing and blameless in the eyes of the church. The church where they have their membership should be one, which maintains baptism by immersion after salvation and is not a participant in the charismatic movement.

3. All the translators must translate the words of Scripture honestly and truthfully, without bias. Each translator must endeavor to produce a translation that is free from private interpretation. "Knowing this first, that no prophecy of the scripture is of any private interpretation" (2 Peter 1:20).

4. The translators must give up any idea of ownership of the translation. Only God owns His Word.

5. The highest financial standards will be maintained. Records will be kept for every donation received and every expenditure made. No money donated for the translation project will be spent for any other reason. If a donor gives a

gift and says it is for a specific purpose, the money will be spent for that purpose only. If the translation leadership wishes to spend the money for a different purpose, they must get the permission of the donor or return the money to the donor. "Avoiding this, that no man should blame us in this abundance which is administered by us: providing for honest things, not only in the sight of the Lord, but also in the sight of men" (2 Corinthians 8:20, 21).

6. The foundation source text of the translation must be the Scrivener edition of the Textus Receptus and the Ginsburg Edition of the Ben Chayim Hebrew text. The King James Bible is to be followed as the primary translation guide. The KJB can be the primary source text when the translators do not know Greek and Hebrew. In that case, the Greek and Hebrews tools mentioned in the previous lesson will be used to gain as much benefit from those languages as possible.

7. The method of translation shall be formal equivalent, which is defined as 1) source language word to the nearest equivalent target language word, 2) source language grammar to the nearest equivalent target language grammar, which in some cases may be different to maintain the same meaning, and 3) source idioms to the nearest equivalent target idioms.

8. The names of the Apostles and Prophets, the writers of Bible books, and the names of the books are to be retained, as close as may be, according to how they are commonly used.

9. The old target language words that are commonly used as translations of doctrinal words such as salvation, grace, justification, propitiation, baptism, church, and others are to be kept if they express the truth of Scripture. Some of them may not correctly express the truth of Scripture. The Chinese Authorized Version maintains this rule, but they have discovered that a new word that more closely expresses doctrinal truth must occasionally be used. John 1:1, in the Chinese Union Version used a term for "word" that was associated with the false religion *Daoism*. It was necessarily to change it.

10. When a Word has various meanings, choose the one that best fits the context of the verse, the general passage, and fits associated cross references.

11. The division of the chapters and verses are not to be altered.

12. Do not add marginal notes in the first edition. Notes can be kept for potential later use, such as creating a future study edition. These notes can include possible alternative translations of certain words and phrases, explanations of the text, and cross references.

13. Each translator should keep a journal that explains his reasons for choosing the words, grammar, and idioms he used in the portion of the translation work he is doing. This journal will be open and available to the other translators. All translators will share copies of their journal with the record keeper regularly and often.

14. An up-to-date copy of the translation should be always kept on a specific computer and a backup copy must be maintained at a different location than the location of that computer.

15. The operation of the translation team will include as much checking and testing of the translation as possible.

16. The churches will be kept continually informed of the progress of the translation effort. The churches will also be trained in the need of a new translation.

7 The Discipline of a Translator

Galatians 6:1 Brethren, if a man be overtaken in a fault, ye which are spiritual, restore such an one in the spirit of meekness; considering thyself, lest thou also be tempted.
Proverbs 24:16 For a just man falleth seven times, and riseth up again:
1 Timothy 3:2 A bishop then must be blameless

Bible translating is slow work, and it mostly takes place behind closed doors in a study. Nevertheless, it is also public work. People will be aware that it is going on and the translators will be in the public eye. Because of this, translators must maintain a blameless reputation, just as a pastor must.   If that reputation is not maintained, it may reflect badly on the translation and the glory of God. In which case, something must be done. Discipline is not pleasant, and we hope it will never become necessary. However, there is the possibility that it will, and you must be ready with as much of a plan as you can.

No One is Exempt from Struggle

God created man in His image. What does that mean? It means a number of things, but I believe one thing it means is that we are a trinity like Him. "And the very God of peace sanctify you wholly; and I pray God your whole **spirit** and **soul** and **body** be preserved blameless unto the coming of our Lord Jesus Christ" (1 Thessalonians 5:23). When we trust the Lord Jesus Christ to be our Savior, our dead spirit (Eph. 2:1) is regenerated, born again (Titus 3:5; John 3:3), and our faith provides the salvation of the soul (Heb. 10:38), but nothing was done for the body. There is a problem with the flesh, due to the fall. "For I know that in me **(that is, in my flesh,)** dwelleth no good thing: for to will is present with me; but how to perform that which is good I find not" (Rom. 7:18). There is a nature in mankind that leads every individual to sin, and that nature is still in the Christian after he receives Christ.

Most of the problems a Christian has are from the flesh. "This I say then, Walk in the Spirit, and ye shall not fulfil the lust of the flesh.

For the flesh lusteth against the Spirit, and the Spirit against the flesh: and these are contrary the one to the other: so that ye cannot do the things that ye would" (Gal. 5:15-16). Even though God has freed us from slavery to sin (Col. 3:1-3; Rom. 6:6-7) and provided all we need to live godly lives (2 Peter 2:2-4). No matter how dedicated we are to Christ, we have a lower nature that struggles to dominate us and lead us into sin. We will either follow the flesh or the Spirit (Gal. 5:16, 18). As long as we live, the possibility of failure lives with us. "Ye have not yet resisted unto blood, striving against sin" (Heb. 12:4).

Personal Discipline

Paul's determination was the keep control of his flesh. "But I keep under my body, and bring it into subjection" (1 Corinthians 9:27). God has made provision for godly living, and He works in you to help you do it (Phil. 2:13), but He doesn't do it for you. Your will and effort play a key part. "Wherewithal shall a young man cleanse his way? by **taking heed thereto** according to thy word. With my whole heart **have I sought thee:** O let me not wander from thy commandments. Thy word **have I hid in mine heart**, that I might not sin against thee" (Ps. 119:9-11).

So, what do we do when we sin. John made it clear that "when" is the right word (1 John 1:8, 10; 2:1) and told us what to do when that happens. "If we confess our sins, he is faithful and just to forgive us our sins, and to cleanse us from all unrighteousness" (1 John 1:9). To confess our sins means that we agree with God's attitude about our sins. Hang in there. When you fall, get up and keep going. "For a just man falleth seven times, and riseth up again" **(Proverbs 24:16).**

Overtaken in a Fault

Sometimes, sin is not just a one-time thing. It can be persistent. "Know ye not, that to whom ye yield yourselves servants to obey, his servants ye are to whom ye obey; whether of sin unto death, or of obedience unto righteousness (Romans 6:13, 16)?" If you yield to sin, you may find it easier to yield to the same type of sin a second time. A third time is even easier. Each time you confess and get up to go on, but the third time leads to a forth and a fifth and a sixth. Finally, it becomes a habit to yield and you find yourself helpless to quit. You may even be addicted. Recovery and victory are possible, but you do not find a way to do it. "For that which I do I allow not: for what I would, that do I not; but what I hate, that do I ... for to will is present with me; but how to perform that which is good I find not. For the good that I would I do not: but the evil which I would not, that I do" (Rom. 7:15, 18-19). This describes a condition in which all too many Christians find themselves.

How does one deal with such a chronic condition, overtaken in a fault? It might be possible for a Christian to find a way to deal with this kind of fault or sin alone, but outside help may be needed. The Scriptures advise us, "Brethren, if a man be overtaken in a fault, ye which are spiritual, restore such an one in the spirit of meekness; considering thyself, lest thou also be tempted. Bear ye one another's burdens, and so fulfil the law of Christ" Gal. 6:1-2). Very often this type of problem will require the help of at least one other person. Remember, that we are to love one another (John 13:34-35) and forgive one another (Eph. 4:32) and bear one another's burdens.

Public or Private?

Whether a translator's sin or fault is public or private makes a difference in how it is treated. If it is a personal sin that is entirely private, I imagine none of us would want to shout it from the rooftop. God clearly sees it. It should be confessed to God and steps should be taken to forsake it. If it is private, but a persistent "fault" that you cannot overcome, then confess it and bring at least one other person into it who is willing to help you overcome it.

However, if the sin is publicly known, it is a different situation altogether. A Pastor is to be blameless in the sight of his congregation and the world (1 Tim. 3:2). How much more should this be true for a person who is translating the Word of God? The Lord said of His Word, "thou hast magnified thy word above all thy name" (Ps. 138:2). The glory of God's name is of utmost importance, but His glory depends on the truth of His Word. God chose *holy* men through whom to inspire His Word (2 Peter 1:21). Surely, He wishes holy people to translate His Word. If a translator is walking openly in sin, it will take away from God's glory and defame His Word. It may cause the public to reject the new translation.

Public sin may be serious enough and the potential damage to the translation and the glory of God great enough that the translator may no longer be allowed to continue as a part of the translation team.

This is especially true if the transgressor is unrepentant. The team may need to ask him to step down.

Something like this happened in Paul's ministry (1 Cor. 5). The sin was especially bad, and the one sinning was unrepentant. Paul advised the church to dismiss him. Later, Paul advised restoration after the individual had repented and forsaken his sin. "Sufficient to such a man is this punishment, which was inflicted of many. So that contrariwise ye ought rather to forgive him, and comfort him, lest perhaps such a one should be swallowed up with overmuch sorrow" (2 Corinthians 2:6). It may be that the translator has damaged his reputation too badly to return to the translation team in the judgement of the other translators and their pastors. Nevertheless, they should confirm their love for him and do all they can to restore him to a fruitful walk with Christ.

Discipline is necessary in the Christian life, especially in personal discipline. Not only that, but for the glory of God, a Christian must be careful to maintain a good name before the world and other Christians. "A good name is rather to be chosen than great riches, and loving favour rather than silver and gold" (Proverbs 22:1). When personal discipline fails, it must be dealt with. Private failure can be dealt with privately. When the failure involves a translator, it can affect the translation negatively if it is not speedily dealt with. When the failure is public, it may require the removal of the translator from the team, and it may have to be dealt with publicly.

8 The Organization of the Translation Team

Every local situation is different. For this reason, there is no single method of organization or operation of the Bible translation team that fits every situation. Whatever type of organization is used, it is imperative that a lot of checking and testing be built into the plan. There are three basic plans of organizing a team and there can be variations of each.

Single Translator Approach

Ron Myers is a missionary to the twenty-two million plus Isan people of Northeast Thailand. The Isan have never had any Scripture in their Isan language until Ron Myers began to translate. The "single-translator" has been his method all along. However, this does not mean he did all his work alone. He had a national translation helper, sometimes two. It is very difficult for a single translator to do his work completely alone.

This method has been used by many translators. Sometimes it is the only way, especially in situations where there is no Bible and few churches. It is always best to have one or more national helpers, who can aid with the language, even if they are unsaved. This method was also used by Robert Patton, who translated the Bible into Sranantongo in Suriname, South America. It was the method used by Adoniram Judson in Burma (now Myanmar). It was often the method used by William Carey and his associates in India. Nevertheless, this method is not the ideal method. More translators can equal more accuracy.

A Single Team Approach

The method of having a single team with several translators is better than a single translator. The single translator method may have national helpers and in that sense is a team. However, there is only one translator. The national helpers aid in checking the accuracy of the translation. In the single team, all the team members are translators, and they all help check the translation. A single team may consist of as few as two translators and may operate in various ways.

The single team is used by the Chinese translation team, of the Chinese Authorized Version, and consists of about 6-8 translators. Two of the team are primary translators. They try to agree on the translation of each verse, but numerous disagreements and difficulties arise. Issues are brought to the entire team for discussion and resolution. Many of these issues are very difficult to resolve and slow down the translation progress, but they work through it.

A Kenyan team translating the Bible into Swahili is a single team. They meet nearly every weekday and translate a certain portion of scripture. All the translating and resolving of disagreements are done together. The team consists of five individuals.

The single team is also used by a Togo team translating the Bible into Ewe. They have about 10 in the team. Each one is assigned a different portion of Scripture to translate and a certain period of time to complete it. After everyone has completed their work, the whole team meets to review it and come to a final translation on each portion.

Multiple Teams Approach

Multiple teams require a minimum total of eight to ten translators to be effective. Ten translators will allow two teams of five. The main advantage of multiple teams is "For by wise counsel thou shalt make thy war: and in multitude of counsellors there is safety" (Proverbs 24:6). Since multiple teams means multiple translators, it also means multiple opinions that can ultimately lead to the best word choices. Also, it means more eyes are checking each word, leading to the greatest accuracy. It can also mean faster progress. It allows the maximum review and checking of a translation with the maximum number of people before the final translation is decided.

Nevertheless, if there are only four, five, or six translators, the best choice is a single team.

A translation team may begin with one team, but, in the course, of time, new translators may be added, and they will transition into a multiple team structure. This happened with a Bukusu translation team in Western Kenya. They started with a single team of six. Later, the team added four more translators and split into two teams. Team one is translating the Gospel of John, and team two is translating Romans.

Since Greek and Hebrew is an important skill in translating, the ideal situation is to have at least one person proficient in those languages in each team. At a minimum, each team needs someone skilled in working with Greek and Hebrew tools in e-sword. Another way to do this is to have the draft translation checked by someone who is trained in Greek and Hebrew. More information on the operation of multiple teams will be given in the chapter on checking and testing the translation.

The King James Bible was translated using a multiple team approach. Originally, 54 men were appointed in 1604 to the "Authorized Version" translation committee. Some died or withdrew before the work began, so the final number of men who worked on it was 47. They were divided into six teams with two teams in each of three locations in England: Oxford, Cambridge, and Westminster. The Bible was divided among the teams in the following manner:

1. **First Westminster Company**, translating from Genesis to 2 Kings:
2. **First Cambridge Company**, translated from 1 Chronicles to the Song of Solomon:
3. **First Oxford Company**, translated from Isaiah to Malachi:
4. **Second Oxford Company**, translated the Gospels, Acts of the Apostles, and the Book of Revelation:
5. **Second Westminster Company**, translated the Epistles:
6. **Second Cambridge Company**, translated the Apocrypha (a group of non-canonical books, some of which presumably depict history during the inter-testament period).

The companies worked on the translation in the following manner.

1. Each translator made his own translation of a passage. Each translated passage or book was reviewed by each of the other members of his team.
2. Differences of opinion were discussed and resolved within the team until each team produced one unified translation of that portion of Scripture.

3.   When the entire team was agreed, they sent the final translated book to the other five teams for review. The other teams would note their differences of opinion, give the place and the reasons why they do not consent to the translation, and send them back to the original team.

4. The differences were reviewed by a special committee of revisors consisting of the chief individuals of the six companies.

5. Any place of especially difficult to understand was to be sent to any learned man in England for his judgement and comment. Any of the clergy could comment on the translation.

6. Nothing was done in secret.

7. Finally, the entire translation was reviewed once again by a "Committee of Two," Miles Smith and Thomas Bilson. After this, the translation was prepared for printing.

Personnel Needed for the Project

There are other jobs besides translating that need to be done. A list of all the jobs follows.

1. The Translators
2. The Churches
3. An over-all director or leader of the whole translation and a leader of each team (if multiple teams approach is used) should be chosen
4. Chief Records Keeper
5. Typists
6. An Expert in the Grammar of the Target Language
7. Checkers
8. Testers
9. Translation Advisor

The Translators

The translators are the persons responsible for moving the words, grammar, and idioms of the source language into the target language. Many say that it is best that the translators be mother-tongue speakers of the target language. This has advantages that should be self-evident. The mother-tongue speaker has knowledge and understanding of the language and culture that others may not have. Also, a mother-tongue speaker does not need a long period of training to learn the target language like a foreigner would. However, a mother-tongue speaker will most likely need extensive training in the source language.

It is not always possible to have a translator who is a mother tongue speaker, especially in pioneer situations or other times when there are no such people available who are qualified. It is not always necessary to have such a translator, if someone else is available, who speaks and reads the target language like a national. Nevertheless, if a foreign national is the translator, he should have one or more mother-tongue speakers available as translation helpers.

The Churches

If you are not in a pioneer ministry where there are no other churches, you will need to get the support of as many churches as you can. Every translation project needs many supporting churches who will be able to give advice, pray for the translators, pray for all other needs of the project, and support the project financially.

The Director

Someone must be the overall director of the translation project. In addition, in a multiple team setting, each team must have a leader. It will be the responsibility of the overall director to appoint team leaders. It is the responsibility of the director to seek out supporting churches and maintain contact with them. He may recruit others to help with these responsibilities.

In some areas, it may be best to form an advising committee made up of leaders from supporting churches. When the translation is controlled by a single church, the committee is made up of leaders from that church. The project director will be a member of this committee. The responsibilities of the committee are below. The director and the translation team share these responsibilities and exercise them in the absence of a committee.

1. To help select the translators and others who will fill other jobs.
2. to help keep the churches informed.

3. To encourage others to pray for the translators and the needs of the project.
4. To help raise finances from the churches.
5. To encourage church members to help check and distribute the translation.
6. To advise concerning the format of the published Bible and choice of publisher.

When working with an international translation ministry, the ministry should be an advisor to the coordinating committee and should be considered a partner in the translation. This is important because such a ministry can provide Bible translation advising on specific challenges the translators will face.

Chief Records Keeper

The Chief Records Keeper should be one of the translators, since he will need to be at all the translation meetings. His job is to keep a master copy of the translation and to maintain a backup copy of it. Additionally, he makes sure that each translator and the translation advisor has an up-to-date copy of the translation. In a multi-team environment, each team should have a record keeper to maintain a copy of the work of that team and to pass on a copy to the chief records keeper.

Typist (s)

Typists may be needed in a couple of situations. Often translation teams will have a shortage of computers. So, some or all of the translators must hand write their translations. One or more typists will be needed to put the translation in digital form in a computer. Secondly, someone will be needed to edit and format the translation. It is most likely that the translators will not have the time to do these jobs. The typist fulfills the following responsibilities.

1. Type the working drafts for the translators.
2. Type the first draft for making copies to be examined by the checkers and used by the testers.

3. Type the drafts after the checkers and testers are finished, and after they have been corrected by the translators.
4. Type, edit, and format the manuscript for publication.

An Expert in the Grammar of the Target Language

Oftentimes, the translators are not expert in the grammar of the target language. This is true, even if the target language is their mother tongue. Sometimes the mother-tongue speaker will speak the target language in a local dialect. That is, some of the words they speak and the grammar they use may not be easily understood by speakers of the same language in different locations. Swahili is an example. The way Swahili is spoken varies in Kenya, Tanzania, and Uganda. Due to this, the translators of Swahili had to study *standard* Swahili grammar, so that their Bible translation work could be easily read by Swahili speakers in all areas. The same is true elsewhere, even in English. I was born in southeastern Kentucky. When I moved to Ohio at nine years old, I encountered some boys who took my hat. As I ran back and forth trying to get the hat back, I yelled, "Givi-cheer! Givi-cheer!" They did not understand me. In standard English, I would have said, "Give it here!" But, I said it with such a heavy accent and strange pronunciation that they did not understand. I found out then that I would have to learn to speak English in a more standard way if I was going to communicate well. Therefore, it is important to have someone available who can be consulted on the standard target language.

The Checkers

These individuals could also be called reviewers. Their responsibility is to proofread the translation and to check portions of it in various ways to find anything wrong in it. They should study it carefully and write out all their observations and the reasons why they think it was translated wrong or could be better. They should include any suggestions for improvements. All their observations and comments should be returned to the translators in a reasonable period of time.

It would not be too many if there were fifteen to twenty of these individuals. They should include different types of people: men and women, young and old, well-educated and less educated, people with a lot of Bible knowledge and people with little Bible knowledge, young Christians and older Christians, pastors and laymen.

Do not wait until a whole Bible book is done to start the checking process. It is best, if it is done in short segments. I suggest that each chapter be checked after the rough draft of that chapter is done. Give it to a few individuals who have agreed to help you check the translation. Let them give you feed back. Checking is easier to do if it is done a chapter at a time.

Be careful to remember that checking is a process that the translators themselves must also do. They should proofread, check the spelling and format, the accuracy, and whether the language flows naturally. Again, it should be done in small increments.

The Testers

Translation testing is just that, putting the translation to the test in the real world. It takes place after a substantial portion of the translation, at least several chapters, are finished to a rough draft or first draft stage. Testing can be done in teaching, preaching, Bible studies, etc. More details will be given on this and on translation checking later.

The Translation Advisor

The Translation Advisor is a professional consultant and minister who is part of an international translation ministry. His job is to give advice, help, and training. The Advisor usually works with projects in various languages. An Advisor can train all members of the translation project. He discusses the translation with the translators, he answers questions that arise, he helps with other issues that come up, he volunteers suggestions and ideas, he helps check the accuracy and quality of the translation, and that it meets the standard for publication. The following are ways that Translation Advisors can help.

1. **Training**: They can give more in depth training in all of Bible translation principles and in each of the practical steps of translating, checking, and testing the translation.
2. **Provide translation consulting by internet conferencing and in person onsite:** They can help the translators to be consistent in applying the translation principles. They can give

guidance and advice in applying the principles of translation, checking, and testing to your particular situation.

3. Provide theological consulting: Having a group that is ready to help with the translator's understanding of the Biblical text is a key element to success.

4. Provide help with accuracy checking: They can review back-translations (explained later) and compare them with the King James Version and the Greek and Hebrew texts. Once again, this can be done via the internet or during personal visits, they can help with accuracy checking and testing of the translation.

6. Representation to churches worldwide: They can represent you and the translation project in churches of the USA and various other churches worldwide.

7. Assist with printing: They can help with formatting for printing, fund raising, and finding printers and publishers.

9 The Operation of the Translation Team

2 Corinthians 8:10 And herein I give my advice: for this is expedient for you, who have begun before, not only to do, but also to be forward a year ago.

11 **Now therefore perform the doing of it;** that as there was a readiness to will, so there may be a performance also out of that which ye have.

Now that you understand the personnel positions you need to fill, it is time to proceed. Once the translators are ready to meet, there are four things to do immediately. **First,** decide if you will have a single translator, a single team, or a multi-team approach. **Second**, the team must choose who will be the team leader or director. **Third**, one of the translators must be chosen to be the chief records keeper. He has the responsibility to keep a back-up copy and help all the translators to stay up to date with their copies. **Four,** discuss who may be able to fill the other jobs, especially the grammar expert. Hopefully you will find many volunteers wishing to do these things for the Lord's sake alone, just as they do many other things in church life.

Before You Translate a Single Word

There is something you should do before you start translating. You should read and study the Bible passage you are about to translate. The better you understand the Bible, the easier your job of translating will be. Study it in English and (if you can) read it in its original language. If you have not learned Greek and Hebrew, you can still look up word definitions in e-sword. I included a chapter full of instruction on studying and understanding the Bible in *A Practical Theology of Bible Translating.*

First Steps to Get Started

First, Create the plan:

1. Decide if you will have one team or multiple teams.

2. If it will be multiple teams, decide who will be on each team.

3. Decide what portions of the Bible each team, or individual if one team, will be responsible to do.

4. Translate John first and then Romans. John is written in a very simple way with simple vocabulary. So, it is an easy book to start with and is easier to translate than Romans. John and Romans can be used for evangelism when they are finished. John/Romans booklets are used for evangelism all over world.

5. Individuals should be assigned the responsibilities to type, proofread, check grammar, and other tasks.

6. Finally, decide on a name for your translation. Two examples are "Traditional Text Korean Bible" in Korea and "The Chinese Authorized Version" in China.

Second, set some realistic goals:

1. Be flexible but not too flexible. The goals may not always be met, but they give you something to work toward and hold the team accountable.

2. Setting goals gives you a way to measure your progress and motivates you to continue. So, do not just set end goals, that is when you will finish a whole book. Set intermediate goals. When will you finish the first five chapters of John, then the next five, and so on.

3. Goals should include how many verses you want to translate per week.

4. When you decide on number 3, you can calculate when you will finish your intermediate and your end goals.

5. Do not be frustrated if you find your goals are not realistic or if things happen that slow your progress.

Third, the members of each team should meet at least once a week.

1. This will ensure each translator is proactive and the burden does not get placed behind other priorities of life.

2.   In the meetings, you will discuss translation questions, exchange translated portions to check, return portions that have been checked, discuss problems or errors that have been discovered, and go over anything else that is of concern.

Fourth, as you progress make a list of key words or terms that all translators need to use.

1. As has been previously mentioned, traditional theological terms should be retained unless they present a false view. Many national speakers may have learned traditional doctrinal terms and should not be required to learn different terms unless necessary. Retaining the traditional terms will result in greater acceptance of the new translation by those who are already accustomed to them. However, each theological term must be considered before being put into the new translation. Any theological terms retained should carry accurate meanings according to Biblical doctrine and agree with the Greek and Hebrew terms in meaning.

2. It is highly recommended that a table of key terms be constructed which shows source language to target language word choices. This will become invaluable in achieving a high level of consistency and accuracy in the translation.

3. Context will dictate changes from time to time but building this list will help in being consistent. The key word list may include the main word you will use in translation but also several synonyms which can be used from time to time, if the context allows it. The list will evolve as you work, but it will help in consistency, proficiency, and speed of translation.

Fifth, as each chapter is completed, it should be proof-read and checked.

The proofreading and checking process should begin as soon as the first chapter is translated. If you wait until a whole book is finished, the proof-reading and checking process becomes almost overwhelming. Also, decide if a person or persons will be assigned the task of doing back-translations (see the lesson on checking and testing the translation). The first group to begin checking is the translation team.

Sixth, preserve the Work Securely.

1.   We strongly recommend that each team use a central computer, removable storage device, or cloud storage for saving their work.

2. The records keeper has the following responsibilities:

a. Make a backup copy after each meeting of the translators. He must do this even if the working copy of the translation is saved on the web. Redundant backups are safer.
b. Make sure each translator who has a computer gets an up-to-date copy of the translation at the end of each meeting.
c.   If the team is working with an international translation ministry, they may want the record keeper to send them a copy of each chapter when it is finished or revised.
d. The redundancy of this plan 1) ensures that the translation work will not get lost in case of an emergency and 2) that no one person will control the translation.

3. If you choose to use cloud storage, we recommend that you use Mega Cloud Storage which offers a generous 20 gigabytes of free storage. This is more than sufficient for the many and varied documents that your teams will generate. Also, the data is encrypted which provides a high level of security for your work (https://mega.io). Also, Windows or Google cloud can be used.

Seventh, format the document.

1. The teams may be working on more than one computer.

2.   Make sure you choose programs, fonts, and document layouts that will be common to everyone.

Eighth, non-conformity to rules.

1. Immediately address any violation of the established rules.

2. Absolutely do not allow *prideful strife*.

3. These will cripple progress, destroy teamwork, and pride will quench the Spirit.

Ninth, become familiar with the copyright laws of your country.

1.   This is especially important when your target language already has a Bible translation. If it does, it is highly likely that the current Bible is from the critical text and that is the reason you are compelled to translate a new accurate Bible from the correct Greek and Hebrew texts or the KJB.

2. If the current Bible is from the critical text, it is also highly likely that you will easily make enough changes to satisfy copyright laws. Nevertheless, be familiar with the law. The specific area of the law in the USA is "derivative copyrights." This is probably the same in many other countries.

Tenth, keep and preserve all written notes you make. These are the history of the translation.

A Suggested Step-by-Step Plan

This plan can be followed for each chapter translated. This suggested plan is based on a four-person single team, having weekly meetings.

1. Four members do the translating and meet weekly.
2. Pastors and the translation advisor give advice on theology.
3.   The translators and several others check each chapter for grammar, spelling, accuracy, etc.
4.   One translator can be the records keeper. The typist can either be one of the translators or a fifth person.
5. Procedure:

Step One: One possible procedure is to divide a chapter or two into portions and assign a portion to each translator. Each translator works on his portion during the week between meetings. Translating one chapter per week will allow you to finish John and Romans in 37 weeks, and you can translate the entire New Testament in about five years. Many chapters are small enough that you can translate two or three in one week, greatly shortening the translation time.

Step Two: After each translator finishes his portion, he should lay it aside for several hours or a day. Then, he should come back to it, proofread it, and check it for errors. If any are found, they should be immediately corrected. He should also mark places that he wants to discuss with the others.

Step three: In the weekly meeting, each translator shares the portion that he translated. Any disagreements should be discussed until agreement is reached. So, ample time should be allowed for this. Each team member should review the whole chapter once more during the week after the meeting. If he decides something should be changed, he should put it forth for discussion in the next meeting. Therefore, each meeting should contain the following activities, at least:

1. Review and discussion of the chapter translated the week leading up to the meeting.
2. Discussion and decision about any proposed changes to the chapter of the previous week.
3. Assignment to individuals of portions of the next chapter.
4. Discuss any other issues.
5. Make backup copies.

Step Four: The translated chapter is checked for spelling, grammar, readability, accuracy, and other such issues by helpers outside the translation team. The translation is revised for any issues found.

Step Five: Accumulate several chapters and submit them to several pastors and church leaders and church members to read and comment on. Pass out copies in a class and use it for teaching. Use any other testing technique you want. If any issues are found, the team should discuss them, and the translation should be revised accordingly.

Step Six: Save the result for later final review by the team and a translation advisor.

This is, of course, only a suggested procedure. It may have to be adjusted for the local situation. The important point is to make a plan and follow it.

10 Financing and Promoting the Translation

Philippians 4:19 But my God shall supply all your need according to his riches in glory by Christ Jesus.
2 Corinthians 11:8 I robbed other churches, taking wages of them, to do you service.
Matthew 6:33 But seek ye first the kingdom of God, and his righteousness; and all these things shall be added unto you.
Psalms 9:11 Sing praises to the LORD, which dwelleth in Zion: declare among the people his doings.

Every translation project has costs, but not every project has to cost many thousands of dollars. In fact, we have seen projects that are done very cheaply. There are some costs, though. These costs are one of the main reasons for developing a group of supporting churches. The churches are the source of the money to meet the needs that cannot be met from self-support. Below, I have listed and commented on some of the main costs of a translation.

> 1. Living expenses for the translation team: In our experience, many of the team connected to the translation are willing to serve as volunteers, e.g., translators, typists, checkers, testers, etc.
> 2. Necessary equipment: Equipment needed includes phones, computers, printers, and copiers. Many times, qualified translators do not have this equipment. Also, there is the cost of internet.
> 3. Supplies such as paper, ink, etc.
> 4. Cost of copies to use for checking and testing.
> 5. Publishing of the finished first draft or final draft.

Financing the Translation

Having mentioned the human source of funds, the real truth is that all supply comes from God. God has access to all the funds that are needed. However, support may not come from the source you think it will.   The Bible is clear that God-called full-time servants of God *should* have full-time support but are not required to have it (1 Cor. 9).

> **1 Corinthians 9:7-14** *Who goeth a warfare any time at his own charges? who planteth a vineyard, and eateth not of the fruit thereof? or who feedeth a flock, and eateth not of the milk of the flock?*
>
> *8 Say I these things as a man? or saith not the law the same also?*
>
> *9 For it is written in the law of Moses, Thou shalt not muzzle the mouth of the ox that treadeth out the corn. Doth God take care for oxen?*
>
> *10 Or saith he it altogether for our sakes? For our sakes, no doubt, this is written: that he that ploweth should plow in hope; and that he that thresheth in hope should be partaker of his hope.*
>
> *11 If we have sown unto you spiritual things, is it a great thing if we shall reap your carnal things?*
>
> *12 If others be partakers of this power over you, are not we rather? Nevertheless we have not used this power; but suffer all things, lest we should hinder the gospel of Christ.*
>
> *13 Do ye not know that they which minister about holy things live of the things of the temple? and they which wait at the altar are partakers with the altar?*
>
> *14 Even so hath the Lord ordained that they which preach the gospel should live of the gospel.*

Paul depended on God to work through the churches. "I robbed other churches, taking wages of them, to do you service" (2 Corinthians 11:8). "Now ye Philippians know also, that in the beginning of the gospel, when I departed from Macedonia, no church communicated with me as concerning giving and receiving, but ye only. For even in Thessalonica ye sent once and again unto my necessity" (Phil. 4:15, 16). However, there were times that he did not use this right to be supported, and he worked at tent-making to support the entire team.

> **1 Corinthians 9:15-19** *But I have used none of these things: neither have I written these things, that it should*

be so done unto me: for it were better for me to die, than that any man should make my glorying void.
16 For though I preach the gospel, I have nothing to glory of: for necessity is laid upon me; yea, woe is unto me, if I preach not the gospel!
17 For if I do this thing willingly, I have a reward: but if against my will, a dispensation of the gospel is committed unto me.
18 What is my reward then? Verily that, when I preach the gospel, I may make the gospel of Christ without charge, that I abuse not my power in the gospel.
19 For though I be free from all men, yet have I made myself servant unto all, that I might gain the more.

Even though Paul determined to make the gospel without charge, God knew he needed help at times and moved churches to help him. God has always supplied the needs of his servants. He supplied guidance and protection to the people in the wilderness after they left Egypt. This He did in the pillars of fire and cloud (Ex. 13:21). He miraculously supplied water, quails, and manna in the wilderness (Ex. 16:13, 35; 17:1-6). He led them into a land flowing with milk and honey (Ex. 3:8). The Lord kept a perpetual supply of oil and meal for the widow, her son, and Elijah in the days of the famine (1 Kings 17:8-16). God commanded the ravens to feed Elijah bread and flesh twice per day (1 Kings 17:1-6). Jesus, who taught us to pray, "Give us this day our daily bread" (Mat. 6:11) and promised, "Ask, and it shall be given you; seek, and ye shall find; knock, and it shall be opened unto you" (Mat. 7:7), also told us this.

Matthew 6:25-31 *Therefore I say unto you, Take no thought for your life, what ye shall eat, or what ye shall drink; nor yet for your body, what ye shall put on. Is not the life more than meat, and the body than raiment?*
26 Behold the fowls of the air: for they sow not, neither do they reap, nor gather into barns; yet your heavenly Father feedeth them. Are ye not much better than they?
27 Which of you by taking thought can add one cubit unto his stature?

28 And why take ye thought for raiment? Consider the lilies of the field, how they grow; they toil not, neither do they spin:
29 And yet I say unto you, That even Solomon in all his glory was not arrayed like one of these.
30 Wherefore, if God so clothe the grass of the field, which to day is, and to morrow is cast into the oven, shall he not much more clothe you, O ye of little faith?
31 Therefore take no thought, saying, What shall we eat? or, What shall we drink? or, Wherewithal shall we be clothed?
32 (For after all these things do the Gentiles seek:) for your heavenly Father knoweth that ye have need of all these things.
33 But seek ye first the kingdom of God, and his righteousness; and all these things shall be added unto you.
34 Take therefore no thought for the morrow: for the morrow shall take thought for the things of itself. Sufficient unto the day is the evil thereof.

Every translation project needs the support of churches in the local area, even if the support is moral and prayer support rather than financial. There may be some foreign financing available, but most financing should be sought from the churches in the local country. Translation ministry is something a person does because of a calling and a conviction. We have encountered circumstances where men wanted to be translators so they could have a job and an income. That is not the reason one should translate. We have also seen many translators who are already full-time in the ministry or have secular jobs, and they have still committed themselves to translate the Bible. It was in their hearts, and they could not avoid it. Therefore, if a translator wants to be a full-time translator, he should raise his own salary through the churches. This is also true for other members of the translation team who wish to be full time. In some cases, one church will take care of the needs by itself, but this is rare.

In some parts of the world, there is an inordinate dependence on the United States. There is far more dependence on the United States to meet the financial needs of other countries than there is dependence on the churches in one's own country or one's own city. There are poor everywhere, even in the US. Some seem to think that everyone in the USA is rich. Let me assure you, that is not the case. It may be that most in the US make a greater amount of money than many in other places, but expenses are also greater. For most in the USA, there is little or no money left at the end of the month. Many live paycheck to paycheck each month. Christians in the USA think of supporting their own local church as a first priority and world missions come second. For centuries, missionaries from the USA and Europe have gone to Africa, South America, Central America, and Asia. At first the new churches were dependent on missions giving by United States Christians. However, many of them are now in a position where they can send and support missions on their own. Some already do.

When foreign missions began with the sending of Paul and Barnabas from Antioch (Acts 13), the USA did not exist. Yet, God still met the needs of missionaries. At one point, Jesus sent out 70 to preach (Luke 10:1). He told them not to take a purse. They were dependent on God to provide individual families to house and feed them. They were well provided for (Luke 10:4-8), but they were totally dependent on God. God was able to give them this provision without the USA. He gave them provision from local resources. God's hand is not shortened or limited that it cannot help.

Promoting the Translation Among the Churches

From the very beginning, you should seek to develop good relationships with churches of like faith and practice. You should let them know what you are doing and why. Concentrate on developing friendships with pastors who are excited by your Bible translation plan. Preach in their churches. Present the burden of your heart. Pray that their burden will match yours. This is something all the translators can do.

First, Keep the Churches Informed:

1. The churches should be kept informed from the beginning of the Translation work.
2. The Pastors could be given regular reports of the progress of the translation.

3. The reports can be done in writing and in person, as often as possible.

3. Encourage the pastors to make it a regular part of the church program to keep the congregation up to date on the progress of the translation.

4. One way to do that is to put a chart in each church building that will track the progress of the translation.

5. Use your imagination and pray for God's guidance for ways to do this.

6. Continually try to recruit other churches. The more churches who are following your progress, the further will be the reach of the new translation.

Second, Train the Churches:

1. You should teach pastors why this translation is important. Give specific reasons. Show them the errors in the current Bible in your language. Not all of them will accept this, but some will. Those who do accept it are your partners.

2. Pastors should explain to their churches why this new translation is important. You can help with this by teaching in the churches.

3. This should include the doctrines of inspiration and preservation.

4. The training should include the history of the Bible text.

5. It should include reasons that the Received Greek Text and Ben Chayim Hebrew text are the correct texts.

Third, Expose the Churches to the New Translation

1. All through the translation process, the churches should continually be reminded of the project and how it is progressing.

2. Pastors and teachers should regularly read portions of the new translation to their churches.

3. Churches should be reminded often and regularly to pray for the project and the translation team.

11 Greek Word Study and Worksheets

2 Timothy 2:15 Study to shew thyself approved unto God, a workman that needeth not to be ashamed, rightly dividing the word of truth.

The purpose of a Greek or Hebrew word Study is to understand the full meaning of a word before you translate it. Although the principles of doing a word study are the same regardless of the tools used, here we will apply those principles to the free computer software "E-sword," at www.e-sword.net. See the chapter on resources for a list of the E-Sword modules we recommend that you download and install. E-Sword is available for I-Pads and I-phones. It is also available for Android phones. For Android phones, I also recommend the similar software, "My-Sword." Also, see the chapter on resources.

Step 1. Choose the word you want to study

Below we are looking at the "Bibles" section of E-sword. This is the "Parallel" view showing the KJB with Strong's numbers (downloaded module KJB+) next to the Scrivener edition of the Received Text with Strong's numbers and parsing codes (downloaded module GNT-TR+). For our example, we will choose *grace*, Greek=χαρις (charis) in Romans 1:7 below. Notice on the KJB side the arrow points to *grace* and on the Greek side the arrow points to χαρις (charis).

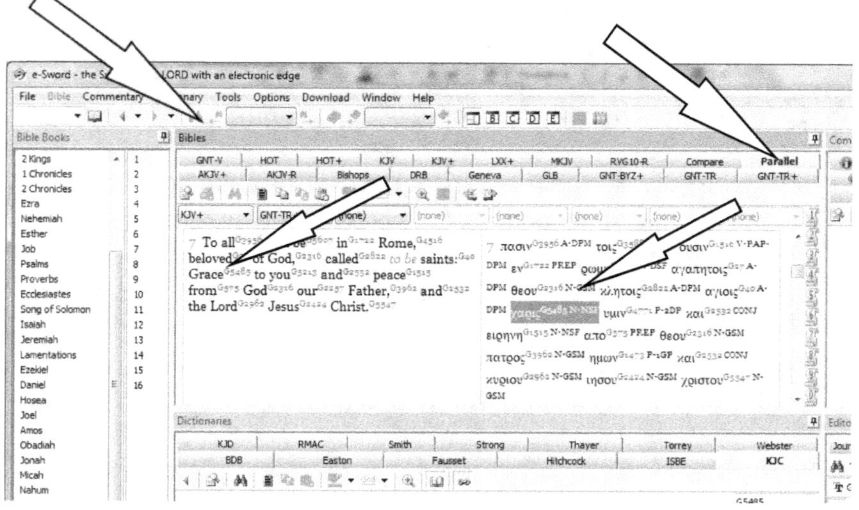

Step 2. Find How the Word was Translated

Click on the Strong's number next to the Greek word, χαρις (or next to *grace)*. Several options will light up in the *Dictionaries* section. In the *Dictionaries* section choose KJC (King James Concordance). This will open the entries in the KJC for that Greek word.

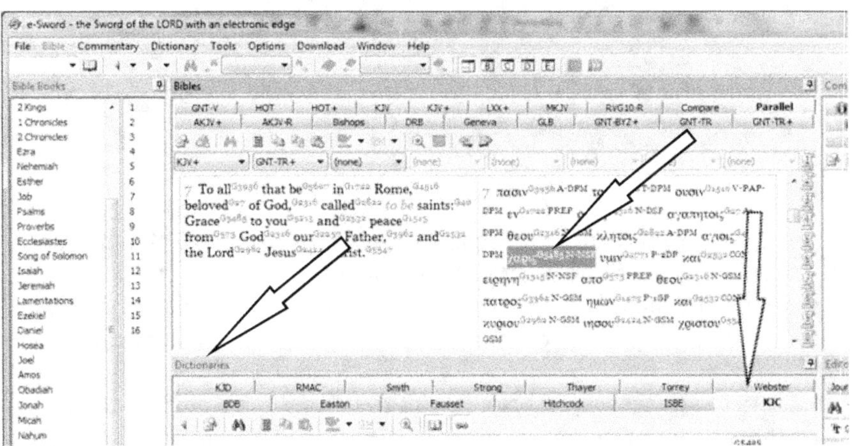

The first image on the next page shows what appears in the *Dictionaries* section when you click on *KJC*. The KJC is designed to show every use of the Greek word in the New Testament and the various ways it was translated in the KJB. The first things it will show are the Strong's number and the Greek word. Below that will be an English transliteration of the Greek word. Next, you will learn how many times the Greek word is used in the New Testament. In the example using grace, it tells us χαρις is used 156 times in the New Testament. Finally, the various ways the Greek word is translated is shown with the verse references where it is used. The first way χαρις is translated is *grace* and we are told that it is translated that way 130 times. By hovering your cursor over a verse reference, the verse itself will pop up and you can read how the word is used. By clicking on the verse reference the Bibles section will go to that verse, allowing you to see the grammar of the Greek text. Unfortunately, the KJC occasionally makes mistakes in that it includes words the KJB did not use to translate a Greek word. The KJC is, perhaps, 98% accurate.

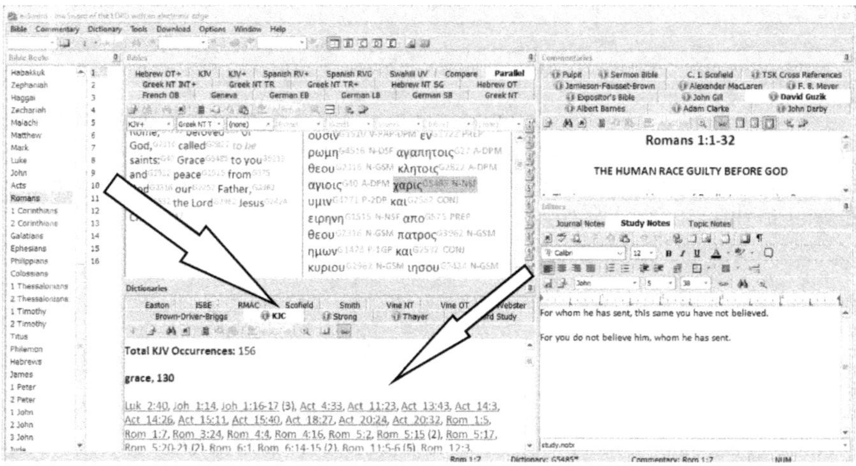

Using the copy/paste function, you can copy all the dictionary information and paste it into a Word document to record your findings, if you wish. Examining the verses where these words are used will give you a clearer view of their meaning in the context and will expand your understanding of the word.

This step shows you how the KJB translated the word and the verses where these various translations occurred. We find that translations related to χάρις are *grace, favor, thank, thanks, pleasure, acceptable, benefit, gift, gracious, joy, liberality, thanked* and *thankworthy*. Thus, the KJC is, itself, a lexicon showing the meanings of Greek words.

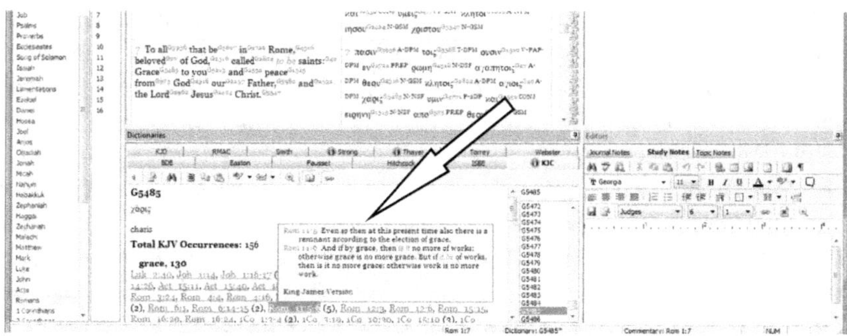

Step 3. Use Greek Lexicons

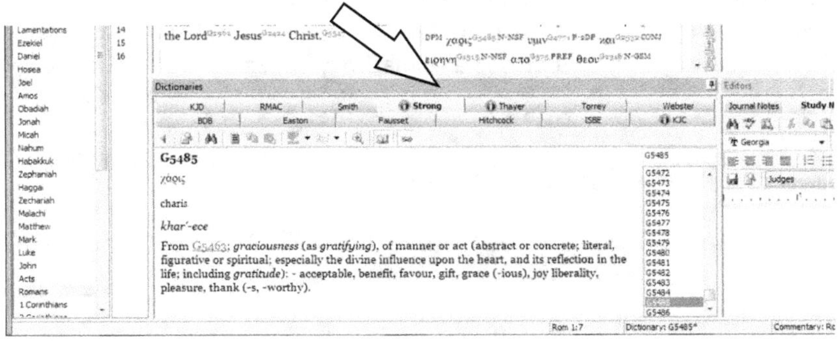

The first Lexicon to use is Strong's and the second is your choice. In our example, we use Thayer's. You are already in the "Dictionary" section with the "KJC" tab highlighted and the word χάρις, charis, showing in the display block. Next click on the "Strong" tab and you will see the information from Strong's Exhaustive Concordance. Here you find six pieces of information, the Strong's number, the word in Greek letters, the word in transliterated English letters, a pronunciation guide, the definition of the word and (after the symbol ":-") ways the word is translated in the KJB listed in alphabetical order.

Next click the "Thayer" tab to display the information in Thayer's Greek Dictionary. In Thayer you will find the same type of information (except for how the word is translated) and sometimes you will find more information than in Strong.

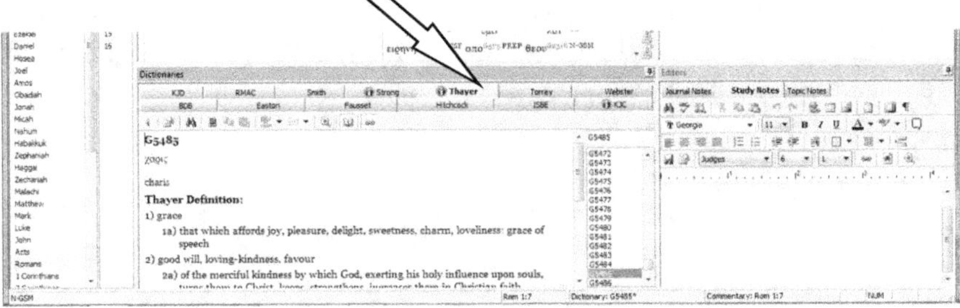

Step 4. Use Webster's 1828 Dictionary

Using the 1828 edition of Webster's English Dictionary has the advantage of seeing definitions that are closer to the meaning of the KJB words. Sometimes Webster 1828 has fuller definitions than many modern dictionaries.

To do this, click the "book" icon next to the search glass (if the look-up box is not there) and click on the "Webster" tab in the dictionaries section of E-sword. Then write the English word (in this case "Grace") in the look up box on the right side. The definition will automatically appear in the information box.

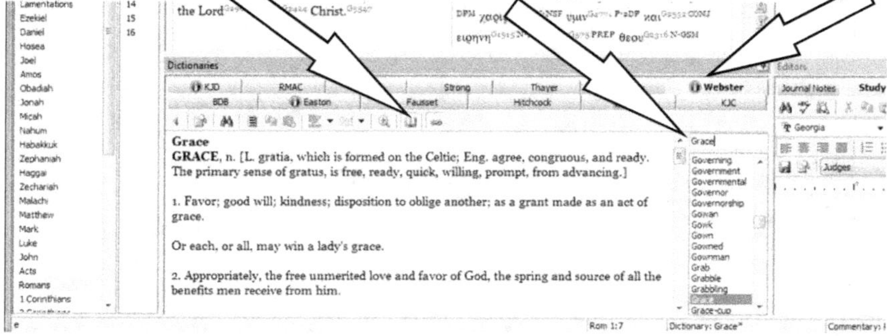

Other dictionaries may also be used.

Step 5. Use Commentaries

There are several commentaries available with E-Sword. Download as many as you think you may need. If you have other commentaries, use them as well. As with all commentaries, be careful. No commentator has all the answers, and they are subject to errors, just as we all are. Choose a verse where you find the word you are studying, such as the verse we started with, Rom. 1:7. Click on the verse reference in the Bible section of E-Sword. This will highlight the commentaries where information can be found. In the "Commentaries" section, click on the commentary you want to start with, such as John Gill's commentary, "Gill."   The place in the commentary relating to the highlighted verse will automatically appear.

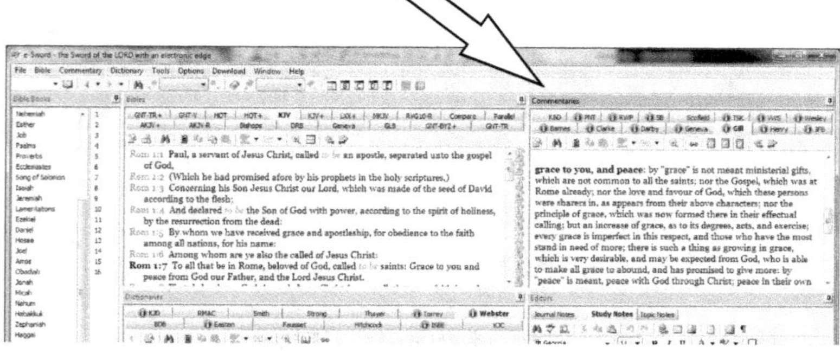

How to Do a Greek Word Study in E-sword

Step 6. Record your findings

E-sword allows you to keep study notes tied to specific Bible verses. You can copy and paste from the other three sections, Bibles and commentaries and Dictionaries.

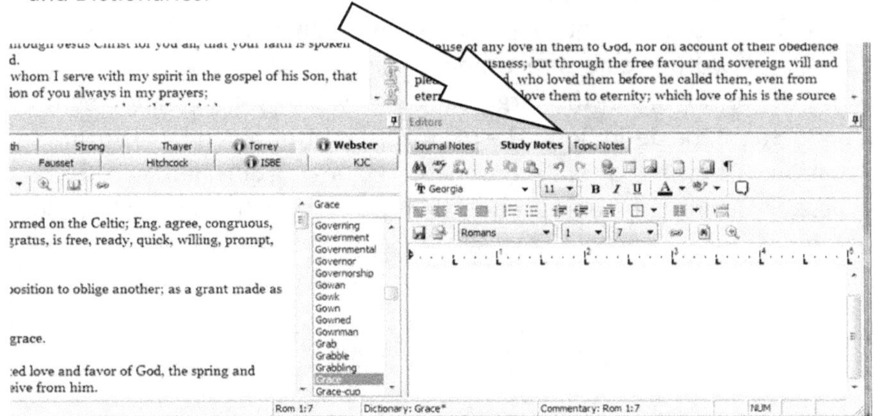

Step 7. Write a Definition of Your Word

The final step is to draw some conclusions based on your research. After looking at all the information you have collected you may understand the word better than most scholars. *You* have done the work, and they may not have. It is best that you write down your conclusions and, perhaps, why you came to them, so that you can refer to them again in the future.

A Worksheet to Track Words

The worksheet on the next page was developed by Dr. Jim Taylor, a member of a Korean Bible translation project. Its purpose is to keep track of how source language words have been translated into target language words. The worksheet will develop step by step as the translation proceeds. As the worksheet develops, it provides a vocabulary resource for the translator. When the translator needs a target language word, from the worksheet he can tell how the source language word was translated before in similar contexts. This will help the translator maintain a high level of consistency, and he can still use a synonym if he wishes. If the translator uses a synonym, he should record the new word along with previous words used for the source word.

You can see the content of the worksheet from the column headings below. The source language is the Greek New Testament. Strong's Dictionary of Hebrew and Greek Words assigns a number to each word. That number is recorded in the worksheet along with Strong's definition of the word. This is followed by the translation chosen for the target language, in this case, it is in Korean. The number of times the word occurs is recorded. It is not an absolute necessity to record the root word of the target language word, but it can be helpful to understand the definition. The root word is often given by in Strong's definition. The part of speech and the Hebrew equivalent word are recorded. Having the Hebrew equivalent can help in translating the Old Testament.

Table 1

Strong's Greek #	Word	Strong's Def	Target Language	Occurrences	Root Word	Part of Speech	Hebrew Equiv
5047	τελειότης	teleiotes (tel-ei-ot'-ace) n 1. (the state) completeness (mentally or morally) [from G5046] KJV: perfection(-ness)	완전		2 τέλειος	noun	תֹּם
5049	τελείως	teleios (tel-ei'-oce) adv. 1. completely 2. (of hope) without wavering [adverb from G5046] KJV: to the end Root(s): G5046	완전		1 τέλειος	adverb	תֹּם
5051	τελειωτής	teleiotes (tel-ei-o-tace') n. 1. a completer, i.e. consummater [from G5048] KJV: finisher Root(s): G5048			1 τελειόω	noun	תֹּם
932 βασιλεία	basileia (bas-il-ei'-ah)	왕국		162 βασιλεύς	noun	מֶלֶךְ

A Worksheet to Aid in Translating

Another worksheet that can be a possible aid to the translator during the translation process, is found below. This worksheet is being used by the Malayalam translation team in Kerala State, India. I have included a copy of the blank worksheet and then an example of a filled in worksheet from John 1:1. It can be used by those who have limited computer equipment, or it can be used on a computer. The verse reference at the top left is self-explanatory. The sentence# and score fields need not be filled in. The date the verse is completed should be recorded. The first column is the information guide. *Word* is for the KJB word and each column contains one word from the verse being translated. Source is for the Greek word. The next three lines are for the part of speech of the Greek word, if Greek is the primary source text, and for the KJB word if Greek is not being used. The next line, translation is for the target language translation. The *use* line is for miscellaneous information. Finally, the last line is for the finished target language translation.

Name______
Page# ___ (or) Scripture Verse ______ Sentence# ______ Date ______ Score ______

word									
source									
tense, voice/ part of speech									
mood / case									
person/gender									
number									
translation									
use									

Full translation:

word									
source									
tense, voice/ part of speech									
mood / case									
person/gender									
number									
translation									
use									

12 A Summary of KJB Grammar

We have seen Bible translation work in Asia, Africa, South America, and in two European languages. Africa and Asia have been particularly instructive regarding knowledge of English. In every place we have gone in Africa and Asia so far, there have been at least a few people who speak English and many people in some countries. Of course, it all depends on what country you visit. The point is that we recommend the Greek and Hebrew texts as the primary source texts, with the use of the King James Bible as a guide in translation work. In some cases, the translators are not well trained in Greek or Hebrew, so the KJB becomes the primary source text. We have seen this in both Africa and Asia. When this happens, I do not feel comfortable hindering them in beginning translation work until they have studied Greek and Hebrew. Why is that, you ask? Aren't you afraid they will misunderstand something in the English KJB and make mistakes in the translation, you ask? Even if that might happen, any possible danger is not enough to stop them from translating. I believe the KJB is so well translated and so accurate that it can be successfully used as the source text for translation. There are ways to avoid the difficulties.

On the other hand, there are important issues that must be considered. In the locations where nationals are trained in English (as is the case in countries like India, China, Kenya, Ghana, Tanzania, and others), there may still be limitations to how well they know English. In one case in Africa, the translators were translating from the KJB and working on Romans 8. They encountered the word "heirs" and could not find a word in the target language to translate it. As we discussed the matter with them, we explained how inheritance works in America and what "heir" means there. They said it was the same with them. When I asked about what word they used to describe it in their language, suddenly the needed words became clear to them. So, we discuss these things with the translators and help them through the issues. One of the issues that may be encountered is the meaning of words in the KJB that are no longer used in English. They are considered archaic or obsolete. Other words have changed meaning in the last four hundred years.

There are English idioms that are not used in the target language, and there is challenging grammar.

However, I have seen people, whose mother tongues are not English, read the KJB all over the world, and I have seen them do it with understanding. Once I asked a German girl if she reads the KJB. She told me, yes. I asked her if she had any problems with it. She said, no. I know of numerous people like this, who are native speakers and readers of Mandarin, Ewe, Twi, Busuku, Luganda, Korean, Spanish, German, Isan, Korean, and others in their home country and who still read the 400-year-old English of the KJB with understanding.

You should also keep in mind the fact that every translator will need to study at least one language that is not their mother tongue. It has often been stated that the best translator is a mother tongue speaker of the target language. This is probably true. However, there are at least two languages involved in any translation project: the source language and the target language. Whoever translates will *not* be a mother tongue speaker of at least *one* of those languages and must learn it. If it is best that a translator be a mother tongue speaker of the target language and it is best to use Greek and Hebrew as the source languages, then the translator must *learn* Greek and Hebrew. The same is true if such a person is using the KJB as the source language. He must learn English and learn to read the KJB with understanding. Such a person can still use the Greek and Hebrew tools we have previously recommended to enhance his understanding of the English text.

In this chapter, I will give a short English grammar tutorial that will hopefully aid in using the KJB in translation work. Along with that, I will also offer some other suggestions that can help. This is also a situation in which the translation advisor is valuable, especially if he is a mother tongue speaker of English. He can help the translator to understand what he is reading in the KJB.

Identifying the English of the KJB

Some have suggested that the KJB is written in a type of English that was never spoken anywhere. I beg to differ with this, although I have no quarrel with those who think this. They, who say this, really have little idea how English was spoken on the street in 1611, the year the KJB was first published. I suspect the reason this is so strongly stated is because of a comparison of the KJB with the English prose of the translator's preface to the KJB. As a young Christian (I was saved at age fifteen), I found reading the KJB to be rather easy. However, the first time I tried to read the preface to the KJB, it was like walking through knee deep mud. To say it was difficult is an understatement! People disagree about what reading grade level the KJB is on. Some say 5th grade (av1611.org) and others say 12th grade (margaretfeinberg.com). I can, perhaps, judge by my own experience. I began reading the KJB at age 13 or 14 as an unsaved non-church going boy. I was in the 7th or 8th grade. I found reading the KJB to be very easy from the beginning. The preface to the KJB is definitely *not* written on a 7th or 8th grade level. It seems to be written on a college level or later. Therefore, the comparison between the KJB and the preface is not a valid one.

The King James Bible was translated using the English of the time, which we now call Early Modern English (roughly 1485 to 1714 [13]). The KJB was translated from 1603 to 1611 and published in 1611. The spelling was very different than current English and was updated in 1769. By then, English had reached a high level of consistency and stability and had entered on the current period of Modern English. The simplicity of the KJB is not due to being an "English that nobody ever spoke", though. It is due to the fact that it was translated from Greek and Hebrew using a formal equivalent method. This gave the KJB the style and simplicity of the original languages. The outstanding literature of the period included the writings of Francis Bacon (1561-1626), the plays of Shakespeare (1564-1616), and the King James Bible (also called the Authorized Version-1611).

English is essentially a Germanic language, having started with Celts who migrated to England before the Romans came. German Anglo-Saxon settlers and invaders arrived in the sixth century. Old English was Anglo-Saxon, the stage of English from roughly 450 to 1100 AD. As the Anglo-Saxons became dominate in Briton, their language began to push out the older Celtic languages. The Anglo-Saxons in England became divided into four independent kingdoms and separate dialects were spoken by each kingdom. The language was changed when the French Normans invaded and conquered England in 1066. Middle English developed from that time until the late 1400's. During that period many French loan words entered the English language.

Since English is basically a Germanic language, it carried many of the same characteristics as German in the Old English period. German is a highly inflectional language. This means that the grammar of nouns, adjectives, articles, and verbs depended on the individual form of the words. Some of these forms look like different words altogether. For example, "the" in German is der, die, das and each of these have a series of differing forms. The grammar of some words depends on special endings. Also, German has a differing word order than today's English. Over time English has almost entirely lost its inflections, and by 1611, almost all the inflections were gone, but some remained. It is those remaining inflections that give many readers difficulty when they read the King James Bible. Below, I have attempted to help you make sense of these and other issues in the KJB. For the sake of convenience and brevity, I will limit the discussion to those areas in which KJB English differs from that of today, with a few relevant exceptions.

Grammar Notes for the KJB

Nouns and Adjectives: Since English had lost most of its inflections by 1611, the nouns and adjectives we find there are in the same form as current English. Possession is indicated the same as today, by using the preposition "of" or using apostrophe s, 's. "And it came to pass, that while he executed the **priest's** office before God ..." (Luke 1:8). In Middle English the apostrophe was not used.

Personal pronouns: The KJB uses several words that all mean *you,* in the second person.   The following chart shows all the personal pronouns as used in the KJB.

First Person (I, we)

Case	Singular	Plural
Subject	I	We
Possession	My, mine	Our
Indirect object	To, with, etc. me	To, with, among, etc. us
Direct object	Me	Us

Second Person (Thou, you)

Case	Singular	Plural
Subject	Thou	Ye
Possession	Thy, Thine	Your, yours
Indirect Object	To, with, etc. thee	To, with, among, etc. you
Direct Object	Thee	You

Third Person (he, she, it)

Case	Singular	Plural
Subject	he, she, it	They
Possession	his, hers	Theirs, their
Indirect object	(to, etc) him, her, it	(to, etc) them
Direct Object	Him, her, it	Them

Many of these forms are the same that are used in current Modern English. Most of the forms that are different are second person pronouns and they all mean you or your. The things to remember are that *thou*, *thy*, *thine*, and *thee* are singular and *Ye, you* is plural. *Thy* and *thine* mean the same. The primary word is thy. Thine is used before a noun that starts with a vowel or h, at the end of a phrase, and other places where thy does not fit. The important thing is that they both are identical in meaning. Another difference is that *mine* is used as a possessive pronoun equal to *my*. *Mine* is also primarily used before a noun that starts with a vowel or h.

The terms thee and thou are used in the Translator's Preface to the KJB. Ye is not used at all and thou is used once in a quote, while thee is used five times outside of a Biblical quote. However, according to the Oxford English dictionary, Ye and thou were no longer used in general conversation.

In the second person, by 1600 ye was a rare alternative to you; no case distinction remained (in earlier English, ye was the subjective case and you the objective). The use of you as a 'polite' form of address to a single person progressively encroached on thou (originally the singular pronoun) until by 1600 thou (and its objective case thee) was restricted to 'affective' (both positive and negative) uses (i.e. so as to be intimate or disparaging). By the late seventeenth century you had become normal in almost all contexts and thou and thee were limited to the Bible and religious use, the Quakers, and regional dialects. [14]

According to this, in 1611, thou was used "disparingly," that is they used it to insult one another ("Don't thou me thou hypocrite!"). However, thou was also used as a familiar term, as between family members, good friends, and married couples. When there are two terms in a language that can be used for *you*, one in a polite or casual relationship and the other in a more familiar or intimate relationship, it is not uncommon for a Bible translation to use the familiar term. German has two terms for *you,* the common term, sie, and the familiar term, du. German Bible translations use Du.

Reflexive pronouns: Words like ourselves, myself, herself, himself, and so on are largely used like they are in current usage. The reflexive pronoun is used as direct object or indirect object when it refers back to the subject. "John poured himself some tea."   The reflexive pronoun is also often used for emphasis. "Behold my hands and my feet, that it is I myself" (Lk 24:39).

In early modern English, the reader will see the base pronoun, without the ending -self or -selves, used for the reflexive pronoun, for example, him instead of himself, them instead of themselves. "Upon the first day of the week let every one of you lay **by him** in store …" (1 Cor. 16:2). The word *him* comes from the Greek word, *eautou*, which is a reflexive pronoun meaning *himself*. The same thing is seen with *them* being used instead of *themselves*. "That the sons of God saw the daughters of men that they were fair; and **they** took **them** wives of all which they chose" (Gen. 6:2). *Them*, today, would be *themselves,* in this verse.   Nevertheless, the normal reflexive pronoun forms are also abundantly used in the KJB. Often the reflexive form (e.g. himself) is used for direct objects and the short form (e.g. him) is used as an indirect object.

Another difference between the conjugation of the reflexive pronoun in 1611 and today is in the second person singular: *thyself* instead of *yourself*.

Relative pronouns, that, which, etc.: Relative pronouns are used to introduce a dependent clause. These include the words who, whom, whosoever, which, that, and what. The words *that* and *which* were common in Early Modern English and were commonly used for persons and things, but now we usually say *who* for persons.

Demonstrative pronouns-this, that, these, those: There is a sequence that was common during the Early Modern English period, demonstrative+possessive+noun, as in Numbers 18:27, "And *this your heave offering* …" and Acts 8:22, "Repent therefore of *this thy wickedness* …" and Luke 15:30, "But as soon as *this thy son* was come …"

The type of construction exhibited in these examples no longer requires the word *this*.

Present tense verb: The second person singular verb retained its inflection, -est, in Early Modern English. However, over time this ending changed, until in current English it is altogether gone. Below are some examples along with how the statements would be expressed in current English. The second person also has corresponding helping verbs, dost and hast. Sometimes the -est ending is shortened to -st, as in hadst.

Reference	KJB-Early Modern English	Current Modern English
Mat. 27:11	And Jesus said unto him, Thou say**est**.	And Jesus said unto him, You say.
Mark 5:31	Thou se**est** the multitude thronging thee	You see the multitude …
Luke 2:29	Lord, now lett**est** thou thy servant depart …	Lord, now let your servant depart …
John 1:50	believ**est** thou?	Do you believe?
John 3:8	The wind bloweth where it listeth, and thou hear**est** the sound thereof	The wind blows where it lists (wishes), and you hear the sound thereof
Mat. 11:25	**thou hast** hid these things from the wise	**you have** hid these things from the wise
1 Cor. 4:7	why dost thou glory	why do you glory
1 Cor. 4:7	as if **thou hadst** not received it?	as if **you had** not received it?

Another present tense verb ending is the -eth ending used with third person pronouns. The -eth ending has corresponding helping verbs, *hath* and *doth*. In later English, the -eth ending became shortened to -s and -es. Below are some scriptural examples.

Reference	KJB-Early Modern English	Current Modern English
Matt. 16:4	A wicked … generation seek**eth**	A wicked … generation seeks
Mark 2:16	How is it that he eat**eth**	How is it that he eats
Luke 3:16	one mightier than I com**eth**	one mightier than I comes

John 3:16	whosoever believ**eth**	whoever believes
Romans 7:2	For the woman which **hath** an husband	For the woman who has a husband
John 2:10	Every man at the beginning **doth** set forth good wine;	Every man at the beginning sets forth good wine;

In addition to these, there is the related construction -ith. When a word ends in y, the y is changed to -i and -th is added. The premier example in the KJB is *saith*. In current English, this is *says*.

Past tense, past perfect, and past participle: Some verbs in the KJB are conjugated differently than the same verbs are now. Among these are the following. The forms molten and sodden are most often used like adjectives.

Help, holp, holpen; melt, molt, molten; seethe, sod, sodden

Luke 1:54 *He hath **holpen** his servant Israel, in remembrance of his mercy;* (he has helped his servant Israel)
Isaiah 44:10 *Who hath formed a god, or **molten** a graven image that is profitable for nothing?* (or melted a graven image)
Genesis 25:29 *And Jacob **sod** pottage: and Esau came from the field, and he was faint:* (Jacob seethed pottage)
1 Samuel 2:15 *Also before they burnt the fat, the priest's servant came, and said to the man that sacrificed, Give flesh to roast for the priest; for he will not have **sodden** flesh of thee, but raw.* (for he will not have seethed flesh-we are more likely today to say "for he will not have boiled flesh")
Lamentations 4:10 *The hands of the pitiful women have **sodden** their own children: they were their meat in the destruction of the daughter of my people.* (seethed their own children)

The past participle verb wont: A past participle is a verb, sometimes used as an adjective, describing action begun and finished in the past, that is, completed action in the past. The archaic verb *wont* is a past participle. It is used nine times in scripture. It means *used to* or *accustomed to*. "And he came out, and went, as he was **wont**, to the mount of Olives" (Luke 22:39). "And on the sabbath we went out of the city by a river side, where prayer was **wont** to be made" (Acts 16:13). "Now at that feast the governor was **wont** to release unto the people a prisoner, whom they would" (Mat. 27:15). "But if the ox were **wont** to push with his horn in time past ... Or if it be known that the ox hath **used to** push in time past ..." (Ex. 21:29, 36).

Perfect tense: For information on how the KJB handles the Greek perfect tense, see chapter thirteen.

Modal and auxiliary verbs-to be and to do: Certain forms of the verb to be, *I be, we be, you be, etc,* were very frequent in the sixteenth century, but started to become rare in the seventeenth century. They were overtaken by *I am, we are, you are, etc.* However, don't assume that *all* "be" forms in the KJB are archaic. They are not. Here are some examples.

Reference	KJB-Early Modern English	Current Modern English
John 12:32	And I, if **I be** lifted up from the earth, will draw all men unto me.	And I, if **I am** lifted up from the earth, will draw all men unto me.
Luke 9:41 (same)	how long **shall I be** with you, and suffer you?	how long **shall I be** with you, and suffer you?
John 8:33	They answered him, **We be** Abraham's seed,	They answered him, **We are** Abraham's seed,
2 Cor. 10:11 (same)	such **will we be** also in deed	such **will we be** also in deed
Heb. 3:13	lest any of **you be** hardened through the deceitfulness of sin	lest any of **you are** hardened through the deceitfulness of sin
1 Peter 5:5 (same)	Yea, all of **you be** subject one to another	Yea, all of **you be** subject one to another

Out of these six examples of *be forms*, three are different in current English and three are the same. Two of the forms that are the same are future tense, but don't assume that all the forms that remain the same will be future. The third example is not future. It is imperative.

Forms of the verb *to do* also present an interesting grammatical structure. You will find Early Modern English constructions like *do set* instead of simply *set, do remember* instead of *remember* alone, *do sin* instead of *sin, doth sanctify, doth command,* and *doth give*. In current English, *do* is usually left out of these constructions. However, do is sometimes still used for purposes of *emphasis,* "I *do* remember." When a translator sees this construction, he would be wise to ask himself if it is being used for emphasis. Once again, do not assume that all uses of the verb *to do* are different in current English. Examples follow.

Reference	KJB-Early Modern English	Current Modern English
Gen. 6:17	I … **do bring** a flood of waters upon the earth	I … **bring** a flood of waters upon the earth
Gen. 19:8 (same)	unto these men **do** nothing	unto these men **do** nothing
Num.36:6	This is the thing which the LORD **doth command**	This is the thing which the LORD **commands**
Deut.10:12 (same)	what **doth** the LORD thy God require of thee	what **does** the LORD your God require of you

The verb *to do* was used often in the KJB, but it became used more and more in later English. Even verbs like *do command* are still used for emphasis, but it was in the eighteenth century when the emphatic use became common. Also, in 1611, you would have read "be not afraid," but now you will more likely see "do not be afraid."

Will versus Wilt: These are used often in the KJB. The two words mean exactly the same thing. *Will* is primarily used in the first and third persons. "And **I will** say to my soul …" (Lk. 12:19). "**He will** make him ruler over all that he hath" (Lk 12:44). However, a small number of times *will* is also sometimes used with the second person. "For where your treasure is, there **will your** heart be also" (Lk. 12:34). *Wilt* is primarily used in the second person. "Lord, if **thou wilt**, thou canst make me clean" (Lk. 5:12). "**Wilt thou** be made whole" (Jn. 5:6)?

Wast versus wert: Was, were, wast, and wert are all the past tense of the verb *to be*. *Was* is the singular of the first and third person singular pronoun. *Were* is the plural of the first and third person plural pronoun. *Wast* is the singular verb of the second person singular pronoun. "**Thou** also **wast** with Jesus of Galilee" (Mt. 26:69). "**Thou wast** altogether born in sins" (Jn. 9:34). Wert is used six times in the KJB. It is also used with the second person singular pronoun. However, it is used with hypothetical or figurative language. "For if **thou wert** cut out of the olive tree which is wild by nature, and **wert graffed** contrary to nature into a good olive tree …" (Rom. 11:24). In this verse, it is used of the metaphorical olive tree.

Art versus are: Once again, both of these words have the same meaning. The word *are* is used with plural nouns. Plural pronouns, and you. *Art* is used with the second person pronoun. "**All things are** delivered to me of my Father" (Lk. 10:22). "**Art thou** a master of Israel, and knowest not these things" (Jn. 3:10)?

The use of *should* and *would*: These two words can possibly cause some confusion with some readers and translators. The word *should* in 1611 carried meanings that it no longer carries in our current form of Modern English. In 1611, one of its meanings was 1) something will certainly take place when certain conditions are fulfilled, and 2) it implies that the fact actually exists without condition. Today, we think of *should* as the equivalent of *ought to,* but at that time it also meant something that would definitely happen. In current Modern English, we are more likely to use the word, *would,* in those cases, instead of *should*.

You ought to also know that the word *should* is most often a translation of the *Greek subjunctive mood*. Because of this, you need to understand some things about the subjunctive. The Greek subjunctive expresses something that is possible in contrast to something that is actually happening. It is not happening now, but it is a definite possibility. It also means that it will definitely happen if certain conditions are fulfilled. In this way, the subjunctive expresses *purpose statements*. A purpose statement is one that tells us what God intends to do. It is sometimes connected with a condition we must fulfill first.

> **John 3:16** *that whosoever believeth in him **should** not perish, but have everlasting life.*

The use of *would* in the KJB is a different story. It is used in the sense of *I intend to* or *I am willing to.* "I asked him whether he would go to Jerusalem" (Acts 25:20). Would is also used in the sense of *I choose to* or *I want to* or *I wish.* For example, "yet I would have you wise unto that which is good" (Rom. 16:19), and "I would to God ye did reign" (1 Cor. 4:8).

Punctuation marks: Most punctuation marks in the KJB are used in the same way as today, such as the period and semi-colon. However, certain differences should be noted. There are a lot of direct quotations in the KJB, but there are no quotation marks. Direct quotations can be recognized by a phrase ending in a comma followed by the first word of the quote capitalized ("And Jesus came and spake unto them, **saying, All** power is given unto me in heaven and in earth" (Mat. 28:18). There are exclamation points and questions marks used the same way as today. However, they are usually followed by a sentence in which the first word is *not* capitalized. "But woe unto you that are **rich! for** ye have received your consolation" (Lk. 6:24). It has been suggested that this keeps the second statement from taking away the emphasis from the first. [15] The colon (:) does two things. First, it adds details and information, "For the LORD giveth wisdom: out of his mouth cometh knowledge and understanding" (Prov. 2:6). Second, the colon gives opposing statements. "Whoso despiseth the word shall be destroyed: but he that feareth the commandment shall be rewarded" (Prov. 13:13).

The Sentence: There are a couple of things a translator should know about sentence structure in the KJB. The first is left over from the Germanic origin of English. The basic English rule of word order is subject-verb-direct object. German word order is the same, *in general*, but it is much more flexible, and it *can be verb-subject-object*. This German word order shows up very often in the KJB. It does not interfere with understanding, but it can seem unusual.

The second thing about sentence structure is the use of multiple negatives. Current English cannot take double negatives. Early modern English could. At that time, one use of multiple negatives was as a literary device to negate different parts of a sentence separately, as in, *"I will **not** meddle with **no** duplicate"* (Stephen Hawes, 1503). In the King James Bible, it is often a device to *emphasize the negation*, just as it is used in Greek. For example, "with such an one **no not** to eat" (1 Cor. 5:11).

Recommended Dictionaries: It is important to have a dictionary that gives definitions matching the meanings of words in 1611, as close as possible. For many years, the 1828 edition of the Webster Dictionary has been used very successfully. It probably has 99% of the definitions that will be needed. Webster 1828 is widely available in paper copies and digitally in places like Google Play. It is available free online at https://webstersdictionary1828.com. When Webster's does not have the definition, as occasionally happens, a Bible program like e-sword is very helpful. You can use it to research the definitions of the Greek word. When webster's has the definition, you can look at the Greek word to verify that you have selected the right definition. See chapters 3 and 4 for more information.

Understanding KJB Words

Languages change over time. New words are created and old words pass out of use. English is no exception and neither are the words in the King James Bible. The great majority of words in the KJB are still used today and mean the same today as they did in 1611. It is also true that some of the words have become archaic or obsolete. They are rarely or never used in current modern English. There are also words that are still used today, but no longer mean what they did in 1611. A translator will need to recognize these words when they are found and determine their meaning in 1611. To do this, he will need to make good use of resources.   So, when comparing Early Modern English with current Modern English, there are several types of words that require rethinking. To recap, see below.

1) **Words or phrases in the KJB that are obsolete or archaic** are rarely or never used in today's English. One such word is *besom* (Is 14:23). It means *broom*. Another obsolete word is *ouches* (Ex. 28:11). An *ouch* is a *clasp* or a *setting*. Another obsolete word is *nought* (Acts 19:27). It means *nothing*. It is only obsolete because the spelling has changed. The modern spelling is *naught*. However, the word *naught* is rarely used today.

2) **Words and phrases in the KJB that are *old*, and may show up sometimes in current Modern English, but are almost obsolete.** Examples are *abode, albeit,* or *amiss*. Another such word may be *appertain* (c.f. Jer. 10:6-7), which is only used seven times in the KJB. We are more likely to say *pertain*, now. Another such word is *beseech*, which means to ask earnestly, but is rarely used.

3) **There are some words in Early Modern English that are still used but have fully or partially changed meaning.** One example is the word *curious*. In Exodus 28:8, the girdle of the ephod, a priestly garment, is called the "curious girdle." At that time, curious had several meanings. One of them was *carefully and artfully made.* You will find that meaning in the Webster 1828

Dictionary and it is the definition that applies in Ex. 28:8. However, today the word curious means "eager to acquire knowledge; inquisitive."[16] It has lost the "carefully and artfully made" definition. For another example, Luke 20:11 uses the word *entreat*. Today *entreat* means to ask or request earnestly. In 1611, one of its meanings was "to maltreat; treat badly."

4) **There are words in the KJB that are understood in current Modern English, but they are not the normal idiomatic words that would be used in the context today.** John 4:48 says, "Then said Jesus unto him, **Except** ye see signs and wonders, ye will not believe." The word *except* here was a perfectly good word in 1611 and it still is. I doubt that anyone makes an issue of it. The only difference is a matter of "normal idiom." Words are used in specific ways in different contexts within a culture. In this context, the usual word used in 1611 was *except*, but today the usual word would probably be *unless*. The two mean the same in this context. Another example comes from 1 Corinthians 1:21, "For after that in the wisdom of God the world by wisdom knew not God ..." The little phrase "after that" is no longer used in the same sense. We use the phrase in the sense of time: "he went to the market and *after that* he went home." However, in 1 Corinthians 1:21, it means *since* or *because*.

How are we to know when we encounter a word like those in this list? The general rule is to always know what a word means. The difficult words in the above categories are few when compared with the entire Bible, but they can cause some challenges. The good thing is that the KJB often defines its own terms in the immediate or wider context. Also, the resources listed in chapter three contain several dictionaries. The most important English dictionary to have on hand is the 1828 edition of Webster, since it contains correct definitions for nearly every King James word. However, there are certain words for which it does not have the correct definition, because the definition had changed by 1828. The word entreat in Luke 20:11, is also an example of this. The Webster 1828 gives this definition "To make an earnest petition or request." As we have seen before, the Greek word used in Luke 20:11, *atimazo*, means "to maltreat or treat badly." In this case, webster did not have the 1611 definition. This shows how important it is to consult the definitions in the Greek lexicons along with English dictionaries. This is one reason we recommend using E-sword and My-sword (see chapter three). Even if the KJB is the primary source text, you must always consult the Greek dictionaries. In this there is safety, "Where no counsel is, the people fall: but in the multitude of counsellors there is safety" (Proverbs 11:14). "For by wise counsel thou shalt make thy war: and in multitude of counsellors there is safety" (Proverbs 24:6).

13 Finding Meaning and Choosing the Right Words

Isaiah 50:4 The Lord GOD hath given me the tongue of the learned, that I should know how to speak a word in season to him that is weary: he wakeneth morning by morning, he wakeneth mine ear to hear as the learned.
Acts 8:30 Understandest thou what thou readest?

The tongue of the learned is not an educated tongue. It is not a tongue with a PhD or any degree. It comes from the Lord, and it is a request every translator should include in his daily prayers, "Grant me the tongue of the learned." A translator needs exactly what is in these verses. Regarding Bible translation, the tongue of the learned is a person who understands words, what they mean and how they are used. The translator needs to thoroughly know two languages at least, the target language and the source language. He needs to know how to find the meaning of words and then he needs the right words to use in the translation, so that his translation will speak "a word in season to him that is weary." This ability comes from God.

In this book, we emphasize being faithful to the Words of God, but that is not enough. Meaning is important too. Each word used in the target language translation needs to have the same meaning as the corresponding word in the source text. Every sentence has to have the same meaning as the sentence in the source text. Every verse must have the same meaning as the verse in the source language. So, the words of the source text must be studied and prayed over until they are clearly understood, then words in the target language must be found which mean the same.

The study of meaning is called *semantics*. Languages were created by God and are spoken by specific groups of people, who have their own identity and culture. All languages and the meanings of the words are inseparably connected with and determined by the culture of the people group. So, languages generally express all the meaning which the people encounter in their culture and experiences. Languages cannot be separated from the culture. Because of this, all languages are different, but they all have certain characteristics in common.

Common Characteristics of Languages

1. No language is perfect. No language includes all possible meanings.

2. Every language can express any meaning any other language can.

3. All languages borrow words and concepts from other languages they are exposed to.

4. Every language uses grammatical forms in its own distinct way. English and Greek make frequent use of passive verbs. Some languages do not use the passive form. Where Greek would use passive, they use active. Therefore, a meaning expressed in a certain grammatical form in the source language may require a different grammatical form in the target language to have the same meaning. One of the key examples of this is the perfect tense in Greek. The Greek perfect tense has no exact equivalent in English. It is not future time. It is neither past time nor present time. It is *both* present and past at the *same time*. The Greek perfect tense describes an action that happened in the past and has results in the present. Sometimes the KJB translates the Greek perfect as present tense, "I **am crucified** with Christ …" (Gal. 2:20). Another example of the KJB using present tense is 1 John 4:2: "Hereby know ye the Spirit of God: Every spirit that confesseth that Jesus Christ **is come** in the flesh is of God…" Other times the KJB translates it as past tense, "For if we **have been** planted together in the likeness of His death" (Rom 6:5). The closest one can come to it in English is a statement like, "The bed is made," which implies that someone made the bed in the past, and it is still made in the present. The same thing is implied in the statement, "The bed has

been made," but not as clearly. However, these statements in English are present tense and past tense respectively.

5. There are no total synonyms between languages or within languages. For example, the Greek word, telos a noun) and teleo (a verb), and the word *end* in English are very close in meaning, but there are slight differences. For example, Teleo does not simply mean to *finish*, *end*, or *complete* a thing. It also means to *pay a tax.* Therefore, it cannot be translated with a single English word in every context. The KJB sometimes translates the Greek words with terms other than *end*: finally, uttermost, finished, accomplished, fulfilled, or custom (payment of a tax), etc. Doing so makes the translation more precise in different contexts.

6. All languages have a vocabulary focus. [17] Every language develops words that express the peoples' experiences within their culture and with other cultures.

7. All languages are living. They develop and change with time and new experiences. Sometimes old words are no longer used, or they may change meaning, while new words are coined to express the same or new meanings. However, major changes usually take a considerable period of time. [18]

Considering all these things, the goal of a translator is to choose words and phrases in the target language, which have the closest equivalent meaning to the words and phrases in the source language. That is the trick, finding and choosing the right words.

The Meaning of Words

The meaning of words is determined by how they are used in their context, regardless of what any dictionary says. That is not to say that dictionaries are often wrong, but sometimes it is easier to understand words in their context than it is to understand an English dictionary or a Greek lexicon.

Let's take John 1:13 as an example. "Which were born, not of blood, nor of the will of the flesh, nor of the will of man, but of God." Let's focus on the word *blood*. What does it mean? It comes from the Greek word *aima*. Studying the context in which aima is used, we find it means literal blood (Mark 14:24), bloodshed, death and killing (Mt. 23:35; Acts 5:18), guilt and punishment (Acts 18:6), kindred and relation, and human being (flesh and blood-Mt. 16:17; Gal 1:16). In English, the word blood is used in all these ways including, "Kindred; relation by natural descent from a common ancestor." [19] This last meaning is illustrated by the phrases, royal blood, prince of the blood, and blue blood.

John 1:13 uses the word blood, but does it mean literal "blood" or does it mean "by birth or descent?" In Greek and English, it would not matter. The translation is the same either way, aima or blood, and the interpretation would be open. However, if we were translating into German, we would have to make a decision as to the meaning of blood in John 1:13. German has two words. One, *blut*, means blood in several senses, but not in the sense of descent. The other word that means descent, kindred, etc.` is *Geblüt.* When Martin Luther translated the Greek New Testament into German, he chose the word *Geblüt.*

There are times when target language speakers have an understanding of a word that is different than the meaning of the source language word. John 4:1 says, "When therefore the Lord knew how the Pharisees had heard that Jesus made and baptized more disciples than John ..." Dr. Turner shared, "In many languages the word *made* is limited to the meaning of 'manufactured.'"   This is a different situation than the cultural problem above. This issue has to do with the meaning of words. If there is only one word for *made* in the target language and it does not mean the same as the source language word, a solution must be found. The word made in John 4:1 comes from the Greek word, poieo, which basically means to make or do in a great variety of applications. Some of those applications in the KJB are as follows: do, bring forth, wrought, to ordain, to shoot out, dealt, bring, to tarry, to provide, to gain, to put, to keep, to spend (time), to perform, to observe, to make (in multiple meanings), to commit, cause, to show, to purpose, to bear, to yield, to continue, to appoint, to hold (a meeting), execute, exercise, to work, to fulfill. As one can see, this word is very flexible. We should allow a translator the same flexibility to find the appropriate word to use in the target language. In the case in question, there are four solutions: choose a synonym for *make* that does express the correct meaning, expand the meaning of their word for *make*, borrow a word, or create a word.

Methods to Find Words

If the translator is a cross cultural missionary coming from another language group in different country, he should begin immediately to develop a written vocabulary in his new language that can be used for translating and communicating Biblical thought. If the translator is of the same language group and culture, then his task is easier, but he still has to choose between words to determine the *best* words to use. It is quite possible that some Scriptural words will not have an equivalent in the target language. The words a language has to express Biblical truth depends on that culture's experience with Christianity. If the Christian religion is strong in a culture, they will have many words to describe Christian experience and beliefs. If a culture has little or no contact with Christians, there will be few, if any, words to describe Biblical concepts. However, languages are very flexible. When people have new experiences or are exposed to new things, they find a way to express their experience or to describe what they have seen.

Though he was a German and was translating the Bible into German, Martin Luther struggled at times to find the right words.

> I have always tried to translate in a pure and clear German. It has often happened that for three or four weeks we have searched and inquired about a single word, and sometimes we have not found it even then. In translating the book of Job, Master Philip, Aurogallus, and I have taken such pains that we have sometimes scarcely translated three lines in four days. Now that it has been translated into German and completed, all can read and criticize it. The reader can now run his eyes over three or four pages without stumbling once, never knowing what rocks and clods had once lain where he now travels as over a smoothly-planed board. We had to sweat and toil there before we got those boulders and clods out of the way, so that one could go along so nicely. The plowing goes well in a field that has been

cleared. But nobody wants the task of digging out the rocks and stumps. There is no such thing as earning the world's thanks. Even God himself cannot earn thanks, not with the sun, nor with heaven and earth, nor even the death of his Son. The world simply is and remains as it is, in the devil's name, because it will not be anything else. [20]

Listen to How People Talk

The Greek language of the New Testament was the ordinary common language the people used in daily life. There is nothing special about the majority of the words used in the New Testament. Paul doubtless heard the same words spoken in the marketplace or by people for whom he was making tents. All he had to do to get a wealth of vocabulary was to get among people and listen to them. Martin Luther found the same thing to be true. He would often listen to people talking. He spoke of this when explaining why he added the *allein,* alone, in Romans 3:28, even though it is not in the Greek text.

> We do not have to ask the literal Latin how we are to speak German, as these donkeys* do. Rather we must ask the mother in the home, the children on the street, the common man in the marketplace. We must be guided by their language, by the way they speak, and do our translating accordingly. Then they will understand it and recognize that we are speaking German to them. (* Roman Catholic critics of his translation-Author). [21]

This is especially true with new Christians. A translator should listen closely to how new Christians express and explain their faith and how they describe their spiritual experiences.

Reading and Writing

Dr. Turner recommends that no one should begin translating until having analyzed at least two hundred pages of text in the target language. The translator should read as much as possible and perhaps write down stories and legends he has heard from native speakers of the language. Doing so will reveal a wealth of vocabulary. If the target language is the mother-tongue of the translator, he should still do this. Native speakers of a language still need to expand their vocabulary.

There are still people groups who do not have a written body of literature. Their literature is their oral traditions, histories, and myths. A translator will need to listen and learn these stories. He should write down as many as possible while looking for words and expressions he can use in the translation. Learning these stories will do more than provide words and expressions. They will explain national culture and why things are done in certain ways. They reveal how the people think and understand the world around them. They may even provide creation and flood stories, which also reveal how and with what words the people communicate these concepts. These things are revealed in both oral and written literature.

Cultures that are based on oral traditions may also be cultures without a written language. Learning the language may be purely an oral task and the missionary translator may find himself with the responsibility of creating a written language for the people. This is a specialized task that is outside the scope of this book. We recommend that translator's from the USA attend the Baptist Bible Translator's Institute in Bowie, Texas. Information can be found on the internet at https://baptisttranslators.com. Below are some statements about the school from the website.

Baptist Bible Translators Institute exists for several reasons. First, there is an unfilled gap in world evangelism. More than 3,000 languages with 380 million people still await the Word of God in their language. BBTI exists to help meet this need. This need exists because missionaries are usually trained to be pastors in the USA but are not trained to deal with crossing language and cultural barriers in remote parts of the world. So those parts of the world that are similar to the USA have been the places to which missionaries have most often gone. This leaves the geographically difficult areas of the world neglected. The people who live there speak a strange language, and their customs are harshly different from anything with which we are familiar.

The principles of linguistics, ethnology, and cross cultural communication that are taught at BBTI are universal to all missionary situations. Missionaries are prepared to meet whatever challenge they will face, whether in the city or the jungle. In either place, missionaries must learn languages and adjust to cultures that are very different from their own.

Although spiritual needs will not be ignored, their training will involve the more practical and technical aspects of missionary work. BBTI can help train missionaries in the technical aspects of phonetics, phonemics, morphology, syntax, language learning principles, cross-cultural communication principles, Bible translation principles, and ethnology. [22]

New Combinations and Expanded Meanings

It is possible to take words that have a clear use and meaning and combine them to make them mean something else. Greek is full of examples of this. The word *krino* means *I decide* and the word *epi* means *upon*. When you combine them into *epikrino*, the new word does not mean *I decide upon*, although it carries that basic idea. It means *I judge*. Other examples involve connecting words, rather than combining them as a single word, but connecting them in a phrase with a single meaning. Greek combines *eis kai eis,* literally *one and one*, but it *means* something a little different, *one and the other* (see Matthew 20:21). The Greek word *eis* means *one*, but it is also a preposition meaning *into*. Also, the Greek word *ena* is the feminine form of *one.* If you combine them into *eis ton ena*, it literally *says* "into the one." However, that is not what it *means*. Its meaning is *one another*.

We do the same thing in English, and I would think it is also done in all languages. In English, we have the word *here*, which means *this location*. Another word is *fore*, which means something that is *located in the front*. We also have the word *to*, which is a preposition indicating a direction. What happens if we combine all three of these words? In English, we have already done this centuries ago. The word is *heretofore*. It means *up to now*, or *until now*. The meaning of each word separately is different than the meaning of the combination of the words.

Since languages have the ability to describe and explain new experiences and new knowledge, they have the flexibility to grow and add new meanings. Often this involves adding meaning to existing words. When the early missionaries and colonists came to Africa, they brought things with them that the Africans had never seen. One thing that eventually came to Africa was airplanes. To the inhabitants of East Africa, who spoke Swahili, an airplane looked like a bird. The Swahili word for a bird is Ndege, and, so, an *airplane* became *Ndege*. This, in turn, became expanded into *airport*. Someone must have looked at several airplanes parked on a grass field and thought it looked like a *field of birds*, "unwanja wa ndege." Regardless of how it happened, uwanja wa ndege became Swahili for "airport."

The same thing can be done for Biblical concepts, when there is no ready target language word that is equivalent in meaning to the Biblical word. Explaining Biblical concepts to those who speak the language often stimulates ideas as to how they can be expressed. When words are chosen, the whole translation team should use them in the translation, in other writing, in teaching, and in other speech. This helps get the people to understand the new combinations and expanded meanings.

Coin New Words

Another method of finding words is to create new words that mean the same as Bible words. This is not the first choice for finding words. It is not the preferred method. However, it is a necessary method in some cases. The Chinese Authorized Version (https://www.bpsglobal.org/chinese.html) translation team has found this to be the case quite a few times. The Chinese Union Version is an error ridden version. That version and other previous versions often do not provide words that adequately express Biblical terms. New terms must be sought, and sometimes new words need to be created. These words will have to be conditioned to the right meaning. Conditioning will be discussed later.

Borrow Words from Other Languages

Every language borrows words from other languages. The English language is considered a Germanic language, because its origins lie in Old Saxon and Angle, German languages. However, current Modern English is far from German today. Many of its words have been borrowed from German, but also from French (massage), Spanish (adios), Latin (bene- as in benefit), Dutch (dollar), Italian (alarm, ballot), Arabic (zero, giraffe), Greek (many words), Chinese (ketchup), Norwegian (ski), Welsch (penguin), African clan languages (banana, zebra, jumbo, yam), Japanese (anime), Native American tribal languages (Chillicothe, moccasin), and more. [23]

The first place to look is a dialect related to the target language. Ekegusii is a language spoken in western Kenya and part of Tanzania. It has subdialects such as the Bunchari dialect spoken by the Suba people of Tanzania. Looking to a subdialect of the target language is a likely place to start in borrowing words. The translator can also look at unrelated languages spoken nearby. Finally, any other language may be consulted. Regardless of which languages provide the words, the translator must teach the target language speakers the meaning of the borrowed word.

Generic Words Verses Specific Words

Generic words represent a general category, while a specific word is one that is a subtopic of a generic word. *Sin* is a generic word and a lot of activities fit within its meaning. *Stealing* is a specific word that comes under the heading of sin. Other words such as adultery, dishonoring parents, lies, hatred, and covetousness are specific words that are part of the generic word *sin*. In the KJB, the word *meat* is most often a generic word meaning *food*. According to the 1828 edition of Webster's Dictionary, *meat* means, "Food in general; any thing eaten for nourishment, either by man or beast." *Meat* is also "animal flesh," which is a specific use of the same word. It is important that a translator knows the difference in the source language and that he finds the proper generic and specific words in the target language. If the translator is not a native speaker of the target language, he will need to talk to native speakers and ask them about which words to use. He can start with a generic word and ask about the specific things that are included within that word. He can also start with a specific noun and ask questions about what generic word it fits.

Ask Hypothetical Questions

If a translator is not a native speaker of the target language and especially if he is in a pioneer situation, he can ask his language helper hypothetical questions to find new words. In order to do this, he will need a good knowledge of the language and culture in which he is working. The translator could propose fictional situations that are culturally relevant and ask for words that describe the situation. Dr. Charles Turner gives us several examples of imagined situations where people were in danger and a gentleman named Roberto rescued them. After sharing the examples, the translator asked the question, "What did Roberto do for these people?" As a result, the translator learned a good target language word for *salvation*. [24]

Contextual Conditioning

Whether you are coining a new word, borrowing a word, combining words, or widening the focus of words, new words will be produced that are not understood by the native speakers of the target language. When it is necessary to make new words or give new meanings to words, the people can be educated on the new meaning over time by a method called *contextual conditioning*. Creating words is easy, but what do they mean to anyone else? The answer is nothing, unless you can do something to make the words a part of the target language and help the people understand them.

The context around a word conditions its meaning. If I use the Greek word *telos*, you may not know what it means. However, you might begin to understand it if I say, "And he shall reign over the house of Jacob for ever; and of his kingdom there shall be no *telos*." You may understand even better if I follow that with, "Who shall also confirm you unto the *telos*, that ye may be blameless ..." And it may confirm your thoughts that telos means *end*, if I also say, "But the *telos* of all things is at hand." But then I tell you, "Render therefore to all their dues: tribute to whom tribute is due; *telos* to whom *telos* ...," and you get the idea *telos* means more than just *end*. A further context helps with this, "of whom do the kings of the earth take *telos* or tribute?" So, you get the idea that *telos* must be some kind of *tax* payment. You learn through the context of Scripture that *telos* means both *end* and *tax.* Meaning is not established by dictionaries, but rather by the contexts in which the words are used. Dictionaries are supposed to reflect that use. However, new words do not have a listing in the dictionary yet, so their meaning must be conditioned by the context. Anything can be given meaning by surrounding it with context. Following are some suggestions about how to condition a word. It can be done in three ways.

1. Make sure the whole translation team and all the helpers know and understand the new terms.

2. Include the terms in the translation.

3. Use portions of the translation that include the new words in as many teaching situations as possible. Use the words in writing and speech. You should use as many ways as you can find to expose the people to the new words in verbal and written forms.

All people are capable of learning new words and understanding new concepts. As Christians begin to read the Bible in their language, they will encounter many new words and concepts. They will have to expand their understanding of words they already know. New words will simply become additional vocabulary to learn, and their knowledge will be expanded.

14 Figures of Speech and Literary Techniques

John 1:29 The next day John seeth Jesus coming unto him, and saith, Behold the Lamb of God, which taketh away the sin of the world.

Literary techniques are methods authors use to get their ideas across and make them stronger. They help authors communicate their ideas, explanations, and arguments more effectively. It is not just human authors who use literary devices. The Almighty Divine Author has also used them. It is good for a translator to know what he is looking at when he sees one in the Bible. In fact, every Christian should be aware of literary devices, because they may help them understand the Scriptures better. A translator may translate literary devices literally in almost every case, but they will help him in translating if they enable him to understand the Bible better.

A type of literary technique that uses words in a non-literal or unusual sense to express a specific meaning is a *figure of speech*. An example of this would be to say, "all the trees of the field shall clap their hands" (Is. 55:12). The trees do not have hands and do not clap, but the waving of the trees in a sudden strong breeze during a significant event may be characterized this way. Nevertheless, when God expresses it as the trees clapping their hands, it should be translated as God said it. In this chapter, we will look at some of the literary techniques and figures of speech in the Bible. [25]

Anthropomorphism

Anthropomorphisms are statements that speak of something as if it were human when it is not human. God is spoken of in this way many times. God made humans in His image, but He is *not* human. It is true that Jesus took upon Himself a human body and was born both God and Man, but Jesus also said, "God is a spirit" (John 4:24). God is so great that he said, "Do not I fill heaven and earth?" (Jer. 23:24). Yet, even in the Old Testament, before the incarnation, the Scriptures picture God as a man, so that mankind may understand Him better.

One example is the use of the word *hand* in relation to God. In 1 Samuel 5:11, great punishment was lowered on the Philistines, and it was the *hand of God* that did it. It was the declaration of the preacher, "There is nothing better for a man, than that he should eat and drink, and that he should make his soul enjoy good in his labour. This also I saw, that it was from the hand of God" (Eccl. 2:24). Job said, "What? shall we receive good at the hand of God, and shall we not receive evil?" (Job 2:10). This same concept carries forward into the New Testament. "And the hand of the Lord was with them: and a great number believed, and turned unto the Lord" (Acts 11:21). Thus, in these verses, the picture of the *hand of God* is used for the *power and work of God*.

So how should anthropomorphisms be translated? The simple answer is to translate them as literally as possible. Each time an anthropomorphism is used it is a picture of something important and that picture should be maintained. Since this type of figure of speech uses the human body for the word pictures, it should be understood universally across languages. If your translation is being done in a culture that does not understand anthropomorphisms, it will be the responsibility of teachers to help the people understand them.

Personifications

A personification is similar to an anthropomorphism. The difference is that it has to do with humans, rather than God. A personification is when one speaks to something non-human as if it is human (see Romans 8:22 above and Revelation 11:8; 16:20; 20:14).

Romans 8:22 For we know that the whole creation groaneth and travaileth in pain together until now.

In this verse, Paul attributes the human characteristics of childbirth to something that is not human. This shows the unnatural condition in which the universe exists because of the fall. It should be translated literally.

Revelation 16:20 And every island fled away, and the mountains were not found.

This verse speaks of islands as if they have sentience and are able to flee away of their own will.

Revelation 20:14 And death and hell were cast into the lake of fire. This is the second death.

The mention of death and hell is probably a personification for those who are dead and in hell.

Anachronism

An anachronism is a statement that is outside its proper time. It is when something that did not exist in Biblical times is introduced into the Bible text. As a rule, this should be avoided. Several examples of what this means and what should be avoided are below.[26]

Luke 12:3 Therefore whatsoever ye have spoken in darkness shall be heard in the light; and that which ye have spoken in the ear in closets shall be proclaimed upon the housetops.

"Proclaimed upon the housetops" should not be translated as "announced on the radio." There were no radios in the first century.

Acts 2:25 For David speaketh concerning him, I foresaw the Lord always before my face, for he is on my right hand, that I should not be moved:

"I foresaw the Lord always before my face" should not be translated "I foresaw the Lord *Jesus* before my face." The statement is a quote from the Old Testament. The name *Jesus*, referring to the Lord, had not been clearly revealed in the Old Testament, so should not be included in a quote from the OT.

Revelation 12:14 And to the woman were given two wings of a great eagle, that she might fly into the wilderness, into her place, where she is nourished for a time, and times, and half a time, from the face of the serpent.

"Two wings of a great eagle" should not be translated "airplane."

Luke 6:44 For every tree is known by his own fruit. For of thorns men do not gather figs, nor of a bramble bush gather they grapes.

The word *peaches* should not be substituted for *figs* in a culture that is ignorant of fig trees. It is anachronistic, because peaches had not yet been brought to the Middle East in the first century. [27]

Beekman and Callow relate the following example in their book, *Translating the Word of God*. [28] It is summarized below with my comments.

Matthew 25:3, "They that were foolish took their lamps, and *took no oil with them*." In Chol, Mexico, there are two words for oil. One type of oil is for cooking, and the other is for fuel (kerosene). Neither of these is olive oil, because olive oil is unknown to them. The Jews used olive oil for both cooking and fuel. The Greek word means "olive oil" and is usually translated in English as simply "oil." So, how should it be translated? The people have no word for olive oil. Should the translator use their word for their type of fuel oil (kerosene) even though the Greek word does *not* mean Kerosene? The answer to this is two-fold. First, Kerosene did not exist in the first century, so to translate the Greek word as kerosene is anachronistic. Second, the Greek word means olive oil and to translate it any other way is a mistranslation. So, my conclusion is that it should be translated olive oil in this situation. How can that be done when the target language does not have a word for olive oil? A new word may have to be created either by combining two or more pre-existing words or making a totally new one. Then, it will be up to teachers to explain the meaning.

Similes

"A simile is a figure of speech in which two essentially unlike things are compared often in a phrase introduced by like or as." [29]

1 Peter 1:24 For all flesh is as grass, and all the glory of man as the flower of grass. The grass withereth, and the flower thereof falleth away:

Human physical bodies are compared to grass. Grass lives for a short time and then turns brown with the change of seasons.

1 Corinthians 3:1 And I, brethren, could not speak unto you as unto spiritual, but as unto carnal, even as unto babes in Christ.

Carnal Christians are compared to babies, using the word *as*. The carnal state is contrasted (also a type of comparison) with the spiritual state, again using *as*.

> **Philippians 3:21** Who shall change our vile body, that it may be fashioned *like* unto his glorious body, according to the working whereby he is able even to subdue all things unto himself.

Someday we will have new bodies. This verse describes our future body by comparing it to Christ's resurrection body. Our new body is said to be *like* His.

Metaphor

A metaphor is a "figure of speech in which a word or phrase that ordinarily designates one thing is used to designate another, thus making an implicit comparison, as in 'a sea of troubles' or 'All the world's a stage' (Shakespeare)." [30]

> **John 1:1** Behold the Lamb of God, which taketh away the sin of the world.

Lamb is a metaphor, since Jesus was not literally a lamb. The comparison expresses the fact that he became the sacrifice for our sins. The sacrificial lambs under the Old Testament were an imperfect foreshadow of His perfect sacrifice.

> **Luke 13:32** And he said unto them, Go ye, and tell that fox …

The metaphor is *fox*, referring to Herod, since the fox is a crafty animal. However, the Greek word is *fox* and should be translated *fox*.

> **John 6:53** Then Jesus said unto them, Verily, verily, I say unto you, Except ye eat the flesh of the Son of man, and drink his blood, ye have no life in you.

Flesh and *blood* are used in a metaphorical sense to picture gaining eternal life by partaking in Christ through faith. Translate it literally. "It is the spirit that quickeneth; the flesh profiteth nothing: the words that I speak unto you, they are spirit, and they are life" (John 6:63).

John 10:9 I am the door

Jesus is not a literal physical door. The meaning is spiritual. However, the translation should say *door,* because He is the way into heaven and *door* is the word God chose to use.

Mark 8:15 … Take heed, beware of the leaven of the Pharisees, and of the leaven of Herod.

The word *leaven* is used metaphorically to refer to doctrine. However, translate the word as *leaven*, not *doctrine*.

Euphemism

A Euphemism is a less offensive word substituted for a more offensive word or a milder word in place of a harsher word.

Acts 13:36 For David, after he had served his own generation by the will of God, fell on sleep, and was laid unto his fathers, and saw corruption:

Death is called *sleep* and should be translated so. Also, the word *corruption* is substituted for *rot*. Translate it the way God gave it.

Luke 7:37 And, behold, a woman in the city, which was a sinner, when she knew that Jesus sat at meat in the Pharisee's house, brought an alabaster box of ointment,

The woman is described as a *sinner*. This is probably a euphemism for the harsher terms *whore* or *harlot*. A translator should retain the word God used, sinner.

Matthew 22:13 Then said the king to the servants, Bind him hand and foot, and take him away, and cast him into outer darkness; there shall be weeping and gnashing of teeth.

"Outer darkness" is a milder (but very descriptive) term used to for *hell,* a place of fiery torment.

Acts 1:25 That he may take part of this ministry and
apostleship, from which Judas by transgression fell, that
he might go to his own place.

Once again, "his own place" is probably a euphemism for hell.
However, never forget that God's euphemisms may actually be
descriptions that teach further truths.

Acts 22:22 And they gave him audience unto this word,
and then lifted up their voices, and said, Away with such
a fellow from the earth: for it is not fit that he should
live.

"Away with such a fellow" is a euphemism for, "Kill him!"

Hyperbole

A hyperbole is a "figure of speech in which exaggeration is used
for emphasis or effect, as in I could sleep for a year or This book weighs
a ton." [31]

Matthew 11:18 For John came neither eating nor
drinking, and they say, He hath a devil.

Of course, this verse does *not* say that John *never* ate or drank.
It is a figurative way of pointing out the hypocrisy of the audience.

Mark 1:5 And there went out unto him all the land of
Judaea, and they of Jerusalem, and were all baptized of
him in the river of Jordan, confessing their sins.

When the verse says "all the land of Judaea" went out to John,
it does not mean every single individual. It is hyperbole to emphasize
the large number of people his ministry affected and how widespread it
was.

Luke 15:24 For this my son was dead, and is alive again;
he was lost, and is found. And they began to be merry.

This is an obvious hyperbole. The man's son was clearly not
dead, he had just arrived back home. The hyperbole "dead' was used to

emphasize the fact that the man's son was gone and lost to him for a while, just as if he had been dead. So, "alive" is also an exaggeration to say that the son was back again.

> **John 12:19** The Pharisees therefore said among themselves, Perceive ye how ye prevail nothing? behold, the world is gone after him.

"The world is gone after him" was not a literal truth. It was an exaggeration, a hyperbole, to say that he was overwhelmingly popular.

> **Acts 17:6** And when they found them not, they drew Jason and certain brethren unto the rulers of the city, crying, These that have turned the world upside down are come hither also;

Paul and Silas had not literally turned every part of world upside down. They had not been everywhere and neither had their converts. However, they had sure made havoc of the silversmith's trade in idols, and the silversmiths felt the devastation. They were exaggerating Paul and Silas' influence in order to persuade the leaders of the city against Paul.

Litotes

A litotes is a figure of speech consisting of an understatement in which an affirmative is expressed by negating its opposite, as in *This is no small problem* [32]

> **Acts 20:12** And they brought the young man alive, and were not a little comforted.

This is a way to express their great comfort. It was not a little comfort, it was a lot of comfort.

> **1 Timothy 4:8** For bodily exercise profiteth little: but godliness is profitable unto all things …

This reduces one especially important thing (exercise) to emphasize something even more important (godliness). It is a communication device that should be translated literally.

> **Acts 21:39** But Paul said, I am a man which am a Jew of Tarsus, a city in Cilicia, a citizen of no mean city: and, I beseech thee, suffer me to speak unto the people.

The city of Tarsus was not a little, insignificant, humble city. Rather, it was a great Roman city. This is an understatement used to emphasize the opposite.

Metonymy

A metonymy is "a figure of speech in which one word or phrase is substituted for another with which it is closely associated, as in the use of "Washington" for the United States government or of the sword for military power." [33]   It can also be defined as "the substitution of a word referring to an attribute for the thing that is meant, as for example the use of the crown to refer to a monarch." [34]

> **Mark 8:34** And when he had called the people unto him with his disciples also, he said unto them, Whosoever will come after me, let him deny himself, and take up his *cross*, and follow me.
> **35** For whosoever will save his life shall lose it; but whosoever shall lose his life for my sake and the gospel's, the same shall save it.

The word "cross" is substituted for the concept of self-denial.

> **Acts 21:21** And they are informed of thee, that thou teachest all the Jews which are among the Gentiles to forsake *Moses*, saying that they ought not to circumcise their children, neither to walk after the customs.

"Moses" is substituted for the Old Testament law.

Synecdoche

This is a figure of speech in which a part of something is used to describe the whole. This may sound like a metonymy, but it is different. In a metonymy, the things that is substituted for the thing that is in view is not necessarily an actual part of the thing. For example, "Washington" is used to mean the US Government, but Washington is not an actual part of the government. It is associated with the government but is not a part of it. In a synecdoche the name of a part of something is used to refer to the whole thing, as in "Taste my steel!" "Steel," the material used to make a sword and is a part of the sword, stands for the sword itself. However, some consider synecdoche to be a type of metonymy.

> **Psalms 44:6** For I will not trust in **my bow,** neither shall **my sword** save me. 7 But thou hast saved us from our enemies, and hast put them to shame that hated us.

The bow and the sword are used to stand for the "force of arms." They are individual weapons in an arsenal of weapons. This is God's way of saying that we should not trust in our weapons or our own might, but we should entirely trust in Him.

> **Romans 3:15** Their feet are swift to shed blood:

The feet are used to point to the whole person.

Irony

Irony is to say one thing but mean the opposite.

> **2 Corinthians 12:13** For what is it wherein ye were inferior to other churches, except it be that I myself was not burdensome to you? forgive me this wrong.

Paul was not admitting he was wrong. He was showing them how foolish their attitude was.

> **2 Corinthians 11:4** For if he that cometh preacheth another Jesus, whom we have not preached, or if ye receive another spirit, which ye have not received, or

another gospel, which ye have not accepted, ye might
well bear with him.
5 For I suppose I was not a whit behind the very chiefest
apostles.

The phrase in focus here is, "ye might we'll bear with him." Why should they bear with a person who preaches another Jesus and causes them to receive another spirit? Paul is not saying they *should*. He is saying they *do*. They will bear with a person like this, but they will not bear with Paul. They will question Paul's apostleship and criticize him, but they will not criticize a false teacher. It is inconsistent and hypocritical.

Apostrophe

This is a figure of speech in which the speaker is addressing something that is not present, is imaginary, or that is not alive .

1 Corinthians 15:55 O death, where is thy sting? O
grave, where is thy victory?

Here Paul is speaking to something that is not alive (death, grave) as though it was. Regardless, it should be translated literally.

Matthew 2:6 And thou Bethlehem, in the land of Juda,
art not the least among the princes of Juda: for out of
thee shall come a Governor, that shall rule my people
Israel.

The Prophet is addressing a city as if it were a person.

Luke 13:34 O Jerusalem, Jerusalem, which killest the
prophets, and stonest them that are sent unto thee;
how often would I have gathered thy children together,
as a hen doth gather her brood under her wings, and
ye would not!

Jerusalem is addressed like a person and it is given the characteristics of a mother. Notice that this verse also includes a simile, "as a hen." Also, when Jesus says that Jerusalem stones those who are sent to it, when it is really *people* in Jerusalem who do this, he is using a metonymy.

Chiasmus

A chiasmus is a series of related phrases or statements that are arranged in an order that emphasizes the relationship, rather than in logical or chronological sequence. The following example is given to help explain this.

> **Matthew 7:6** Give not that which is holy unto the dogs, neither cast ye your pearls before swine, lest they trample them under their feet, and turn again and rend you.

The first two phrases are the first part that emphasize swine and dogs and the two phrases of the second part show the relationship. They are not arranged in logical order, but according to which one the author wants to emphasize. The dogs (A) come before the swine (B) in the first part. However, in the second part the relationship with the swine (B) comes first ("trample them under their feet"), followed by the relationship of the dogs (A) (rend you). It is arranged in an AB-BA order. Dr. Turner gives this paraphrase if you remove the chiasmus. "Do not give dogs what is holy, lest they turn and bite you, and do not throw your pearls before swine, lest they trample them under foot." [35]

Collocational Clash

Collocational clash happens when you put words together that are not supposed to go together. *Collocation* is to place words together in determined and natural order. The words in that order *clash* when they are in an unnatural order or connect in unnatural ways. Dr. Turner gives the following example. "English allows us to say, 'a flock of geese,' but requires us to say, 'a herd of cows.' One cannot say, 'a herd of geese.' The words clash and do not belong together." [36]

Collocational clash must not be confused with *cultural* clash. Matthew 9:9 speaks of Matthew collecting money for the Roman government. Beekman and Callow mentioned how Australian aborigines have been receiving money from the government for many years, and one translation helper could not conceive of someone collecting money *for* the government. [37] Dr. Turner gives an example from Romans 9:17, "For the Scripture saith unto Pharaoh ..." He then explained that putting the word *says* with Scripture is a clash in many cultures, because books cannot speak. Only people speak. Therefore, the suggestion was made that Romans 9:17 could be translated, "It is written in the scripture that God said to Pharaoh ..." [38] However, this type of accommodation to cultural understandings should be viewed with extreme caution. The statement about Scripture speaking is not limited to Romans 9:17. It is also made in Galatians 3:9, where the Scriptures *preach* the gospel and have the power of *foresight*. These statements give us additional insight into the nature of the Word of God. Whenever God speaks words that eventually get written down, those spoken words are Scripture when He speaks (see Mat. 4:4). The words of Scripture are a part of God, just like your words are part of you. The words not only proceed out of His mouth but also from His heart and mind and nature. If Romans 9:17 and Galatians 3:9 are retranslated to accommodate the culture, these truths will be erased from the Bible.

Hendiadys

A hendiadys is a "figure of speech in which two words connected by a conjunction are used to express a single notion that would normally be expressed by an adjective and a substantive, such as grace and favor instead of gracious favor." [39] The conjunction used in the New Testament for this is usually *and*. Normally, two nouns connected by *and* represent two connected ideas, but sometimes they represent a single modified concept.

> **Acts 1:25** That he may take part of this ministry and apostleship, from which Judas by transgression fell, that he might go to his own place.

The "ministry and apostleship" are not two separate ministries. These two words represent one unified concept expressed with two nouns connected by *and*, instead of saying *apostolic ministry*. Apostleship is the ministry.

Luke 21:15 For I will give you a mouth and wisdom, which all your adversaries shall not be able to gainsay nor resist.

Mouth and wisdom does not represent two ideas. Rather, it represents one idea: A mouth that speaks wisely or a wise mouth.

How should you translate a hendiadys? Expressing these concepts by using a hendiadys is not the usual way such things are expressed in English. Normally we would use a noun and adjective. However, the Jews did use hendiadys often. The New Testament is not only the revelation of Jesus Christ and the gospel, but it is also a Jewish book. We should keep its Jewish flavor in our translations. It is my belief that we should translate a hendiadys the way God originally wrote it. Leave it to teachers to help believers understand why it is written as it is.

Rhetorical Questions

A Rhetorical question is a "question asked for effect, to which no answer is expected, such as 'Whatever happened to good manners?'"[40] There are many questions in the Bible, about 1000. Of these, about 70 percent are rhetorical questions. [41] Rhetorical questions are not asked for the purpose of gaining information. They are actually used to impart information. Rhetorical questions have several functions in the New Testament. The translator must understand the meaning, function, and use of a rhetorical question in the source language. He also must understand the meaning, function, and use in the target language if he translates the question literally, because the literal translation may not mean the same in both the source and target languages. Rhetorical questions in the NT are used to emphasize the negative or positive aspects of a statement, to show the certainty or uncertainty of a statement, to express an evaluation of a situation, to give a command or exhortation, to introduce a subject, to focus on certain conditions, to prohibit or condemn or rebuke an action or attitude, and to express surprise. [42]

1. A rhetorical question may emphasize the negative or positive aspects of a statement.

Matthew 7:22 *Many will say to me in that day, Lord, Lord, have we not prophesied in thy name? and in thy name have cast out devils? and in thy name done many wonderful works?*

These people are not asking for information or trying to convince the Lord they did these things. They are emphasizing action they consider to be true and already known by the Lord.

John 18:35 *Pilate answered, Am I a Jew?*

Pilate did not expect an answer. He asked this question to emphasize the fact that he is not a Jew. It means, "I am not a Jew."

Notice that in English a negative question, "have we not …," implies a positive answer, "yes, we did," and a positive question, "Am I a Jew," implies a negative answer, "No, I am not a Jew."

A note from Greek is appropriate here. The TR includes the Greek word *mete, not,* in this question. It is correct and appropriate to translate the Greek statement into English as a Rhetorical question, "Am I a Jew," as the New King James Version and the New International Version also do. However, in this case, since the Greek text includes the word *mete* or *not,* the Greek language allows the passage to be translated as, "I am not a Jew," in a language that does not use rhetorical questions.

2.   A rhetorical question may express the certainty or uncertainty of a statement or condition. Indeed, this is one of the most frequent uses of rhetorical questions.

Matthew 6:31 *Therefore take no thought, saying, What shall we eat? or, What shall we drink? or, Wherewithal shall we be clothed?*

The questions here are meant to emphasize the fact that we are uncertain where we will get food, drink, and clothing.

1 Corinthians 12:17 *If the whole body were an eye, where were the hearing? If the whole were hearing, where were the smelling?*

These questions are asked to express the certainty that seeing, hearing, and smelling are all necessary. It means all the gifts are equally necessary.

3.   Rhetorical questions are also used to evaluate certain situations or issues or attitudes.

Matthew 7:3 *And why beholdest thou the mote that is in thy brother's eye, but considerest not the beam that is in thine own eye?*

This rhetorical question is meant to say that it is not right to judge your brother for a minor fault when you can't even see your own large fault. Or, as Dr. Turner says, "You should judge your own greater faults before you judge your brother's minor faults."

4.   Rhetorical questions may be used to give commands or exhortations.

Mark 14:6 *And Jesus said, Let her alone; why trouble ye her? she hath wrought a good work on me.*

Jesus is using a rhetorical question to tell them, "Stop troubling her!"

Romans 14:10 *But why dost thou judge thy brother? Or why dost thou set at nought thy brother?*

These questions are given to authoritatively direct them to not judge their brother. They are commands in question form.

5. Rhetorical questions are also used to introduce new subjects or to introduce new information about a subject.

Matthew 11:16 *But whereunto shall I liken this generation?*

Jesus asked this question, because he was about to tell them what the generation is like.

Luke 7:44 *And he turned to the woman, and said unto Simon, Seest thou this woman?*

Jesus was introducing the topic of servanthood to his host.

6. Rhetorical questions are used to prohibit, discourage, rebuke, or advise against an action or attitude.

Mark 4:40 *And he said unto them, Why are ye so fearful? how is it that ye have no faith?*

This is a rebuke for their lack of faith during a time of danger.

1 Corinthians 6:16 *What? know ye not that he which is joined to an harlot is one body? for two, saith he, shall be one flesh.*

This question is meant to condemn the sin of fornication, because of its evil effect, and to warn believers against it.

7. Rhetorical questions may focus on a certain condition or several conditions, especially when giving advice on how to handle the condition.

James 5:13, 14 *Is any among you afflicted? let him pray. Is any merry? let him sing psalms. Is any sick among you? let him call for the elders of the church; and let them pray over him, anointing him with oil in the name of the Lord:*

Romans 13:3 *For rulers are not a terror to good works, but to the evil. Wilt thou then not be afraid of the power? do that which is good, and thou shalt have praise of the same:*

8. Rhetorical questions can be used to express surprise.

Mark 6:2 *and many hearing him were astonished, saying, From whence hath this man these things? and what wisdom is this which is given unto him, that even such mighty works are wrought by his hands? Is not this the carpenter, the son* *of Mary, the brother of James, and Joses, and of Juda, and Simon? and are not his sisters here with us? And they were offended at him.*

These questions express their reaction to the surprise they experienced in seeing Christ's power. It is an expression of their astonishment and confusion that an ordinary person could do such things. Ultimately, it revealed their unbelief.

Determining Whether a Question is Rhetorical or Real:

A real question is one which expects an answer. A rhetorical question does not. How do you determine whether a question is real or rhetorical, whether it expects an answer or does not expect an answer? The method to do this simple. If someone other than the one who asks the question responds, the question is real. The response does not have to be an answer. When Jesus was asked by what authority He did things, He responded with another question. Since He responded, it is clear He took the question to be a real one. In other questions, the context makes it clear that a question is real. The women on their way to the tomb had a question, "Who shall roll us away the stone from the door of the sepulchre" (Mark 16:3)? No one could answer, but it is clear that it was a real question. If the question is rhetorical, it is answered by the one who asked the question, or it is not answered at all. Many rhetorical questions are found in the epistles. In that context there is no way someone else except the writer could answer the question.

The Problem with Rhetorical Questions:

Rhetorical questions were very common among the Jews, Greeks, and Romans. They are common and understood among English speaking people. However, this is not true for all people and all languages. Most languages use rhetorical questions, but they do not always have the same functions as you see above. They may have some functions and not others.   Some people groups may only use rhetorical questions for very limited purposes. Therefore, it's possible that a rhetorical question that is expressed in another language the same way it is expressed in English will be misunderstood. The translator must be aware of how things are understood in the target language.

Misunderstandings can abound. John Beekman and John Callow give us the example of the Cora Indians of Mexico regarding Mark 4:30, "Whereunto shall we liken the kingdom of God?" The readers took this to be a real question and decided Jesus was seeking the help of the audience find illustrations to use to explain the Kingdom of God. Should the translator change the rhetorical question into a statement so the people would understand better? Should the translation read, "I will compare the Kingdom of God to ..." The Textus Receptus Greek text uses a question word here, showing that Jesus asked a question. He did not make a statement. If the translator changes it into a statement, he will leave out the word *tini, to what*. Would that be to take away from the Word of God? Mark 4:30 does not exist alone. It has a context which clearly shows that Jesus follows the question with several illustrations, which did not come from the people listening. A little study and some teaching can clear up the confusion without the necessity of changing the Word of God.

If it is necessary, there are some verses where the Greek text can be translated as a rhetorical question or as a statement. Let me give you an example. In Mark 13:2 Jesus said, βλέπεις ταύτας τὰς μεγάλας οἰκοδομάς; "Seest thou these great buildings?" In the printed Greek texts, this is punctuated as a question, but in the first century, Greek did not have punctuation marks. The word, βλέπεις, can be translated *do you see* or *you see.* So, it is possible to translate it as a statement, *You see these great buildings.* So, there are some places where the Greek text allows a translation as a question or a statement.

Changing a rhetorical question into a statement or changing a negative question into a positive (or vice versa) is not recommended. Suppose a culture does not use certain types of rhetorical questions that the Bible uses or suppose a culture does not use rhetorical questions at all. Should we accommodate the Bible to the culture, or should we allow the Bible to elevate and illuminate the culture? When the Bible was translated into English and introduced into English culture, the Bible had a profound effect on English culture and education. When I started reading the Bible as a teen, it challenged me. I learned new words, learned how to think, and even how to write, but to accomplish this I had to listen to teaching and do considerable study. Much confusion can be cleared up by good teaching and diligent study. The people can learn new ways of thinking and communicating.

How to Translate Figures of Speech

The first choice is always to translate as closely as possible to what is actually said in the source text, no matter what kind of figure of speech it is. It will be the responsibility of teachers to make the people understand the meaning of the figurative language. "So they read in the book in the law of God distinctly, and gave the sense, and caused them to understand the reading" (Nehemiah 8:8). There are many things in Scripture that are hard to understand. It is not the job of the translator to explain all of these or to make their meaning plain. It is his job to translate the words of God. It is the job of teachers to explain. So, the first rule is to translate as closely as you can.

A figure of speech that is firmly rooted in a major doctrine or in the historical context of the Bible *must* be translated literally. This is the case with "lamb of God." It was these animals that were prescribed to be sacrificed for sin in the Old Testament. A translator can never translate this as some other animal familiar to the people who speak the target language. In many tribes of Papua New Guinea, the main food animal is the pig and the lamb has historically been unknown. However, we cannot translate the Bible to say, "Behold! The pig of God!" without doing violence to the entire Bible and destroying a great picture of Christ's sacrifice on the cross. The idea of blood sacrifice for sin goes back to Genesis 3 and the idea of a lamb as that sacrifice goes back to at least Genesis 4. In the New Tribes film, Ee-Taow, the missionary to Papua New Guinea used a large stuffed lamb to show the nationals what a lamb is. Therefore, these figures of speech should be kept intact and translated literally, even if the translator must create a new word or borrow a word that is unknown to the national people.

On the other hand, there are target language figures of speech that can mean something contrary to the source language meaning. One example can be found in Matthew 24:31. "And he shall send his angels with a great sound of a trumpet, and they shall gather together his elect **from the four winds**, from one end of heaven to the other." The figure of speech in question is highlighted. This metaphor is unknown is Swahili. However, that is no problem, because the meaning of the metaphor is explained in the next phrase of the verse, "from one end of heaven to the other." Therefore, it should be translated literally.

However, there is a further problem. The Greek word translated wind, *anemωv, anemone*, means *winds*. But, the plural Swahili word *pepo* can mean *winds* or it can mean *demon*. This can be a serious problem and a solution must be found. The following suggestions have been made.

1. Translate it idiomatically as "four corners" or similar. This is not recommended because the word God used was *winds* not *corners*.

2. Translate it literally, just as it is. Dr. Jim Taylor pointed out that the terms Spirit and wind in John 3:5-8 are the same Greek word, yet the context points out the difference clearly.

Could the translators have said, "Except a man be born of water and of the wind"? After all, Jesus later used the wind as an example in verse 8. But when we couple the doctrine of theology with the context and then look at the possible translations, we are driven to exactly what the translators used. Context is what they used to drive their translation.

Personally, because the context defines the word, as you pointed out, I would just use a literal translation. It would be very hard for a reader to misunderstand it because the context so clearly defines it. [43]

3. Introduce some additional information into the verse that will drive interpretation toward *wind* and away from *demon*. The KJB translators also used this technique in 1 John 3:17, "bowels *of compassion*." They added *of compassion* in italics so the reader would know that the words are not in the Greek text. One possibility for Matthew 24:31 is "the four *blowing* winds..."

The translator must be aware of what a figure of speech means to target language speakers. Figures of Speech are a type of idiom and are often unique to a language. The rules regarding idioms in chapter four apply to figures of speech also. Even if a language does not use figures of speech, they should still be translated as God said them. Remember that every language has the ability to express the same meanings as any other language, although the people may not understand them at first. However, as teachers explain the meaning of Scripture, the culture will be expanding in its literary capability and in the ability of the people to communicate person to person. Since the

Bible was translated and published in English many of its previously unknown expressions have become well known English idioms. Examples are broken heart (Ps. 34:18), a cross to bear (Lk. 14:27), a fly in the ointment (Eccl. 10:1), a person is known by the company he keeps, (Job 34:8), and a house divided against itself cannot stand (Mat 12:25).[44]

15 Translation Challenges

2 Timothy 2:1, 3 Thou therefore, my son, be strong in the grace that is in Christ Jesus … Thou therefore endure hardness, as a good soldier of Jesus Christ.

Translating is hard work. It takes a lot of time and there will be temptations to give up and quit. There will be many questions and challenges. You will have to study and pray to understand what you're reading. You will have to look at the smallest details. What does "of" mean? Is it possessive or does it mean "by." It is not possible in this book to list all the questions that may arise, but this chapter contains various types of issues we have encountered.

Implied Information

The question, "Are you that prophet?" (John 1:21), carries a lot of *implied information*. Implied information is information the original participants in the Biblical narratives would likely have known beforehand, but it is not in the immediate context. This goes beyond simply adding a word or two to make the translation clear. John 1:21 brings up the question of who is being referred to as "that prophet"? The question, "Are you that prophet," assumes John knew of whom they are asking. The prophet referred to in the verse was foretold in Deuteronomy 18:15, "The LORD thy God will raise up unto thee a Prophet from the midst of thee, of thy brethren, like unto me; unto him ye shall hearken." Many modern readers in many countries where the gospel is well known and readers among unreached people may not know this information. Should a translator provide the implied information in the translation? One suggestion for this verse is to translate it, "Are you that prophet *who was promised*?" Although the KJB translators did sometimes include implied information, most of the time they did not. They did not include it in John 1:21, thereby leaving the reader to discover it for himself or for teachers to inform believers. *The general principle of Bible translation is that the translator is to translate, not interpret or explain.* So, generally, implied information should *not* be inserted into the text. However, the translator will have to prayerfully decide this issue each time it comes up. There are some general guidelines as to when implied information may be inserted.

1) It may be required by the grammar or the word structure of the target language.

2) Consistent misunderstanding caused by the structure of the target language may require it. For example, Acts 2:15 says, "For these are not drunken, as ye suppose …" In English, it is implied that Peter also is not drunk. In some languages, the word "these" may be understood to exclude Peter, implying that Peter was drunk.

One notable example of the KJB translators inserting implied information is in Matthew 1:6. The Greek text literally says, "David the king begat Solomon of her of the Urias." English grammar requires more. Therefore, the KJB translators gave us, "David the king begat Solomon of her *that had been the wife* of Urias."

Ambiguities

Ambiguity means "the possibility of interpreting an expression in two or more distinct ways" [45] The Scriptures contain several ambiguities. Below are some examples offered by Dr. Turner.

1) Matthew 9:13 *But go ye and learn what that meaneth, I will have mercy, and not sacrifice: for I am not come to call the righteous, but sinners to repentance.*

Does this mean that God wants us to show mercy or that God would rather give us mercy than to have us come to Him through sacrifices?

2) Romans 6:3 *Know ye not, that so many of us as were baptized into Jesus Christ were baptized into his death?*

Does this mean water baptism or the Baptism of the Spirit? Arguments have been made both ways. Paul did not specify which it was.

3) 2 Corinthians 5:14 *For the love of Christ constraineth us; because we thus judge, that if one died for all, then were all dead:*

Does this mean the love Christ has for us or the love we have for Christ?

4) Ephesians 5:25 *Husbands, love your wives, even as Christ also loved the church, and gave himself for it;*

Does the word *church* mean the local church or all Christians as a whole?

These are not ambiguities because of the meaning of the Greek or English words. They are ambiguities in interpretation. Nevertheless, they can affect the translation. The translator may be tempted to add explanatory words, such as the word *water* or the word *spirit* in Romans 6:3. *However, it should not be done.* If God inspired a portion of the Scriptures so that the interpretation was ambiguous, it is because He wanted it that way. Therefore, the translator should allow the ambiguity to remain, if it is possible given the grammar and structure of the target language. Do not add words to clear up ambiguities when those words are based on nothing more than the interpretation of the translators.

In some cases, a literal translation will create an ambiguity in the target language. Beekman and Callow in their book, *Translating the Word of God,* gives us the following example of that difficulty. [46]

Mark 10:38 *can ye drink of the cup that I drink of?*

In one culture of West Africa, this statement is what a drunkard says to his fellows to challenge them to drink as much and as strong liquor as he does. The translator may determine that this question must be translated idiomatically. A translator should translate as literally as possible, but in some cases, he may find that he has no choice except to translate idiomatically (see Matthew 1:23 for reference). One solution to this problem might be to add information that is implied by the verse: "can you drink of the cup *of suffering* that I drink of?" However, "this would be adding to the text something not necessary for understanding. The responsibility falls on the reader to study, not the translator to clarify." [47] The phrase can also be clarified by teaching.

Use of Italics

Much of the information in this section was provided to the author by Dr. Jim Taylor, a colleague in Bible translation ministry and a missionary pastor in Korea. He was a translator of a new Korean Bible translation.

We have already seen that there may be reasons to add words to the translation to make it read smoother or to explain something. Words should only be added by the translator when it is absolutely necessary. When a translator finds that added words are needed, they should be added in such a way as to make it clear to the readers that they are not in the Greek or Hebrew text. In the KJB, any added terms are italicized to indicate a difference from the source text. The purpose of italicized words is to more clearly reflect the source text. It is to differentiate between words that have the force of inspiration, and words that are simply linguistic necessities in translation.

When Italics Should be Used:

Italics should be used when there is no corresponding Greek or Hebrew word, and the word is not implied in the form of the Greek word, but the word is necessary for understanding or clarity. Example: "Whatsoever he saith unto you, do *it*." "It" has no corresponding Greek word, directly or indirectly, but the sentence would not be grammatically correct without it.

When Italics Should Not be Used:

First, italics should not be used for subjects of verbs implicit in the Greek personal ending. For example, the Greek word, *echo*, means either *have* or *I have*, depending on the need of the sentence. Greek verbs automatically include the appropriate pronoun.

Second, italics should not be used for generic words modified by adjectives, when the Greek adjective is used as a noun. The exception would be where there is a possible debate about what that word should be. An example is that a Greek word can literally say, "the seeing me" as a noun/adjective, but it directly implies (and can be translated) "those who see me." "Those who" would not require italics in this instance.

Masculine nouns generally can be translated with "men, people, those"; feminine nouns with "women", and neuter nouns with "things".

Third, italics should not be used for other words that are directly demanded by the form of the Greek words. For example: Greek does not have a word for "a," but it is directly implied by the lack of the definite article.

Fourth, there can be many instances where there is not a one-to-one word equivalence, where italics still may not be required.   For example, "given by inspiration of God" translates one Greek word, but no italics are necessary.

Italics can be a challenge. Bear in mind that a translator is allowed to question whether he needs to follow KJB italicized words in the current translation he is engaged in.   One translator, who is committed to the KJB, gave this testimony: "When adding words (the italics words in English), we ask ourselves, Do I need this, or can I say it without the word and be understood?" [48] Is the italicized word needed in the target language translation. This is a valid approach to translating. Any given language may not need some of the italicized words in the KJB but may need other italicized words, because languages are different.

Polysemy and the Meaning of Words

Polysemy is the principle that some words have several meanings. For example, in Isaiah 7:14, the word, *Almah*, was translated virgin. However, in Hebrew, it also means *young woman.* Over the years the right translation has been repeatedly debated. Liberals favor *young woman*, while conservatives and fundamentalists prefer *virgin*. Regardless, when Isaiah 7:14 was quoted in the New Testament, the issue was settled by the inspired word, παρθένος, *parthenos*, used in Matthew 1:23 and translated *virgin*. The Greek word can *only* be translated *virgin*.

The same issue arises around the word, τέκνον, *teknon*. The word τέκνον means several things. The primary meaning is *a child,* and this is often the translation. The KJB has been severely criticized for translating the word in various ways: child, children, son, sons, daughters. However, the fuller meaning of τέκνον is "to bring forth, bear children. A child, male or female, son or daughter ... a child ... Specifically a son." [49] The word can be translated child, children, son, or daughter.

Consistency in Translation – or Not

In verse 19, the KJB translated the word, μαρτυρία, *marturia*, as *record*. In verse 7, the same word was translated *witness*. This is only one small example showing that the translators did not hold themselves to a standard that required translating the same Greek word by the same English word every time. Translators should have flexibility in this regard. Since Greek words most often have several meanings (see the discussion on polysemy), translators must use the definition that is most appropriate for the context in which the word is found. A single target language word does not necessarily fit in every context. On the other hand, if two contexts are the same, one target language word could be used in the first and the same or a synonym in the second. Let's allow the KJB translators to explain why they translated the *same* Greek word by *different* English words from the original preface to the KJB.

> Another thing we think good to admonish thee of, gentle reader, that we have not tied ourselves to an uniformity of phrasing, or to an identity of words, as some peradventure would wish that we had done, because they observe that some learned men somewhere have been as exact as they could that way. Truly, that we might not vary from the sense of that which we had translated before, if the word signified the same thing in both places (for there be some words that be not of the same sense everywhere) we were especially careful, and made a conscience, according to our duty. But that we should express the same notion in the same particular word; as, for example, if we translate the *Hebrew* or *Greek* word once by *purpose*, never to call it *intent*; if one where *journeying*, never *travelling*; if one where *think*, never *suppose*; if one where *pain*, never *ache*; if one where *joy*, never *gladness*, &c.; thus to mince the matter, we thought to savour more of curiosity than wisdom, and that rather it would breed scorn in the atheist than bring profit to the godly reader. For is the kingdom of God become words or syllables? Why should we be in bondage to them, if

we may be free? use one precisely when we may use another no less fit as commodiously?

As a result of this approach, one may examine how the KJB translated the same Greek word in different contexts and, by doing so, obtain a fuller understanding of the meaning of the Greek word. The KJB translators used different translations of words in different contexts, but they always translated in agreement with the correct definitions of the Greek word.

The opposite is also true at times. Different Greek words can be translated with the same word in the target language.

Though there is flexibility in translating, there are certain situations where consistency is important. Major theological terms should be kept consistent in most places. These words include salvation, justification, redemption, sanctification, propitiation, atonement, forgiveness, and such like. A record should be kept on these and other words as to how the source text words are translated into target text words.

Flexibility in Greek Prepositions

Greek prepositions have a great deal of flexibility in how they are translated. The actual translation depends on the use of the preposition in the sentence and the translator should feel some freedom and latitude in choosing what word to use in the translation. The rule for translation should be to translate a preposition in the source language into a preposition in the target language that is appropriate to the meaning of the context. What preposition is chosen for the target language should be guided by the general meaning of the Greek preposition in combination with the context.

An example of this is the preposition προς, *pros*. The basic teaching on this preposition is as follows.

1) It takes the genitive, dative, and accusative for the object of the preposition. The preposition means something different depending on the case of its object.
2) Most of the time in the New Testament it takes the accusative.
3) It is important to learn the words the vocabulary gives

as the basic ways to translate the preposition.

4)   Those words for the accusative are: toward, to, against, and with.

However, in actual translation, there is more flexibility, as this table will illustrate. The table shows many of the various ways the KJB translated this preposition. Translators should be aware of this flexibility because it will be necessary to apply it when translating.

Ref.	Greek Phrase	English Translation
Jn 1:1	πρὸς τὸν Θεόν	**with** God
Mt 4:6	πρὸς λίθον	**against** a stone
Mk 8:16	πρὸς ἀλλήλους	**among** themselves
Mk 11:1	πρὸς τὸ ὄρος	**at** the mount
Lk 24:29	πρὸς ἑσπέραν	**toward** evening
2 Co 5:10	πρὸς ἃ ἔπραξεν	**according to** that he hath done
Mt. 19:8	πρὸς τὴν σκληροκαρδίαν ὑμῶν	**because of** the hardness of your hearts
Rom. 4:2	πρὸς τὸν Θεόν	**before** God
Lk 23:12	πρὸς ἑαυτούς	**between** themselves
Mk 5:11	πρὸς τῳ ὄρη	**nigh** unto the mountains

The importance of correctly translating the prepositions cannot be overestimated. The New Testament is incomprehensible without them. So, when translating prepositions, look closely at the meaning of the context.

Cultural Substitutes

A cultural substitute is an item in one culture that is substituted for an item in another culture, when both have the same *function*. Both items do not necessarily have the same meaning. An extreme, example is to substitute *pig* for *lamb* in Papua New Guinea for a tribe which knows nothing about lambs. There are other examples of more minor items, however. A few examples of items that could potentially give rise to cultural substitutes are below.

The following examples are some places that may tempt one to do a cultural substitute: [50]

> **Luke 11:11** *If a son shall ask bread of any of you that is a father, will he give him a stone? or if he ask a fish, will he for a fish give him a serpent?*

It has been suggested that in some cultures one might wish to do a cultural substitute for the serpent, because in some areas of the world snake flesh is considered more delicious than fish. Therefore, the people would say that the father would give the son a snake, even though he asked for a fish. For this reason, the translator should substitute some equivalent item for the serpent, something undesirable to the people of the target culture. However, this allows the culture to determine what you make God say in the translation, it misses the point of the lesson, and it ignores the first question, "If a son shall ask bread of any of you that is a father, will he give him a stone?" In the first question, the answer is obviously that the father would give the son what he asks for. That he would be certain not to give the son a stone would be obvious in any culture. So, the second question would be answered the same way. The father would give the son what he asks for. That is the main point of the lesson. God listens to and answers our requests (v.10).

> **Luke 18:13** *And the publican, standing afar off, would not lift up so much as his eyes unto heaven, but smote upon his breast, saying, God be merciful to me a sinner.*

In some cultures, beating the breast indicates anger or a show of strength. Therefore, some suggest that we substitute an act in the target culture that signifies repentance. That would help the target people to easily see the meaning of the act. However, this is not necessary. The act is explained in the verse itself. When the publican says, "God be merciful to me a sinner," the act of beating the breast can be understood to express repentance so no substitute is needed.

Acts 14:14 *Which when the apostles, Barnabas and Paul, heard of, they rent their clothes, and ran in among the people, crying out,*

In some cultures, this would seem extremely strange, because the target people would never consider tearing their clothes. Clothing is much too expensive to tear. Yet, we understand the significance of tearing the clothing in first century Jewish culture. Also, historically rending the clothing in distress goes all the way back to Genesis 37:29. All of this can be understood by reading, study and teaching.

On a personal note, when I was a young Christian, I did not understand such things as rending the clothes, sitting in sack cloth and ashes, and striking oneself on the chest. All these things were strange to my American culture. Beating the breast was an indication of anger or bravado in my culture. However, I studied, read, and listened to teaching. I learned what these things really mean. After that, I have had no problem with them. This is also the way it is in other cultures. Every culture can learn new things, so the Bible does not need to be changed to accommodate the culture. Any culture is ignorant of Biblical truth until they read the Bible and learn. If we change the Bible, they will never learn the culture of the Bible and the meaning of Biblical events.

The KJB and Cultural Substitutes: The KJB does occasionally employ cultural substitutes, mainly in matters of weights, measures, and money. In many of these, there is no exactly equivalent to English weights, money, and measures. Some examples are listed below.

John 2:6 *And there were set there six waterpots of stone, after the manner of the purifying of the Jews, containing **two or three firkins** apiece.*

The Greek word translated *firkin* is μετρητής, *metretes*. This is the only place in the New Testament it is used. The Greek, μετρητής, *metretes*, contains about 8 3/8 gallons. It was translated into the closest British measure available. The *firkin* is a real British liquid measure now containing 9 English gallons according to the Webster 1828 and Collins English dictionaries. On the other hand, Martin Luther translated it with a German word, *Maß*, which simply means *measure*.

John 6:19 *So when they had rowed about **five and twenty or thirty furlongs**, they see Jesus walking on the sea, and drawing nigh unto the ship: and they were afraid.*

The Greek word translated **furlong** is στάδιον, *stadion*. It is a Greek measure of length that is 600 Greek feet, but that measurement varied over time and by location. The Roman Stadion was 625 Roman feet or 606.9 English feet or 185 meters. There is a good chance the Roman measure is in view here, since it was a Roman controlled world. Once again, the KJB translation is the nearest British measure to the Greek or Roman stadion, the furlong. The English Furlong is 660 feet, 220 yards, and 201 meters.

Matthew 20:2 *And when he had agreed with the labourers for a **penny** a day, he sent them into his vineyard.*

A penny is the Roman δηνάριον, *denarion*, equivalent to the Greek Drachma. It is translated *penny* and *pence*. There is not any real equivalence between the denarius and the English penny. However, the denarius was the standard gold coin of the Roman Empire in the first century, just as the penny is the basic coin of the English and American monetary systems.

Matthew 5:26 *Verily I say unto thee, Thou shalt by no means come out thence, till thou hast paid the uttermost **farthing**.*

A farthing is the translation of two Greek words ἀσσάριον, assarion, (Matthew 10:29; Luke 12:6) and κοδράντης, kodrantes, (Matthew 5:26; Mark 12:42). The first is the Roman coin As, valued at 1/10 of a denarius or about 1.5 cents. The second is the Roman coin quadrans, valued at 1/4 of the As or about .375 cents. According to the 1828 Webster dictionary, a farthing was ¼ of an English penny at that time. None of these are an exact match, but each of the Roman coins is a fraction of the denarius and in that way match the farthing, which is a fraction of the penny.

Mark 12:42 *And there came a certain poor widow, and she threw in two **mites**, which make a farthing.*

Mite is a translation of the Greek word λεπτόν, lepton, the smallest Roman copper coin. Two leptons make a Quadrans. Therefore, a lepton is equal to about 0.1875 cents. A mite is something that is very small or tiny. The lepton is the smallest Roman coin, so the word mite is an apt description of it. In addition, the mite was also a coin in 1611 and apparently dated back to the time of Chaucer. It was the smallest copper coin, so it matches the lepton in that way also.

Luke 19:13 *And he called his ten servants, and delivered them ten **pounds**, and said unto them, Occupy till I come.*

This is a money measure. The Greek word μνᾶ, *mna*, pound, refers to a silver coin that consists of one hundred δραχμή, *drachmas*, and is 1/60 of a talent. The closest functional match was the British Pound, which was equal to 240 pence in the past. Now, the Pound is worth 100 pence.

John 19:39 *And there came also Nicodemus, which at the first came to Jesus by night, and brought a mixture of myrrh and aloes, about an hundred **pound** weight.*

This pound is a measure of weight. The Greek word is λίτρα, *litra*. The Roman pound was about twelve ounces, a close match to the British pound (16 ounces).

How to Translate Cultural Substitutions:

First, avoid cultural substitutions if it is possible. Most substitutions are not true translating. They are an accommodation to the target culture. They also do not recon with the teaching ministry, which is designed to clear up the confusion that cultural differences can cause. Cultural substitutions also downplay the ability of believers in every culture to understand that the Scriptures describe a culture different from their own. There are many cultural items in the Bible that are foreign to current cultures outside the middle east, but they can be understood with study and teaching.

Second, there are often no terms in languages that are an exact translation from Greek of terms referring to money, length, and weight. The translator's choices are limited to 1) choose a term in the target language that has the same or a similar function or a close value, or 2) transliterate the Greek words, that is, put the Greek names into target language letters. This would make a translation use lepton, denarius, assarion, quadrans, mina, etc.

Third, when a term is imbedded in the historical context of the Bible or history, leave it alone. When a term is necessary for doctrinal truth, leave it alone. No substitute is acceptable in these cases.

Forth, it is important that readers of the Bible recognize the Bible is embedded in the Jewish and Graeco-Roman cultures of the day. It is important to understand that Christianity arose out of Judaism. To preserve this important connection a translation must remain faithful to that culture. Doing this will not compromise truth, and the doctrinal truth of the Bible will still be clear.

Last, the conclusion is that any cultural substitution should be rare and only be done in extreme circumstances. The goal of the translator should be to refrain from cultural substitutions.

The Historical Present

The historical present is a Greek idiom that views a past event with the intensity of a present event. The events and statements made in John 1:29, for example, were past events when they were written. Yet, John writes them in present tense, "John sees Jesus coming unto him and says…" In John 1:29, John also prophesied a future event in present tense, "which taketh away the sin of the world." John frequently uses present tense and often mixes present tense and past tense in one sentence.

Shifts in Verb Tense:

There are differences in verb tense in both the KJB and the Greek text in the same verse or set of verses. In John 1:41, the present tense is used in the words "findeth" and "saith." This is followed in John 1:42 with the past tense "brought" and then by another past tense, "said." This shift in verb tense is typical in the gospel of John and elsewhere in the NT. It is an inconsistency that was acceptable in Greek and in the Early Modern English of 1611. However, it is not always acceptable in other languages. If the KJB had been translated into current Modern English, the tense would have to be more consistent, especially in the narrative of a historical occurrence or story. Writers sometimes employ tense shifts for certain purposes, but the general rule in current English grammar and literature is: "Do not shift from one tense to another if the time frame for each action or state is the same."[51] Any translator must be careful about the grammatical rules of the target language, while being prayerfully sensitive to truths that the Holy Spirit may want to bring out by shifts in verb tense.

Genitive Structures

Genitive structures are translations from the genitive case in Greek. In English genitive constructions are expressed by two nouns connected by the preposition *of*. Genitive structures are extremely common. They are often thought of as expressing possession as in *this is the book of John* or John's book. However, genitives have very wide meanings. That same phrase *the book of John* can mean *John's book* or the *book by John* or the *book about John*. It is important for a translator to understand the meaning of a genitive. Below are some samples and what they mean.

> **Matthew 27:54** Truly this was the Son of God = possession, God's son
>
> **Mark 1:1** the gospel of Jesus Christ = the gospel *about* Jesus Christ
>
> **Romans 1:1** the gospel of God = the gospel *that comes* from God
>
> **Romans 2:16** my gospel (Lit. the gospel of me) = the gospel I preach
>
> **Matthew 1:18** the birth of Jesus Christ = when Jesus was born
>
> **Matthew 13:35** from the foundation of the world = from the time God founded or created the world
>
> **Matthew 21:25** The baptism of John = The baptism John performed.
>
> **Ephesians 1:1** by the will of God = because it is God's will
>
> **Ephesians 1:13** the word of truth = the word that is true

Ephesians 1:13 the holy spirit of promise = the Holy Spirit that was promised

"Of" expressions will help you discover the relationships between nouns and make it clear who does what action. The examples above can help you do this, but bear in mind, they are not intended to tell you how you should translate them. Deciding how they are to be translated will also depend on the full context of the verse and the passage you are translating.

Genitive Structures in the Greek New Testament:

1. The Genitive of Possession: The Basic function of the genitive case is to show possession. For example, Luke 5:3 says "And he entered into one of the ships, which was **Simon's** …"

2. The Genitive of Separation: Two elements in a sentence which are separate can be expressed by a genitive and translated using the preposition *from*, for example Eph. 2:12, "being aliens **from the commonwealth** of Israel …"

3. The Genitive of Place: Sometimes the genitive case tells us where an action took place. Luke 16:24, "… send Lazarus, that he may dip the tip of his finger **in water** …" The word, ὕδατος, udatos, water, is in the genitive case. The first thing we would think of is possession and to use the preposition "of." However, it is clear this does not work in this sentence. The water is clearly the place where the finger is dipped, expressed as a genitive. Therefore, the correct way to translate the genitive is "in water."

4. Genitive of Content: A genitive can modify a noun to show its contents and be translated using the preposition with. John 21:8, "… dragging the net **with fishes** …"

5. The Genitive of Time: John 3:1, "The same came to Jesus **by night** …" The genitive case is sometimes used to express the time of action. However, it describes a specific time rather than a point of time (expressed by the dative) or duration of time (expressed by the accusative). It speaks of this time rather than that time. Such is the use of νυκτός in this verse: night time as opposed to daytime.

6. The Genitive of Comparison: Comparisons can be made using the genitive case. John 1:50 says, "thou shalt see greater things **than these**."

As you can see, the Greek genitive case is not always translated into English using the preposition *of*. In these examples, it is translated using *of*, *from*, *in*, *with*, *by*, and *than*. How you translate it will depend on the meaning the sentence as a whole.

Subscriptions to the Epistles

The subscriptions are the notes at the end of New Testament epistles in some manuscript copies that give information on the writers and place of writing. For example, the end of 1 Corinthians has the following note: "The first epistle to the Corinthians was written from Philippi by Stephanas and Fortunatus and Achaicus and Timotheus." An article was written about these subscripts by M. H. Watts and published in the Trinitarian Bible Society 2009 Quarterly Record. Below is a quote from the article that shows some of the subscriptions are inaccurate, and therefore, not inspired.

> The subscriptions are thought to have been added about the middle of the 5th century by Euthalius, Bishop of Sulca in Egypt ... The First Epistle to the Corinthians is stated to have been written from "Philippi", even though the Apostle writes in 1 Corinthians 16:8 that he intends to "tarry at Ephesus until Pentecost" and then, in verse 19, sends greetings from "the churches of Asia"... The Epistles to the Thessalonians are said to be written "from Athens", but they were clearly written at Corinth. Silvanus and Timothy, who are mentioned in the salutations (1 Thessalonians 1:1; 2 Thessalonians 1:1), joined Paul at Corinth according to Acts 18:1, 5 ... The First Epistle to Timothy carries a subscription which cannot possibly be correct or even early, because it states the Epistle was written from "Laodicea, which is the chiefest city of Phrygia Pacatiana" but (to our knowledge) Paul never was at Laodicea and, in the Epistle itself, Paul writes of having left Ephesus for

> Macedonia (1.3) ... The Epistle to Titus is said to have been written from "Nicopolis of Macedonia" but there was no Nicopolis belonging to that Province (but there was one in Epirus and in Cilicia) ... The Epistle to the Hebrews, apparently (from the subscription), was written "from Italy by Timothy", but this is wholly without foundation and plainly contradicts the inspired writer's own words in 13:23 - "Know ye that our brother Timothy is set at liberty; with whom, if he come shortly, I will see you". [52]

Just this small amount of information clearly shows that these subscripts cannot be inspired and, so, are not part of the Scriptures. The conclusion can only be: do not translate them and include them with the Bible.

Beware of Presuppositions and Bias

2 Peter 1:20 says, "Knowing this first, that no prophecy of the scripture is of any private interpretation." A private interpretation of Scripture is a personal view of Scripture that is not necessarily justified by a reading of the Biblical text. At times it has been called a presupposition or a bias. A presupposition is a belief that one holds before coming to the Bible to find the truth. Presuppositions may come from denominational doctrine, Sunday school training while growing up, or some other source. Translators must not let preconceived ideas unduly affect their translation. A translator may be charismatic, but he must not make verses promote speaking in tongues when they have nothing to do with tongues. A translator may be a convinced Calvinist, but he must resist the temptation to push Calvinistic doctrine through how he translates. He may do this by choosing words or adding words that slant the meaning toward Calvinism. The same is true for a translator who holds Arminian doctrine. He cannot hide words that teach eternal security by re-interpreting them. The KJB was translated by both Calvinists and Arminians, by Puritans and Anglicans, but they translated honestly. None of them were premillennial in doctrine, but they translated a New Testament that is thoroughly premillennial. They let God speak for Himself. Their goal was to translate God's words as honestly and accurately as possible and let them do the teaching.

16 Other Issues in Translating

Proverbs 2:1 ¶My son, if thou wilt receive my words, and hide my commandments with thee; 2 So that thou incline thine ear unto wisdom, and apply thine heart to understanding; 3 Yea, if thou criest after knowledge, and liftest up thy voice for understanding; 4 If thou seekest her as silver, and searchest for her as for hid treasures; 5 Then shalt thou understand the fear of the LORD, and find the knowledge of God. 6 For the LORD giveth wisdom: out of his mouth cometh knowledge and understanding.

There are many individual issues and questions that will arise in the course of a translation project. Some of them will be one-time issues, but you will be faced with others repeatedly. With some of the recurring issues, you will have to work through your process again every chapter. It is doubtful that any textbook or set of lessons could cover them all. Looking at some of them can help you prepare for the various types of issues that will come up. Many of the following are issues that arise in the first chapter of the Gospel of John. Some will be from the Greek New Testament and some from the English Bible. When the examples are from the Greek NT, it is assumed the translator has studied Greek. However, they should still be of some benefit to the translator who has not studied Greek.

Issues from John 1 in the Greek NT

Predicate Nominative (John 1:1): The verb ειμι, *eimi*, *I am*, takes a **predicate nominative**, not a direct object. A predicate nominative is an object of the verb *to be* that restates the same person, place, thing, or idea that the subject expresses. Ἐν ἀρχῇ ἦν ὁ λόγος, καὶ ὁ λόγος ἦν πρὸς τὸν Θεόν, καὶ **Θεὸς ἦν ὁ λόγος**. "In the beginning was the Word, and the Word was with God, and **the Word was God**." The emphasized portion of John 1:1 contains this predicate nominative. The verb "ἦν," *en*, is the imperfect tense of ειμι, and means *was*. The *word* and *God* are the same person. So, "God" is the predicate nominative of "Word."

Θεὸς ἦν ὁ λόγος, *the word was God*. The New World Translation mistranslates this clause. It says, "the word was a god," because Θεὸς, *theos*, does not have an article. (In Greek, a word without an article is generally understood to have *a* or *an* in front of it, but not always.) It is an error to assume John 1:1 should be translated *a god*. The fact that both nouns are in the nominative case makes one of the nouns a predicate nominative. So, the subject and the object are the same. The noun that carries the article is the subject of the clause and if the subject has an article, the article also applies to the predicate nominative. The translation *a god* is incorrect. The Word is *the* God.

Abstract Nouns (John 1:17): In verse 17, νόμος, *the law*, is a concrete noun. It refers to a specific law that you can touch and read, the law of Moses. The nouns, χάρις and ἀλήθεια, *grace* and *truth*, are abstract nouns. Abstract nouns can be difficult to translate in some languages. English and most European languages are full of easy-to-understand abstract nouns. That is not so in some languages. When these two words were combined with "came" in Trique (Mexico) they were understood to be the names of two angels. This only occurred because of the combination with "came." [53]

How should a translator react to such a situation? It depends on the verse and the words involved. First, a translator might find an accurate way to translate the difficult word that conveys the proper meaning while avoiding the misunderstanding. Second, if this is not possible, the translator should avoid paraphrasing the verse or changing the words. If there is no way to avoid a misunderstanding without inaccurate or paraphrased translation, then the verse may be clarified in teaching.

The Preposition εἰς (John 1:18): The basic meaning of εἰς is often given as *into*. However, it can be translated several ways. According to Dana and Mantey, the root meaning is *within* or *in*. [54] It may be used with verbs of place (into, to, toward, upon), time (to, up to, until), or purpose (in, unto, for).

Information Regarding the Attributive and Predicate Positions of Adjectives (John 1:18): *Attributive position* means the adjective is preceded by an article. *Predicate position* means the adjective does not have an article. An adjective in the attributive position, such as ὁ ἄδικος κριτής, *the unjust judge*, describes a quality of the noun it modifies. An adjective in the predicate position makes an assertion about the noun it modifies: ὁ κριτής ἄδικος means *the judge is unjust*. While it is typical that the article appears in front of the adjective in the attributive and the predicate does not have an article in front of the adjective, there are exceptions as we can see from verse 18. In the phrase, ὁ μονογενὴς υἱός, μονογενὴς is a typical attributive adjective and the phrase means *the only begotten son.* However, in the phrase Θεὸν οὐδεὶς, οὐδεὶς looks like a predicate adjective, but it is not. The phrase certainly does not mean *no man is God.* While that statement is true, it is nonsense in the context. The translator will have to look at the context carefully to determine which rule applies with each adjective. The article is not always the final determiner.

In the phrase, Θεὸν οὐδεὶς, the adjective is fulfilling three functions. It is an attributive adjective, but without the article. Οὐδεὶς means *not one, not at all, no one,* etc. However, it is masculine and means *no man* in this sentence, with the force of *not any man at all.* Due to this, the adjective is used as both an adjective and a noun. Finally, the adjective is in the nominative case and is used as the subject of its clause. Θεὸν is accusative and, so, is the direct object of the clause. Therefore, the phrase, Θεὸν οὐδεὶς ἑώρακε, means *No man has seen God.*

The Conjunction ὅτι (John 1:20): The form of this conjunction is the relative pronoun ὅ τι. There are several ways in which ὅτι is used.

> 1. It is used as a causal particle meaning *because* or *for* (See Jn. 1:30).
> 2. It is commonly used as a conjunction to introduce a clause.
> 3. It can be translated as *why* in some instances (e.g. Mk. 9:11, 28).
> 4. Finally, it introduces direct quotes. In this use, it is equivalent to our quotation marks. There are no such marks in Koine Greek. When it is used in this way, ὅτι does not need to be translated. This is the case in John 1:20. The KJB does not translate the word in the latter half of the verse, "but confessed, I am not the Christ."

The Article Translated as a Pronoun (John 1:21): Sometimes, in English, we will use the definite article to indicate something unique or special. An example of this is in the following conversation. "Who are you?" "I am George Bush." "Do you mean, you are ***the*** George Bush" (former President of the US)? In verse 21, we have a similar use of the article in Greek. "Ὁ προφήτης εἶ σύ?" "Are you *the* prophet?" In Greek

"Ὁ προφήτης" is first in the sentence indicating the writer is emphasizing it. The question is about a special prophet foretold by Moses (Deut. 18:15). Therefore, the article was translated as a pronoun (that) so that the English translation would also indicate the fact that a unique prophet was in view, *that prophet.*

εἰ Verses εἶ, the Importance of Accent (John 1:25): These words have the same letters, but they mean very different things. εἰ is a particle meaning *if.* εἶ is a verb, present active indicative second person singular of εἰμί, I am. The only difference between the spelling of these two words is the accent. The first has no accent and only a smooth breathing. The second has the smooth breathing and a circumflex accent. Some words are distinguished only by their accent. It is important to notice the accent on words.

Personal Pronouns Used for Emphasis (John 1:25): In the phrase, εἰ σὺ οὐκ εἶ ὁ Χριστός, the word εἶ, being second person, implies the word *you* and means *you are.* Nevertheless, the Biblical writer included the personal pronoun, σὺ. By contrast, the word βαπτίζεις is a second person verb and includes *you* in its meaning, but the personal pronoun, *you*, is not written separately in Greek. When the personal pronoun is written separately, it is very often done for emphasis. When the verb is used without a separate personal pronoun, the translation can often be made without a personal pronoun. However, when the personal pronoun is there, look carefully to see if it needs to be expressed in the translation.

Preferred or was made? (John 1:27): Why is "is preferred before" a good translation in verse 27. In this verse, the word ἔμπροσθέν is used closely with γίνομαι. According to Strong, one of the meanings of ἔμπροσθέν is *placed in front of.* According to the 1828 edition of Webster's Dictionary, the definition of *preferred* is "Regarded above others; elevated in station." [55] In other words, *preferred before* is a perfect translation of ἔμπροσθέν. In verse 27, γίνομαι was translated simply as *is.* This construction is also found in verses 15 and 30.

Uses of ἐν with the Dative (John 1:33): In verse 33, the preposition ἐν is translated *with* two times. Ἐν always takes its object in the dative case. The root meaning is *within.* When ἐν refers to location it means *in, into, on, at, within, among us, etc.* It is sometimes used with elevated objects, such as mountains, and means *in, on, and upon.* It sometimes refers to an instrument or means by which something is accomplished. In that case, it means *with, through,* and *by means of.* It may imply contact or close proximity and, therefore, means *near, with, at, on*, and *by*. It may refer to time with similar meanings. Some other ways it is translated are *throughout, because of, toward, under, about, after, against, besides, and between*. Many of these last meanings are used only once in the New Testament. The exact word you use in your target language depends on being consistent (even loosely) with the basic meanings in the context of the verse, your knowledge of the target language vocabulary, and your creativity. This is generally true with other prepositions. Seek God's guidance and carefully study the context.

Uses of the Conjunction δὲ (John 1:38): στραφεὶς δὲ ὁ Ἰησοῦς is translated in the KJB as, *"Then Jesus turned …"* The conjunction δὲ is translated *then* in verse 38. δὲ has several functions.

1) It is used as a conjunction that expresses *opposition* or *antithesis*. As such it can be translated *but, howbeit, however, yet, on the other hand*, and such like.

John 2:21   ἐκεῖνος **δὲ** ἔλεγε περὶ τοῦ ναοῦ τοῦ σώματος αὐτοῦ.
KJB: **But** he spake of the temple of his body.

John 3:18   ὁ πιστεύων εἰς αὐτὸν οὐ κρίνεται· ὁ **δὲ** μὴ πιστεύων ἤδη κέκριται
KJB: He that believeth on him is not condemned: **but** he that believeth not is condemned already,

John 6:23 ἄλλα **δὲ** ἦλθε πλοιάρια
KJB: **Howbeit** there came other boats

2) Δὲ is also used as a *continuative* or *transitional* conjunction and can be translated *and, moreover, then, now*, etc. When δὲ is translated *now*, it often is used to introduce an *explanation*.

John 4:6 ἦν **δὲ** ἐκεῖ πηγὴ τοῦ Ἰακώβ
KJB: **Now** Jacob's well was there.

Acts 11:12 ἦλθον **δὲ** σὺν ἐμοὶ καὶ οἱ ἓξ ἀδελφοὶ οὗτοι,
KJB: **Moreover** these six brethren accompanied me,

3) At times it is used *emphatically* or *intensively*. In those instances, it can be translated *indeed, yea, really, in fact, etc.*

Acts 3:24 καὶ πάντες **δὲ** οἱ προφῆται ... προκατήγγειλαν τὰς ἡμέρας ταύτας.

KJB: **Yea**, and all the prophets ... have likewise foretold of these days.

Grammar and Meaning (John 1:38): The word, στραφείς, is passive participle that is translated as active voice in the KJB, "Jesus turned." The passive voice indicates that the subject (Jesus) is receiving the action not performing the action. So, the literal meaning of the Greek seems to be that Jesus was turned by something outside of Himself. However, that is not what it means and to translate it as *Then Jesus was turned and saw them* is awkward and incorrect English. It is also historically wrong. In the context, it was Jesus who was doing the turning. No one turned Him. So, the context shows the action to be active rather than passive.

This goes to reemphasize a major point that a translator must keep in mind while translating: *A meaning in the source language that is expressed in a certain grammatical form may have to be translated into a different grammatical form in the target language to retain the same meaning.*

Word Order Rearranged (John 1:40): Sometimes it is necessary to rearrange words to make the translation have the same meaning as the Greek text.

Greek: <u>was Andrew the brother of Simon Peter</u> <u>one of the two who heard</u> <u>from John</u> <u>and followed him</u>

KJB: <u>One of the two which heard John *speak*, and followed him, was Andrew, Simon Peter's brother.</u>

As you can see, the words were rearranged. In Greek, the arrangement of words in a sentence is very flexible. Greek is an inflectional language, that is, the meaning of sentences depends on the various endings and prefixes of words, not word order. Many languages, such as English, are not inflectional and meaning depends on words being arranged in the proper order. The word order of the Greek text in verse forty is confusing in English. It must be rearranged to have the same meaning in English.

Παρά with the Genitive of Person (John 1:40): Another issue in verse 40, is that the word παρά seems to not be translated in the KJB.

The object of the preposition, παρὰ, in verse 40 is Ἰωάννου. The preposition basically carries the idea of *with, beside, near*, but can be translated in a number of ways depending on the context. When παρὰ is used in the genitive case with persons, it carries the meaning of *going forth from* or *proceeding from the vicinity* of someone. Verse 40 speaks of the disciples hearing something that *proceeds from* John. The context reveals that what *came from* John was speech. Therefore, it was speech they heard. Literally, "who heard from John …" Since *from John* is awkward and not idiomatic in English, the KJB translated παρὰ Ἰωάννου according to the actual *meaning* of the prepositional phrase, that *John spoke*. Therefore, ἀκουσάντων παρὰ Ἰωάννου was translated as "*which heard John speak*." The word, speak, was placed in italics to indicate to the reader that the Greek word for speak was not present. However, the meaning is present in παρὰ Ἰωάννου, so it was translated correctly though somewhat idiomatically.

The Word *Would* (John 1:43): The translation of the word, ἠθέλησεν in verse 43, aorist active indicative of θέλω, is *would*. The Greek word θέλω means *to will, desire, wish, etc.* [56] The English definition of the word *would* includes *intent, desire, wish.*[57] Therefore, *would* in the context of verse 43 expresses a desire and an intent. Jesus wished to go to Galilee and, therefore, intended to do just that.

The Only Begotten Son (John 1:18; 3:16)

The next issue involves the use of the term "only begotten" and two verses where it is used. The King James says it is the "son" that is begotten. The UBS text says, "only begotten god."

Arianism teaches that the Lord Jesus is *a god* that was created by God the Father as the first act of creation. Yes, they say, He is God, but He is of a different substance than the Father and is less than and subordinate to God the Father. It is a form of denying Jesus' divinity. I restate this, because John 1:18 is another passage affected by this belief.

In 381, the creed of the Council of Constantinople was formulated. It was based on the Nicene Creed, but it added a phrase in regard to the Lord Jesus. It stated that Jesus was "begotten of the Father *before all worlds.*" This statement was doubtless an attempt to completely destroy Arianism and to clarify the doctrine of the trinity. However, it introduced an additional heresy that was even recognized by the Reformers. The 1646 Westminster confession of faith says that

Jesus, the Son, was "eternally begotten of the Father." To be "eternally begotten" means begotten in eternity past. The heresy is that "begotten" means that the Son had a beginning and, if so, He is *not eternal*. Therefore, He is not equal to God, the Father. John 1:18 was likely changed in the background of the Arian controversy and the change in the Nicene Creed. The phrase "only begotten god" refers to the Lord Jesus and implies that He, as God, had a beginning.

The phrase "only begotten God" has very little manuscript evidence behind it. According to the critical apparatus in the UBS Greek text, it is seen in Papyrus 66, Papyrus 75, the Vaticanus and Sinaiticus manuscripts, three other manuscripts, one Syriac manuscript and the margin of another, a Coptic manuscript, a Georgian manuscript, Origen (in two places out of four), Cyril, and seven other church "fathers."

Next to that, the evidence in favor of "only begotten Son" is overwhelming. The entire Byzantine or Traditional Text of thousands of manuscripts includes it.

Is Jesus the only begotten? What does μονογενής, monogenes, really mean? (John 1:14, 16)

The NIV translates the word, μονογενής, "one and only." Others translate it similarly. Nathan Lawrence, in *"Is Yeshua the Only begotten…?"* says this.

> Why is this latter translation a better though not a perfect one? This is because Greek scholars originally thought that *monogenes* was derived from two Greek words: *mono* (only) and *gennao* (to beget, to bear). Greek scholars have now discovered that *monogenes* actually derives not from *gennao*, but from *genos* meaning 'one of a kind or class' and therefore means 'unique, the one and only, the one and only of a family' " (*The Unseen Realm*, pp. 36–37, by Michael S. Heiser; see also *The Complete Word Study Dictionary* pp. 995–996, by Spiros Zodhiates). [58]

He is wrong in this. The word γενος (genos) means *family, offspring, race, nation, and kind, sort, or class* (A Manual Greek Lexicon of the New Testament, by G. Abbott-Smith). [59] The full definition from the Word Study Dictionary is as follows.

génos; gen. génous, neut. noun from gínomai (G1096), to become. **Offspring, posterity** (Act 17:28-29; Rev 22:16; Sept.: Jer 36:31). **Family, lineage, stock** (Act 4:6 where some translate it as "sect" or "order"; Sept.: Jer 41:1; Act 7:13; Act 13:26; Php 3:5); **nation, people** (Mar 7:26; Act 4:36; Act 7:19; Act 18:2, Act 18:24; 2Co 11:26; Gal 1:4; 1Pe 2:9; Sept.: Gen 11:6; Est 2:10); **kind, sort, species** (Mat 13:47; Mat 17:21; Mar 9:29; 1Co 12:10, 1Co 12:28; 1Co 14:10; Sept.: Gen 6:20; Gen 7:14; 2Ch 4:13). (Emphasis-SC) [60]

Γενος is a noun that comes from γινομαι, a very versatile verb. Regarding persons, things, or circumstances, Γινομαι means to *come into being, be born, arise, come on* (G. Abbott-Smith). Since γενός is referring to a person, when it points to Jesus Christ, this definition applies. Therefore, μονογενής, referring to Jesus Christ, means the Son of God entered this world as a human being by the process of begetting and birth. Γινος definitely carries the idea of birth.

Uses of Γενος:

> Kindred-Acts 7:14
> Born-Acts 18:2, 24
> Offspring-Rev. 22:16
> Nation-Gal. 1:14 (an ethnic people)
> Stock-Phil. 3:5 (still an ethnic people)
> Country-Acts 4:36 (may refer to the people)
> Countrymen-2 Cor 11:26 (Paul's countrymen-the Jews)
> Diversities-1 Cor 12:28 (kinds of tongues)
> Generation-1 Peter 2:9

Although in some contexts the word carries the idea of a *kind* (as in Mt. 13:47; 17:21; Mk. 9:29; and 1 Cor. 14:10), this is not the case when it applies to a person entering the world. In the context of entering the world, it means a birth and a begetting.

Doctrinal significance of "only begotten":

The begetting prophesied: I will declare the decree: the LORD hath said unto me, Thou art my Son; this day have I begotten thee. (Ps. 2:7)

The begetting was on a *day*. Since there were no days in eternity past, the begetting must have occurred during time and history. It would be impossible to have the begetting prophesied, but not at all mentioned in the New Testament, as might be the case if every use of monogenes is to be translated as "only," "unique," or "one and only" rather than "only begotten."

The Begetting Described: "Then said Mary unto the angel, How shall this be, seeing I know not a man? And the angel answered and said unto her, The Holy Ghost shall come upon thee, and the power of the Highest shall overshadow thee: **therefore** also that holy thing which shall be born of thee shall be called the Son of God" (Luke 1:34-35).

Jesus is the only human being ever to enter the world through having been begotten by God the Father. He was certainly unique and one of a kind, but He was far more than that. He was begotten by the almighty, divine power of God the Father, creating a fertilized egg in a woman's womb. That is the *reason* He is called the Son of God.

The Importance of the Begetting: Behold, a virgin shall be with child, and shall bring forth a son, and they shall call his name Emmanuel, which being interpreted is, God with us. (Matt. 1:23)

> *The next day John seeth Jesus coming unto him, and saith, Behold the Lamb of God, which taketh away the sin of the world. (John 1:29).*

He was the Son of God, God manifest in the flesh, born of a virgin, a lamb without spot or blemish, fit to be the eternal offering for sin. The translator must include the begetting in John 1:18 and John 3:16. His translation there must match his translation in Psalms 2:7. The begetting is a necessary part of the virgin birth, by which Jesus became flesh and dwelt among us, was born sinless, and was fit to be the offering for sin. Eternal life depends on the doctrine of the begetting. It must be clearly presented in any accurate Bible translation.

Questions and Answers

Finally, I will share a few questions and comments that have come up in the course of translation ministry and the answers. These may help when you are translating the same or similar passages, but, once again, there are many other challenges you will face as you translate the Word of God.

Question: What does "purifying" in John 2:6 mean? Many scholars take it to refer to the cleansing of the hands that the Jews did. This seems a little odd since there would have been over 100 gal. of water there. Here is a thought. What if the water itself was being purified (it is thought that being in stone the water is purified). And the water was rotated after 2-3 days to the next and then again to the third set. They do something like that in Africa called the three-pot system. Then from the last group of pots they could dip a pitcher and pour it over the people's feet and hands. Thus, having clean water for everyone. It is hard to wrap our minds around how they use these big pots to wash in. It looks like this was done back then for washing guest's feet also.

Answer: The waterpots contained 2 or 3 μετρήτας of about 8 3/8 gallons each or 16.66 - 25 gallons per waterpot. It makes sense that the water was for the cleansing of the hands and feet of the wedding guests. Whatever term is chosen for the cleansing should also be used for other instances where Jewish cleansing customs and laws are referred to such as John 3:25. A hundred or more gallons of water may not be too much to cleanse the feet and hands of a large number of guests. They did not wash in the waterpots. The water was drawn out by the servants and carried to the guests. That was what Jesus said after the water was turned into wine. "Draw out now, and bear unto the governor of the feast" (John 2:8). So, they did not wash in the pots themselves and would not have contaminated the pots by washing. It seems to me this wedding was a big one, so a wedding with a large number of guests would require a lot of water. I'm not sure of the exact procedure, so a system like you described may have been used. The purifying or cleansing customs of the Jews are written about in Mark 7:3-4. The water wasn't there just for hands and feet, but for washing hands, feet, cups, tables, and all kinds of vessels both before and after the wedding.

Question: Do you have any thoughts on Greek Strongs numbers 227 (alethes) and 228 (alethinos). It is the Greek adjective for true or genuine. I'm not seeing any difference. It seems that they are the same word with a slightly different spelling.

Answer: There is overlap in the meaning of these two words, but each word has a different emphasis. Both words mean true in the sense of factual, not false. In that sense, they are synonyms. Here is how I see it.

Ἀληθής (227-alethes)
> Meaning 1: to be true, ie. factual, according to reality.
> Meaning 2: one who speaks the truth

Ἀληθινός (228-alethinos)
> Meaning 1: genuine, pure, real, not counterfeit, not pretended, as in "the true God."
> Meaning 2: truthful, trustworthy, honest, one who cannot lie, one who loves truth.
> Meaning 3: to be true, ie. factual, according to reality.

Question: Please give an opinion on several things.

Romans 1:4 - spirit of holiness = Holy Spirit or something different. It seemed to be the Holy Spirit.

Romans 1:5 - Obedience to the faith = Paul's obedience to the faith (a body of beliefs) among all nations, or something different? The Union version talks about all nations obeying the faith and another translator says *obedience of faith among all nations*. If we take his way, we are saying his faith caused his obedience. However, the KJB seemed to think of this as obedience to the faith instead. The difficulty seems to be that this is a genitive and which genitive use should we take here? Any thoughts would be appreciated.

Answer:

Romans 1:4 – I agree this is the Holy Spirit.

Romans 1:5 - I don't think Rom. 1:5 is a special kind of genitive. I've reviewed the various uses of the genitive, and nothing seems to specifically fit this. I think the preposition "to" was chosen because it more clearly expresses the thought *in English*. I don't believe it is referring to Paul's obedience to the faith. Instead, it is describing the *purpose* of Paul's apostleship. His purpose was to produce "obedience **to** the faith" among the nations. The key to understanding this is Rom. 10:16, "But they have not all **obeyed the gospel.** For Esaias saith, Lord, who hath **believed** our report?" *"The faith"* often refers to the *gospel* (see some examples below). According to Rom. 10:16, the gospel must be *obeyed*. According to the same verse, the way you obey the gospel is to *believe*, have faith. Paul's purpose is to preach the faith, the gospel. The response of many in the nations is to obey the gospel, i.e., believe. I don't think we should translate by paraphrase, but if I might paraphrase to show what I think Rom. 1:5 means I would say, By whom we have received grace and apostleship, for *belief in the gospel* among all nations, for his name. Obedience = belief, the faith= the gospel.

The faith equals the gospel: Below are several verses that indicate the phrase "the faith" means "the gospel" in some contexts.

1) Acts 9:20 *And straightway* **he preached Christ** *in the synagogues, that he is the Son of God.*
Galatians 1:23 *But they had heard only, That he which persecuted us in times past now* **preacheth the faith** *which once he destroyed.*
(to preach the faith=to preach Christ)

2) Acts 6:7 *And the word of God increased; and the number of the disciples multiplied in Jerusalem greatly; and a great company of the priests were* **obedient to the faith.** (i.e. believed the gospel)

3) Acts 24:24 *And after certain days, when Felix came with his wife Drusilla, which was a Jewess, he sent for Paul, and heard him concerning* **the faith in Christ**. (the faith = faith in Christ)

4) Philippians 1:27 *Only let your conversation be as it becometh the gospel of Christ: that whether I come and see you, or else be absent, I may hear of your affairs, that ye stand fast in one spirit, with one mind striving together for* **the faith of the gospel**;

Question: Romans 9:28. Do you know why the KJB translators translated the word *logos* as *work* here? Second, would you understand the Greek word for "cut short" to mean to be completed, ended, finalized, finished?

Answer: Logos means several things. It is used over 2/3 of the time according to the major definition, "word," but it is also used idiomatically in Greek. It seems to me, though, that all the uses have something to do with speech or writing, either spoken of, written about, or declared. Below is a lexical definition based on the usage of the word. [61]

> **Λόγος, ὁ - 1.** The Word (God the Word), the Word of
> God (the Bible), a word (of men);
> **2.** A saying, an account (either given or taken),
> communication: speech, utterance, talk, tidings,
> treatise, doctrine, fame (i.e., wide report), a message, a
> report, preaching, a rumor;
> **3.** A thing (that is reported or spoken of, or a question
> asked), a matter, (i.e. "Subject; thing treated; that
> about which we write or speak; that which employs
> thought or excites emotion;… Affair; business; event;
> thing; course of things"-Webster 1828);
> **4.** Reason (logical thinking), a reason (cause or ground
> of something), cause;
> **5.** Work, action taken, (when God speaks, His work is
> done- "And God said … and it was so." Gen. 1.9);
> **6.** Intent;
> Mat 5.32, 37; 12.36; 22.15; Mar 1.45; 11.29; Lu 1.3-4;
> 7.17; Jn 1.1,14; 7.36,40; Ac 1:1; 8.21; 10.19; 11:22;
> 15.6; 18.14; 19.38, 20.7, 24; Ro 9.28, 2Co 8.7; Eph 4.29;
> 6.19; Col 1.18; 2.23;Tit 2.8; He 6.1; 1Pe 3.15; 4.5
>> **εἰς λόγον,** as concerning, Phi 4.15
>> **πρὸς ὃν ἡμῖν ὁ λόγος,** with whom we have to do,
>> He 4.13
>> **διήρχετο ὁ λόγος,** went there a fame abroad (lit.
>> the word went out), Lu 5.15
>> **τίνι λόγῳ,** for what intent (lit. for what word or
>> reason), Ac 10.29
>> **διὰ λόγου,** by mouth (lit. by word), Ac 15.27

συναίρει μετ᾽ αὐτῶν λόγον, to recon with, Mt 25.19

ἡγούμενος τοῦ λόγου, chief speaker, Ac 14.12

οὐδενὸς λόγον ποιοῦμαι, (lit. not one saying moves me) idiom "none of these things move me" Ac 20.4

It struck me that when God speaks, something happens, as definition 5 says. When he speaks, His work is done (Gen. 1:9). In Romans 9:28 the term "word" does not fit the context, but "work" does. His work is based on the words He declared in verses 27-29. So, the verse is telling us that the Lord will utterly complete the *action* in the *word* spoken in verse 27 and He will do it speedily. I think using the term logos is an idiom to refer to the work spoken of in verse 27.

Question 2: "cut short" - I think this means to *speedily finish* it.

Question: We are having a discussion about Romans 11:7. We have some who think that Israel in this verse is Jacob and others who think that it is the nation of Israel referred to as a person. In Swahili countries are never referred to as people and therefore do not take personal pronouns but rather the pronoun of "it." This is the reason for the heated discussion.

Answer: I also believe "Israel" in Romans 11:7 is the nation of Israel. Romans 11:1 says God is talking about *His people*. I think part of the issue here may be the definitions you are using. A "nation" in the Scriptures is only partly the same as what we call a nation or country today. The word nation in the Bible is an ethnic word. The nations in Genesis 10 were descendants of the sons and grandsons of Noah. These nations were people, not countries with geographical boundaries, and the nations were named for the founder of the nation, who was a person. For example, in Hebrew Egypt is Misraim (the founder of the nation). In the Bible, a nation has 1) a common founder or forebear, 2) a common language, 3) common laws or traditions, and 4) a place where they live. If we look at it Biblically, which we should because we are translators, what we call a nation today may be one country with legally recognized boundaries, but within its borders it may have many *Biblical nations*. Kenya is a superb example of this. It is one country, but it has many clans who have their own language and their own identity. I bet, if the history of each clan was traced back far enough, it would be found that there was a founder and the clan was originally called by his name. As far as calling Israel "he" goes, that may only be because the verb is third person singular and Israel is masculine. So, there may be flexibility based on target language grammar.

Further Challenges

Currently, a project has been ongoing in Africa to translate the Bible into Swahili. Typical of all translators, those working on the Swahili translation have encountered numerous challenges. Certain issues are encountered repeatedly. The following three are among the most important they have faced.

1. Meanings of participial phrases: The participle is one of the most frequently used constructions in Greek grammar. It is one of the most versatile verbal constructions, and because of this, it is sometimes difficult to translate. The participle is a verbal adjective, but it can also be used as an adverb. In English, a participle is often a verb ending in -ing. Some languages use many participles, but other languages have difficulty with them or rarely use them. The Swahili project leader gave this example from Romans 5:1, "Therefore being justified by faith ..."

> English speakers understand this means because/since we have been justified by faith. However, it is not possible to say "being justified" in Swahili. The translators tried to say it, but it ended up meaning "when" we have been justified by faith. Close, but not the same. [62]

> This is the reason we acknowledge that grammar in one language does not always convey the same meaning in another language. In this case the quote itself has the answer to how this should be translated. Since, Swahili cannot translate the verse with a participle, it can translate with an active verb. Instead of, "Therefore, being justified by faith, we have peace

with God," one can say, "Therefore, because we have been justified by faith, we have peace with God."

2) East Africa currently has a bible translation, the Swahili Union Version. It is a bad version, but it is some help in finding words for the new translation. Every day the project team has to ask the question, "What reason do I have for changing this word in the CUV?"

3) Finally, the Swahili team is using the King James Bible as a translation guide. The KJB occasionally added words, and those added words are in italics. When the translators encounter italics, they ask themselves, "Do I need the italicized word, or can I say it without the word and be understood?" If you can translate it accurately and clearly without the italicized words in the KJB, you should.

The issues in this chapter are examples of some of the challenges encountered by translators every day. May they give you ideas about how you can translate other challenging places.

17 Choosing a Name for God

Matthew 3:3 For this is he that was spoken of by the prophet Esaias, saying, The voice of one crying in the wilderness, Prepare ye the way of the Lord, make his paths straight.

There are nearly four thousand languages that have no published Scripture, as far as is known. That means they do not have the name of God in written scripture. How should a translator handle translating the name of God? This can be a difficult, especially if a people group is not yet reached with the gospel. Let's begin by looking at how *God* Translated His *own* name.

How God Translated His Name

There are many quotes in the New Testament that come from the Old Testament. Some of these quotes are paraphrases. They are like the way some of us preach, saying, "The Bible says … ," then we paraphrase what the Bible teaches. Other quotes are partially paraphrased and partially exact quotes. Others are almost entirely exact quotes. These quotes sometimes contain the sacred name of God, taken from Hebrew, Jehovah, and put in Greek. Both the Hebrew Old Testament and the Greek New Testament were inspired by God. Obviously, they are two different languages. When someone takes a word in Hebrew and puts it into Greek, it is an act of *translation*, regardless of who did it. So, when God took words He inspired in Hebrew and put them into Greek, He also was translating. How, then, did God translate His Holy name from Hebrew into Greek? Let's look at both the Hebrew names Elohim and Jehovah.

In Hebrew, Elohim is a noun that means God. It is used in Genesis 1:1 and many times afterwards. Look at the following examples of Old Testament quotes in the New Testament.

1)   <u>Ezek. 37:27 with 2 Cor. 6:16</u>
Ezek. 37:27 - I will be their **God** (עֲלֵיהֶם Elohim), and they shall be my people.
2 Cor. 6:16 - … I will be their **God** (θεός Theos)

2)   <u>Ps 45:6 with Hebrews 1:8</u>

Ps. 45:6 – Thy throne, O **God** (אֱלֹהִים Elohim), is for ever and ever

Hebrews 1:8 - Thy throne, O **God** (θεός Theos), is for ever and ever

When God translated Elohim into Greek in the New Testament, He chose to use the Greek word, θεός, *theos*. *Theos* is explained in Acts 17:23 where Paul told the philosophers on Mars Hill, "For as I passed by, and beheld your devotions, I found an altar with this inscription, TO THE UNKNOWN GOD" (θεός theos). From this, we learn that theos was a general or generic religious term the Greeks used to designate a god, just like the English word *god* is a general word for deity. Secondly, we also learn that theos was a name applied to pagan gods and no wonder, because the Greeks were pagans. Nevertheless, rather than transliterate the Hebrew name into Greek letters, or make a new name altogether, God chose the pagan Greek name θεός, the name of the "unknown theos," when He inspired the New Testament.

How about God's name, Jehovah? Below are three examples of how God translated that name into Greek.

1)   <u>Isaiah 40:3 with Matthew 3:3</u>

Isaiah 40:3 - Prepare ye the way of the LORD (יְהֹוָה Jehovah)

Matthew 3:3 - Prepare ye the way of the Lord (Κυρίος, Kurios)

2)   <u>Deuteronomy 6:16 with Matthew 4:7</u>

Deuteronomy 6:16 - Ye shall not tempt the LORD (יְהֹוָה Jehovah) your God

Matthew 4:7 - Thou shalt not tempt the Lord (Κυρίος, Kurios) thy God

3)   <u>Ps. 118:26 with Luke 19:38</u>

Psalms 118:26 - Blessed be he that cometh in the name of the LORD: (יְהֹוָה – Jehovah)

Luke 19:38 - Blessed be the King that cometh in the name of the Lord (κύριος Kurios)

Here are three examples showing how God chose to translate His own Hebrew name, Jehovah. How could it be any clearer? God did not inspire the New Testament writers to write Jehovah. He did not inspire them to write Elohim, either. He inspired them to use the Greek name Theos for Elohim and He inspired them to use Kurios for Jehovah. Not only that, but when he wanted the world to know that His Son has a *name that is above every name*, He inspired them to write the Greek name Iesous (Ἰησοῦς), or Jesus. Jesus' Hebrew name is Yeshuah, which means *Jehovah saves*. However, God did not inspire the New Testament writers to use the name Yeshuah. He inspired the Greek name Jesus, which also means *Jehovah saves*!

How Should We Translate His Name?

We've seen how God handled translating His name from Hebrew to Greek. Can we learn anything from this about how to translate from Hebrew or Greek into other languages? I think it teaches us exactly how to do it. Since God translated Jehovah into Kurios and God into Theos, let us first understand a little more about Theos and Kurios.

Theos was not just a generic word for God, it was also the name of a specific god that the Athenians worshipped. His nature and name were unknown to them. They called this god, the *unknown god* (Acts 17:23). The word *theos* was a generic name for a god in general. Zeus was a theos, Ares was a theos, Apollo was a theos, etc. The generic nature of the word and the unknown aspect of the *unknown god* made *theos* the perfect name to represent the God of the Bible. Before Paul's time the Greeks had been prepared for this. Three Greek philosophers, Xenophanes, Plato, and Aristotle had used the term *Theos* as a personal name for *one Supreme God* in their writings. So, God led the Apostles to appropriate the word as the personal name of the Supreme Creator God of the Scriptures. [63]

Kurios means several things. It is clearly used to refer to Jehovah of the Old Testament (Mt. 1:20, 21) and it refers to the Lord Jesus Christ (Acts 16:31). However, it also refers to people in different ways. It is the title of the owner of a vineyard (Mt. 20:8), of the master of a house (Mk 13:35), of a master of servants (Mt. 24:45-46; Eph. 6:5), and of husbands (1 Peter 3:6). It is used for the title *sir* and applied to masters (Mt. 13:27; Jn 4:11, 15), fathers (Mt. 21:30), the Roman Procurator (Mt 27:63), and as an address of respect (Jn 12:21; Jn 20:15; Act 16:30). Kurios is used in similar ways in Standard Modern Greek and is also used for the direct address, mister. So, the word Kurios means Lord (God), lord (a ruler), master, and sir. In other words, kurios is a word that speaks of one who is in authority.

Seeing that these are the meanings of theos and Kurios, how do we go about deciding on a name for God in other languages? God declared His name to be Jehovah in Hebrew and, as God, He is called Elohim in Hebrew. However, when He inspired His Word in Greek to reach those who speak and read Greek, he chose to call Himself by Greek names, Theos and Kurios. Does He have names in the other languages of the world?

Principle 1: Choose a Name from the Native Culture

God has revealed himself to all nations. Remember, after the waters of the great Flood receded and the earth dried, only Noah and his three sons and their wives were still alive out of all the billions (probably) on earth. They began to multiply right away. Instead of scattering to refill the earth, they began to migrate to find a new home. By the time their migration had brought them to the valley of Shinar (Genesis 11), they had grown into a large number. At that time, they all knew several things about God.

1) They knew God is the supreme being.
2) They knew God is the creator of all things.
3) They knew what sin is.
4) They knew God demanded righteousness.
5) They knew God judged the entire world for sin in a great world-wide flood.
6) They knew God accepts the sacrifice of a lamb.
7) They knew about God's covenant with Noah (Gen. 9).

Up to that time they had always had one language. God divided their one language into many. Surely, He did not leave His name to only one language. Without doubt, He gave each group His name in their language.

After God divided their single language into many and disbursed each nation/language group, they still had the knowledge of things above strongly in their hearts. They had enough knowledge to believe in Him and worship Him. God "hath made of one blood all nations of men for to dwell on all the face of the earth, and hath determined the times before appointed, and the bounds of their habitation; That they should seek the Lord, if haply they might feel after him, and find him, though he be not far from every one of us" (Acts 17:26-27). If God wanted each new ethnic language group to continue worshipping Him, then *surely He planted in each language the name by which He wanted to be known, so they could worship Him by name.* He did not want all nations to know Hebrew, but He wants the entire world to know His name (Ps. 148:11-14). After Babel (Gen. 11), God led each migrating nation to a land where they could live separately from other nations. They still had all the knowledge they needed to trust and worship Him, including His name in their language. All these nations began as monotheistic, and only later did many of them sink into idolatry. Others remained monotheistic. Not all have completely forgotten what they learned in the days of the flood and following. God describes it this way.

> *For the wrath of God is revealed from heaven against all ungodliness and unrighteousness of men, who hold the truth in unrighteousness; Because that which may be known of God is manifest in them; for God hath shewed it unto them. For the invisible things of him from the creation of the world are clearly seen, being understood by the things that are made, even his eternal power and Godhead; so that they are without excuse: Because that, when they knew God, they glorified him not as God, neither were thankful; but became vain in their imaginations, and their foolish heart was darkened. Professing themselves to be wise, they became fools, And changed the glory of the uncorruptible God into an image made like to corruptible man, and to birds, and fourfooted beasts, and creeping things.* (Rom. 1:18-23)

These verses reveal the existence of general revelation. Not all revelation is restricted to the Bible. Some of it comes from God's creation. This revelation goes out to all nations without exception (Ps. 19:1-6; Rom. 10:18). The nations not only had knowledge of God from God's works in the flood and the pre-flood world, but they were reminded of much of that information from the world around them. From the creation, the nations learn of the existence of an invisible creator who is eternal and all powerful. They learn enough that they can know of Him, find Him, glorify Him, and be thankful. God has not left Himself without a witness among the many peoples of the world. "Nevertheless he left not himself without witness, in that he did good, and gave us rain from heaven, and fruitful seasons, filling our hearts with food and gladness" (Acts 14:17). It seems reasonable to believe that God has also revealed His name in each of the many languages of the world.

In addition to the information about God they learn from creation, the nations have the witness of their conscience.

> *14 For when the Gentiles, which have not the law, do*
> ***by nature*** *the things contained in the law, these,*
> *having not the law, are a law unto themselves:*
> *15 Which shew the **work of the law written in their***
> ***hearts, their conscience also bearing witness,** and their*
> *thoughts the mean while accusing or else excusing one*
> *another;) (Rom. 2:14-15)*

Though the nations sank into sin and error, many retain enough knowledge that the gospel can touch their hearts when they hear it. That knowledge includes the name God gave them. *One of the ways missionaries can decide what name to use when translating the name of God into various languages is to follow the example of Paul.* As we have seen, he took a pagan name of a god and, under the leading of the Holy Spirit, adopted that name to be the name of the God of the Bible and added teaching that refined the name to make it mean all the Bible teaches about God. The peoples of the world use various names to describe their gods. Many of these peoples have a name for a true supreme creator God who created all things. In many cases, their belief in this name is pure enough to allow it to be adopted as the name of the God of the Bible. Any misunderstandings the people have about this god can be corrected through Bible translation and teaching. Next, we will see some examples of the adoption of the name.

The Santal:

In 1867 two missionaries, Lars Skrefsrud and Hans Borreson, found a people north of Calcutta, India called the **Santal.** They learned that the Santal believed in a deity called **Thakur Jiu** (which means "genuine god"). After hearing the missionary messages, Santal sages insisted that Thakur Jiu was the right name for God. To the Santal this God represented the supreme God that their people worshipped in ancient times. However, they no longer worshipped Him at the time the missionaries came. They had served Thakur Jiu at first, but later turned to spiritism and became captive to the worship of demons. As they studied the history of the beliefs of the people, the missionaries found that "Thakur Jiu" did not have any disqualifying beliefs attached to Him. They found Thakur Jiu to be in the "theos" category. Their acceptance of this name had a great and positive effect on the Santal people. It led to great interest and widespread conversions. [64]

The Gedeo:

Several million people in tribes of south-central Ethiopia have a common belief in **Mangano,** the benevolent creator of all that is. One of these tribes is called the **Gedeo** Tribe. Few of them actually worshipped Mangano. They were more concerned about appeasing an evil being named Sheit'an. They did this because they felt so separated from Mangano that they could not renounce Sheit'an. In 1948, missionaries, Albert Brant and Glen Cain, came among the Gedeo. They found there several who claimed to have been told of their coming in visions from Mangano. They also found Mangano to be in the same category as Thakur Jiu. There was a great response of the Gedeo to the Gospel. Many were thankful for the opportunity to be reconciled to Mangano through Jesus Christ. Three decades later there were more than 200 churches among the Gedeo averaging more than 200 members each. [65]

The Mbaka

A similar story can be told about the **Mbaka** of the Central African Republic. The designation of the creator in several Bantu languages is *Koro*. Many of the Mbaka were already prepared to respond to the gospel when Ferdinand Rosenau and his Baptist colleagues preached to them in the early 1920's. The Mbaka not only believed that Koro was the supreme creator God, but they also believed that Koro had sent His Son to do *something* wonderful for mankind. They were resolved that whenever Koro's messengers arrived, they would listen and believe their message. Koro was a logical choice of a word for God. [66]

Swahili

The **Swahili** language is one of two official languages of the seven countries of the East African Community and is a common trade language of others. It is the mother tongue of the Swahili people. The name for God in Swahili is **Mungu**. It is a derivative of the ancient name of the creator God **Mulungu**, which is used in the Yao, Nyamwezi, Shambaa, Kamba, Sukuma, Rufiji, and Turu languages. Mulungu or Mungu was known as the great creator god and became the name of the God of the Bible in these languages and in Swahili. [67]

The Kikuyu

The **Kikuyu** people of Kenya worshipped **Ngai**, along with the Embu, Meru, Maasai and Kamba groups of Kenya, and the Maasai of Tanzania. Ngai was the omnipotent creator of the universe and everything in it. Ngai is now the God of the Bible and worshipped by believers among these people groups. [68]

The Bukusu

The **Bukusu** people of Kenya are one of the twenty tribes of the Luhya Bantu people, and they speak a language called Busuku. In pre-Christian days, they believed **Wele** is the creator of all (Wele Khaumbi). After he created, he divided all things (Wele khakaba). In their tradition. Wele created the first man (Mwambu, the inventor) out of *mud* at a place called Mumbo, which means "west." In the Genesis account, God created man from *dust* and drove man out of the garden of Eden toward the east (Gen. 3:34). So, when Adam looked back at the garden, he was looking *west*. [69]

The Luo

There is in Kenya and Tanzania near Lake Victoria a people known as the **Luo**. They are the fourth largest tribe in Kenya and speak a language known as Dholuo. The traditional name of their God is **Nyasaye**. The Luo belief about Nyasaye is described in the following way.

> The Luo recognize a supreme being whose common name is Nyasaye. He is described as Nyakalaga, the one who dwells everywhere. Legend attributes to

Nyasaye an anthropomorphic form. He works and continues to support the universe he created in the totality of his creation. Nyasaye is considered to be without matter. He is powerful and intervenes directly in the daily activities of man. He can create and destroy man. He can send various sicknesses, disasters, and punishment when he is angry. He is also the source of man's blessing ... [70]

All of these and many other people groups have a traditional name for a god who is considered the supreme being of the universe and the creator. In many cases, missionaries have determined that this god is in the same category as theos was among the Greek speaking people of the first century and, therefore, the traditional name qualifies as the name of the great creator God in their languages.

Kurios:

There is great similarity in how Kurios is used in Greek and the uses of the English word *Lord*. In Modern American usage, *Lord* is limited to Deity for the most part, but not in British and early American usage. *Lord* was used for a ruler, a governor, a husband, a father, a nobleman, and the owner of a house (e.g., lord of the manor). [71] In these things, the English word *lord* is a good match to Kurios and, therefore, to Jehovah.

The conclusion is simple. Since God chose Kurios in Greek to equal Jehovah in Hebrew and the definitions and usage of Kurios reasonably match the English word *Lord, then the English Lord is the proper and correct translation of the Hebrew name Jehovah.* Lord is also the right word to translate kurios when it refers to Jesus Christ.

Is this true in other languages also? When I was in Germany, I went often to a German Christian youth center, in the early days. There was an older man there several times, who would walk by me and say, "Preis den Herr" (praise the Lord). The German word for the Lord was *Herr*. However, the word Herr means more than that. It also means sir, mister, gentleman, master, and ruler. It is a very good match to Kurios.

Other European languages follow the same pattern. The **Spanish** words for "the Lord" are "El Señor." Señor also means other things, similar to what Herr means. In **Swedish**, *herre* means gentleman, lord, sir, master, mister, and (when capitalized) the Lord. In **Slovene**,

Gospod means Lord, sir, mister, and gentleman. The **Portuguese** *Senhor* means Lord, master, sir, mister, and gentleman. Romanian has *domnul*, which means Lord, mister, and gentleman. The word *Kungs* in **Latvian** has a similar range of meanings as does the **Italian** word *Signore,* Lord, lord, master, gentleman, and mister. The **Icelandic** term *drottinn* means lord, king, Lord, god, master. The **Dutch** word *Heer* means Lord, mister, and gentleman. In **Danish**, the word Herre is used to mean Lord, master, mister, gentleman, and sir. Some of the same meanings accompany the word *Gospodin* in **Croation,** such as lord, mister, and gentleman. In **Hungarian**, it is Úr, meaning lord and gentleman.

All these European languages have a word that is clearly a match for Kurios. For some of them this is no wonder because of the influence of Greek and Latin, and some of them influenced each other. Nevertheless, there are languages in Africa that are similar without the influence of Latin and Greek. In **Swahili**, the word ***Bwana*** is used for the Lord and sir. The **Kikuyu** of Kenya say ***Mwathani***, which means Lord, master, ruler. The **Luo** tribe of Kenya and Tanzania use the word ***Ruoth***, meaning lord and king. When it applies to Jehovah and Jesus Christ, the translation of the term *Kurios* requires a word that speaks of authority, rulership, power and is a term commanding respect.

Principle 2: Contextual Conditioning

In spite of the provision God made for groups to know and understand Him, there may be people groups where God's name has been lost or corrupted beyond the ability of a missionary to use it. They may have names for gods and spirits, and all of them may be irreparably filled with meaning that is more closely associated with demons rather than God. What is the missionary to do then? How does he translate the name of God in a situation in which there is no pre-existing name for God? The answer is *contextual conditioning*.

Contextual conditioning is based on helping people learn new meanings for words. This is done by a combination of teaching and reading the word in the Scriptures. Teaching is important even if the language has a good word for God and the Lord. But, teaching is especially important if a missionary has to give a meaning to a word that is different than its current meaning in the general culture. It is also necessary to translate the Bible to give the people the opportunity to read the new word in the Scriptures.

There are certain ways to choose a word that the missionary can condition in its cultural context. *The first is to choose a word from another language.* The English word *God* originally came from another language, probably from old Germanic and some trace it back to Sanskrit. As seen in the examples above, several languages in Africa share a name for God, all of whom speak diverse mother tongues. A name may possibly be chosen from a neighboring group barring any prejudice or enmity between the groups.

Another possibility is to coin a word for God. One example involves the Yagaria of Papua, New Guinea. Dr. Charles Turner explained it this way.

> In the Yagaria language of Papua, New Guinea, the word *God* was transliterated as "Got." Yagaria phonemic structure does not allow this word to end in a consonant, so an "I" was added, and the name for God became *Goti*.
>
> Naturally, this word did not mean much the first time the Yagaria people heard it. Through the translation of the New Testament and many years of teaching, the word *Goti* has come to mean the God of the Bible.
>
> The word *Goti* became the nearest formal equivalent of the word God by contextual conditioning of the word in many experiences; some of which were real life experiences and others were those recorded in Scripture. New Testament vocabulary can be developed primarily in this way. One can make a word like *Goti* and condition it to mean *God* by surrounding it with sufficient contexts that cause it to mean exactly that. [72]

Another method is to widen the meaning of old words. This happens often in languages, such as the earlier given example of airport in Swahili. An airport is "uwanja wa ndege." These words literally mean "a field of birds." If the people can be made to understand a concept, such as the concept of God, they themselves may suggest the word or combination of words to use.

We have already seen that Theos had a pagan background. Kurios also had pagan associations. The ultimate "lord" in the Roman

Empire was Caesar. He was considered to be a god. Refusing to accept this was one of the things that got Christians in trouble. The New Testament and the preaching of the gospel declared Jesus Christ to be the Lord of all, king of kings and Lord of lords. Eventually it was the New Testament view that prevailed.

Dr. Turner describes how this worked out with the Kaka people of Cameroon, who had a god named Ndjambie.

> They considered *Ndjambie* to be a venerated spider that, having spun the web that supports the universe, became submerged in the universe and lost all interest in it. He was not immoral, but amoral. He did not care about whether people did right or wrong and was the epitome of unpredictable fate. How is it possible that such a word as *Ndjambie* could ever be used to represent the God of the universe? The process of development went like this:
>
> (1) The missionaries learned the Kaka culture in order to understand what *Ndjambie* meant to the people. This gave them a basis for making changes in the people's concept of God.
>
> (2) The missionaries used the word *Ndjambie* in many biblical contexts. The things said about *Ndjambie* in these new contexts caused this word to take on new meanings. By teaching history as recorded in Scripture, but using the word Ndjambie in the places where God is mentioned, the people began to realize that he was not a cosmic spider who had spun the universe, but a loving person who had created the world and mankind.[73]

Conclusion

The method we should use to translate the name of God is clear. The foundation of our understanding was laid by God Himself when He chose to translate His Hebrew name, Elohim, into Greek as Theos and His great name Jehovah into Greek as Kurios. He has chosen to have many names in many languages. God Himself is the cause of the more than 7,000 languages that exist on earth. He confused the languages at

Babel. Since it is not His will that all nations speak the same language, it is not His will that all nations speak Hebrew. So, His Hebrew name should not be transliterated into other languages, except in those few places the KJB did it (Exodus 6:3; Psalms 83:18; Isaiah 12:2; Isaiah 26:4), so that all will know what that name is.

It seems God has placed a name for Himself that He seems pleased to use. There are words in various languages that closely match the meaning of Kurios. These words are well suited to use for Jehovah and the Lord Jesus Christ. When a missionary cannot find a word for God or Lord in the mother tongue, there are ways to combine or create words that can be used. However, these will most likely need to be conditioned through Bible translation and teaching.

18 Adding to and Taking Away from the Scriptures

Deuteronomy 4:2 Ye shall not add unto the word which I command you, neither shall ye diminish ought from it, that ye may keep the commandments of the LORD your God which I command you. **3** Your eyes have seen what the LORD did because of Baalpeor: for all the men that followed Baalpeor, the LORD thy God hath destroyed them from among you. **4** But ye that did cleave unto the LORD your God are alive every one of you this day.

Proverbs 30:5,6 Every word of God is pure: he is a shield unto them that put their trust in him. 6 Add thou not unto his words, lest he reprove thee, and thou be found a liar.

Revelation 22:18, 19 For I testify unto every man that heareth the words of the prophecy of this book, If any man shall add unto these things, God shall add unto him the plagues that are written in this book: **19** And if any man shall take away from the words of the book of this prophecy, God shall take away his part out of the book of life, and out of the holy city, and from the things which are written in this book.

We have been priviledged to work with numerous translators in Africa, Asia, South America, and North America. The translators we have worked with are very conscientious and concerned about being faithful to the word of God and producing true, faithful, trustworthy, and accurate translations that are so well done that they are truly the Word of God, with nothing added and nothing taken left out. The possibility of taking something from God's word or adding something to it is one of the greatest concerns of translators. The Word of God warns us sternly to never take from God's words and never add anything to them. This is a legitimate concern. Three times the Scriptures command us not to do this, in Deuteronomy (the law), Proverbs (the writings), and Revelation (the New Testament). Each time the command comes with a warning of judgement.

Modern theology and translation philosophy would restrict the "word" of Deuteronomy 4:2-3 to the message only. Many modern teachers of translation techniques are less concerned with the words of Scripture than they are with the meaning. To them the words are not set in stone but can be exchanged for other words if the meaning is maintained. Who determines the meaning of the Scriptures, and when the meaning has been successfully transferred into the new translation? Why, the translator of course. Look at the following example to see how far we have come in English Bible translating by letting translators change words based on their personal understanding of the meaning.

> **KJB: Psalms 23:1-3** The LORD is my shepherd; I shall not want.
> 2 He maketh me to lie down in green pastures: he leadeth me beside the still waters.
> 3 He restoreth my soul: he leadeth me in the paths of righteousness for his name's sake.
> **The Message: Psalms 23:1-3** God, my shepherd! I don't need a thing.
> 2 You have bedded me down in lush meadows, you find me quiet pools to drink from.
> 3 True to your word, you let me catch my breath and send me in the right direction.

There are many differences between the KJB and The Message in Psalm 23. There are many changes in meaning, "don't need" vs. "shall not want," "a thing" is added, "bedded me down" vs. "lie down," "leadeth me" vs. "find me," "quiet pools" vs. "still waters," "you let me catch my breath" vs. "He restoreth my soul," and "send me in the right direction" vs. "leadeth me in the paths of righteousness." The whole phrase "true to your word" is added in the Message. What makes the translator think that "waters" is the same as "pools?" In Psalm 1:3, the waters are "rivers." The *message* in *The Message* does not mean the same as the *words* in the KJB. Does The Message take away from the Word? Does it add to the Word? Does the King James Bible? Do they both faithfully communicate the message of the Scriptures? Do the words really matter? Can we change the words to communicate the message to this generation, or is the message imbedded in the words? If you change the words, do you change the message?

In Deuteronomy 4:2, the phrase, "Ye shall not add unto the word which I command you," seems to refer to the entire law. However, the

Lord followed that statement up with this, "neither shall ye diminish ought from it." The Lord communicated the law to Israel in specific words when He inspired it. To remove a single word is to diminish something from it and, therefore, to violate God's command. Proverbs 30:5-6 and Revelation 22:18-19 are more specific. The commands not to add to or take from Scripture refer to "his words" and "every word." Revelation 22:19 speaks of specific words in a book. It is followed up by this prophesy about those who remove God's words, "God shall take away his part out of the book of life" (Rev. 22:19). To play with God's words is to endanger the soul.

Satan's Original Strategy: Genesis 2, 3

In Genesis 1, God created the heaven and earth. He made man on day six. It was a good creation and Adam and Eve had a perfect environment in the Garden of Eden. All was well. They had a happy relationship with the Creator, and they had full provision. There was only one thing prohibited to them. "And the LORD God commanded the man, saying, Of every tree of the garden thou mayest freely eat: But of the tree of the knowledge of good and evil, thou shalt not eat of it: for in the day that thou eatest thereof thou shalt surely die" (Gen. 2:16-17). The devil tempted Eve to eat the forbidden fruit in Genesis 3.

> 3 And he said unto the woman, **Yea, hath God said**, Ye shall not eat of every tree of the garden?
> 2 And the woman said unto the serpent, We may eat of the fruit of the trees of the garden:
> 3 But of the fruit of the tree which is in the midst of the garden, God hath said, Ye shall not eat of it, neither shall ye touch it, lest ye die.
> 4 And the serpent said unto the woman, Ye shall not surely die:
> 5 For God doth know that in the day ye eat thereof, then your eyes shall be opened, and ye shall be as gods, knowing good and evil.
> 6 And when the woman saw that the tree was good for food, and that it was pleasant to the eyes, and a tree to be desired to make one wise, she took of the fruit

thereof, and did eat, and gave also unto her husband with her; and he did eat.

The first violation of God's will on the part of the newly created man and woman was not disobedience to God's direct command in Genesis 2:16-17. The disobedience was preceded by doubt and misuse of God's Word. The incident established a step-by-step pattern Satan has used ever since.

1. Doubt caused by questioning God's Word "Yea, hath God said...?" (v. 3).
2. Subtract from God's Word: "freely" is gone in Eve's quote (verse 4).
3. Add to God's Word: Eve added "neither shall ye touch it" (verse 3).
4. Twist the meaning of God's Word: "ye shall surely die" became "lest ye die" (v. 3). (Different words equal different meaning.)
5. Once Eve had gotten to the point where she questioned God's Word, added to it, subtracted from it, and changed its meaning, she was ready for open denial of God's Word: "Ye shall not surely die" (v. 4)
6. Finally, Satan delivered the final blow: direct heretical teaching: "ye shall be as gods, knowing good and evil" (v. 5)

Who Can Add or Subtract?

Although translators are among the primary culprits in adding to or subtracting from God's words, they are not the only ones who can do it. Eve was not a translator and she did it. Adding to God's words and taking from them go hand-in-hand with twisting the meaning just like Eve did. Pastors and other teachers can do this easily. In fact, anyone can do it, if they are not careful with how they tell others "what God says." Take heed that you do not add something or take away something that changes the meaning of God's Word.

Even though anyone can repeat what Eve did, it has been done in a very destructive way for a long time. It is particularly grievous in the new English translations starting in the late nineteenth century through the early twenty-first century. Ever since 1881 when the Revised Version was published, new English Bible versions have been translated and published on the average of about two per year. [74] When new English Bibles are printed they are called "derivative works" under copyright law. A copyright will not be granted for a derivative work unless certain requirements are met.

> Section 101 of the federal Copyright Act defines a derivative work as a "work based or derived from one or more already existing works." To be copyrightable, a derivative work must incorporate some or all of a preexisting work **and add new original copyrightable authorship to that work**. Courts evaluate the originality requirement for derivative works no more stringently than any other copyrighted work. The requisite level of originality is extremely low and simply requires "**independent creation plus a modicum of creativity**." *Fiest Publ'ns, Inc., 499 US 346.* Thus, a derivative work can be sufficiently original for purposes of copyright law, even though it **closely resembles** preexisting works. [75] (Author's emphasis)

This requirement means that every English "Bible" that is published must be *different* than all those that came before. If a new version were to be published today, it would have to contain new creative content different than the more than 250 previous versions. Something must be added, taken away, or changed to get a copyright. So, we are going to focus on how a translator can add to the Word of God, and how he can take away from it. Doing this will help you to see how modern Bibles have been changed.

When One is *NOT* Adding or Taking Away

What does it mean, then, to add to or subtract from the Word of God? First, let's look at two situations that are *not* violations of God's commands in this matter.

Christians are merely human. They make mistakes. No matter how dedicated and sincere they are, no matter how hard they try, they are still prone to error. *When a teacher or translator makes a mistake, he is not guilty of adding to or subtracting from the Scriptures.* The prohibitions in Deuteronomy, Proverbs, and Revelation describe someone who is *deliberately* altering God's Word. However, if a translator becomes aware of his mistake and deliberately chooses not to correct it, he may be guilty of adding to God's word or diminishing something from it.

Secondly, *a translator does not violate those commands when he pays attention to the grammatical requirements of the target language.* There are over 7,000 languages and God is the author of them all (see Genesis 11). All languages have similar components: nouns, verbs, adjectives, etc. However, they differ in how those components are used to express meaning. I say, "What is your name?" A German says, "How are you called?" I say, "My car doesn't work." A German says, "Mine auto goes not." These differences exist between Greek, Hebrew, and English, also. Translators must translate so that the translation is accurate, but also good grammar and idiom in the target language. John 1:1 is a perfect example.

> **Greek:** In beginning was the word and the word was with the God and God was the word.
> **KJB:** In the beginning was the word, and the word was with God, and the word was God.

There are differences between the literal Greek translation and the KJB. A definite article was added, "In *the* beginning." A definite article was left out: "the word was with *the* God," vs. "the word was with God." The last phrase in the KJB, "the word was God," is in a different word order, but this is perfectly accurate according to Greek and presents no problem. So, did the KJB violate the commands not to add or subtract, when it added an article and subtracted an article? The answer is no. Why not? The differences are required by the rules of the English language. No two languages are the same. A single word in one language may require two or more words in another language to express the same meaning. The opposite is also true. Two or more words in the first language may be translated by only one word in the next language. These things are not in violation of the passages in Deuteronomy, Proverbs, and Revelation. The actions listed above do not violate the prohibitions, because the grammar and syntax of the languages involved require them. No two languages can be translated exactly literally. God made languages and these matters are God-made characteristics of languages. The goal of a translator is to make a translation that reads smoothly and accurately according to the rules of the language that is receiving the Word of God

Taking Away From the Words of God

How does one take away from the Scriptures, then? Below are five ways one may take away from the Words of God.

First, a translator may take away from God's words when he fails to translate words of the Bible that are necessary to convey the meaning of the Biblical text. We are looking at words beyond "the" and "a." God used the words He wanted to use. It is not up to me or you to decide which are important and which are not. Notice this comparison.

> **Matthew 1:25 KJB** - And knew her not till she had brought forth her **firstborn** son: and he called his name JESUS.
> **Matthew 1:25 NIV** - But he did not consummate their marriage until she gave birth to a son. And he gave him the name Jesus.

The NIV leaves out the very important doctrinal words "her firstborn."

Second, You may take away from God's words when you translate the Hebrew and Greek words of Scripture into words that inadequately communicate the meaning.

> **Matthew 6:1 KJB -** Take heed that ye do not your **alms** before men, to be seen of them:
> **Matthew 6:1 NIV** - Be careful not to practice your **righteousness** in front of others to be seen by them.

The NIV changed the word "alms" to "righteousness." The two words do not mean the same thing. "Righteousness" is to obey the law of God, while "alms" is to give love gifts to the poor. Righteousness includes giving alms, but it is not specific enough to communicate the right meaning. When the NIV changes the Biblical word into a word that means something different, it is hiding the word God chose from people.

In reality, this difference is not there because some translator decided to use a different word. It is based on two rival Greek New Testaments, which is discussed elsewhere in this book and in *A Practical Theology of Bible Translating.* However, that simply means that one of those Greek texts changed the Word of God. You had better be careful which Greek New Testament you use, if you do not want to take away from or add to God's word. Do not simply accept a modern scholar's word for it.

On the other hand, the words "do" (KJB) and "practice" come from the same Greek word. The meaning of the Greek word is basically to do or make something. The two different words used in the KJB and the NIV do not mean the same thing. "Practice" involves a repeated or habitual action, while "do" may be a one-time action. So, it's ok to give alms to get glory from men as long as it's only once or twice and not as a practice? Changing the word can change or confuse the meaning and is, in reality, both taking away the right word and adding the wrong word.

Third, a translator may take away from God's words when the words he uses convey a different meaning than the original words. When this is done, the new translation says something God did not say. *Such a translation is not God's word in that place.* It is hiding God's word from people and giving them the words of the translators instead.

> **Matthew 6:27 KJB -** Which of you by taking thought can add **one cubit unto his stature?**
> **Matthew 6:27 NIV -** Can any one of you by worrying add **a single hour to your life?**

The two highlighted statements are obviously not the same. This difference does not come from differences in the Greek New Testament. The United Bible Societies Greek text, the Nestle, the Westcott and Hort, the SBL, the Tyndale, and the Textus Receptus *all read the same.* They all say, "one cubit unto his stature." This was deliberately changed by the translators. God did not say "a single hour to your life." Those are the words of the translators not the words of God. Those words were added after the words "one cubit unto his stature" were taken away and hidden from the readers.

Fourth, a translator can take away from God's word when he creates a confusing translation. Examples of poor translation have often come to light. In an airport in India, a sign boldly proclaimed, "Eating carpet strictly prohibited." In an Arab country, a marketplace was selling "Syrian Paralysis Cheese." In Asia, a handicap pathway was marked, "Deformed Man Passage." This is one of the reasons that a translation must go through a rigorous checking process with native speakers of the language. The translator's job is to do all he can to avoid confusion.

> **Job 6:6 KJB** - or is there any taste in the white of an egg?
> **Job 6:6 RSV** - or is there any taste in the slime of the purslane?

> Who killed Goliath? David did! Or, did he? See 1 Samuel 21:9.

> **2 Samuel 21:19 KJB** - Elhanan the son of Jaareoregim, a Bethlehemite, **slew the brother of Goliath the Gittite**
> **2 Samuel 21:19 NCV** (New Century Version) - Elhanan son of Jaare-Oregim from Bethlehem **killed Goliath** – Dito the Message, the ASV, the NASV (1995), the Christian Standard Bible, etc.

Fifth, a translator may be taking away from the word of God by using or promoting a Greek New Testament text or a Hebrew text that removes words from the Textus Receptus or the Ben Chayyim Hebrew text.

Adding to the Words of God

First, one can add to the Words of God by adding words that are not warranted by the source text, whether those words change the meaning or not.

> **Matthew 24:36 - KJB** But of that day and hour knoweth no man, no, not the angels of heaven, but my Father only.
> **Matthew 24:36 - NIV** But about that day or hour no one knows, not even the angels in heaven, **nor the Son**, but only the Father. The NIV adds the words "nor the son."

Second, a translator can add to the Words of God by adding words that change the meaning of the source text.

> **Matthew 19:17 KJB** - And he said unto him, **Why callest thou me good**? there is none good but one, that is, God:
> **Matthew 19:17 (NIV)** "Why do you **ask me about what is good?"** Jesus replied. "There is only One who is good…"

The man did not ask about what is good. The concept of the "good" was an ancient Greek philosophical discussion. Once again this comes from a faulty Greek text. Centuries ago, someone decided to add

Greek philosophy to the New Testament by *removing* "why callest thou me" and *adding* "ask me about what is" in front of "good," thereby changing the meaning.

Third, a translator can add to Scripture by adding words that reflect his own bias or translating according to his own ideas or private interpretation of Scripture.

> **Psalm 1:1** KJB - Blessed is the man that walketh not in the counsel of the ungodly, nor standeth in the way of sinners, nor sitteth in the seat of the scornful.
>
> **Psalm 1:1** "God's Word" - Blessed is the person who does not follow the advice of wicked people, take the path of sinners, or join the company of mockers.
>
> **Psalm 1:1** The Message - How well God must like you— you don't walk in the ruts of those blind-as-bats, you don't stand with the good-for-nothings, you don't take your seat among the know-it-alls.

The so-called "God's Word" and The Message placed the personal interpretation and teaching of the translators in the text, in place of the actual words of God. In this way, the meaning of the text can be twisted according to private interpretation. The answer to bias is simple. It is exemplified by the KJB translators. Some of the KJB translators were Calvinists and some were Arminians. Some were Puritans and some Anglicans. Nevertheless, they all translated honestly, letting the Scriptures speak for themselves.

Fourth, a translator can add to the Word of God if he tries to translate in such a way that explains the meaning of Scripture. This is exhibited by several of the examples above, especially with the Message. The translator is not writing a commentary. He is translating what God said. Commentaries and explanations are the job of teachers, not translators.

Fifth, a translator can add to the word of God by using or promoting a Greek New Testament text or a Hebrew text that removes words from the Textus Receptus or the Ben Chayyim Hebrew text.

What a Translator Needs

I think most translators want to do a good job. Many of them fear taking words away from Scripture or adding words to it. How can they avoid doing that? Here are some suggestions.

1) The translator must understand the meaning of the source language words as well as he can.

2) The translator must know what words in the target language convey the same meaning as the words in the source language and how to use target language grammar and syntax to precisely convey the Biblical meaning.

3) The translator must choose the target language words that are closest in meaning to the biblical words and arrange them in a final translation, translating as literally as possible.

4) The translator must convey to target language speakers and readers the exact same meaning that is in the source language with equivalent words.

Being a Bible translator is an extremely serious thing. So, care must be taken not to add to or take from God's Word. In *Biblical Bible Translating*, Charles Turner has some encouragement to give translators.

> What is a translator to do then? Many missionaries have faced this dilemma, and rather than taking the risk of adding to or taking away from the Bible, they do not translate any Scripture at all. These missionaries take away more of God's Word from the people than anyone else! They do not give them any portion of God's Word … A translator who has done his best to study the meaning of the Bible and learn the native language and culture will not be adding to Scripture or taking away from it. [76]

19 Checking and Testing the Translation

Proverbs 11:14 Where no counsel is, the people fall: but in the multitude of counsellors there is safety.
2 Corinthians 13:1 In the mouth of two or three witnesses shall every word be established.
Proverbs 18:17 He that is first in his own cause seemeth just; but his neighbour cometh and searcheth him.

Once a chapter or a book has been translated the job is not done. The same book or chapter must go through a rigorous checking and testing process. *Checking* means that the translation is proofread for grammar and typing errors and examined to determine its accuracy. This should be done in small segments while the translating is being done. *Testing* is different. In testing, we put the translation to use in real-world situations, such as teaching, preaching, etc. This checking and testing is performed by a number of different individuals. It results in gaining insight into the quality of the translation, finding errors, and refining the choice of words. The purpose is to produce the most accurate and excellent translation possible. The more times it is checked and tested, and the more people involved, the greater the chance that the translation will be completely accurate.

A translator should check his own work but should not depend on himself alone. The Scriptures above teach us several important things about that. We may think our work to be fine, maybe even perfect, but then someone else views it and finds several errors. "He that is first in his own cause seemeth just; but his neighbour cometh and searcheth him." "In the mouth of two or three witnesses every word shall be established." In fact, the more checkers and testers there are, the better it is. The Bible uses the word *multitude*, "in the multitude of counsellors there is safety."

Begin with a Translator Self-Check

The very first person who should check the translation is the translator himself. When you have finished translating a chapter or portion of a chapter, you should set it aside for a day or so. Then, you can come back to it with a fresh mind. This will help you to see things you missed the first time through. If the translation is handwritten, this first check is performed *before* it is typed. Further checking will be done *after* the manuscript is typed.

First, proofread it for spelling, punctuation, grammar, and capitalization. Are proper names correctly and consistently spelled? Is punctuation used properly? Are periods and commas where they should be? Are direct quotations shown properly according to the rules of the target language? Are the chapter and verse numbers correct? Are any verse numbers left out? Have you consistently used italics for added words?

Next, check the quality of the translated text. Review each verse for accuracy. Did you choose the right word? Is the grammar correct? Is it clear and understandable? Does it read naturally as in the usual written and spoken target language. You want it to be the normal target language, but not a dialect of the language that is used by only one segment of the culture. To explain, Swahili is a language spoken in different dialects in Kenya, Tanzania, Uganda, the DRC, etc. Additionally, the street language is different than standard Swahili. Yet, standard Swahili is clear to all who speak the various dialects. It is the standard language that should be used for the target translation.

Checking in a Team or Single Translator Setting

When there is only one translator there may be limitations on how many people can be found to help check the translation. Regardless of that, a thorough job of checking can still be done. An example of this comes from Dr. Robert Patton, medical doctor, missionary to Suriname in South America, and translator of the Bible into Sranantongo.

My plan was as follows. First, I studied the text carefully, and usually read a conservative commentary on the section to help me understand it clearly. Then I made a preliminary translation. This translation was given to two assistants, who would independently correct and modify the translation. I would incorporate both their suggestions into a revised translation. The revised translation was given to two additional language helpers, who each revised the revision working independently. These revisions were worked again into a corrected copy, which was then given to a third pair of language helpers, who repeated the process. Thus the text was gradually refined with six nationals working on it independently along with myself. [77]

Another example comes from Ron Myers, missionary to the Isan people of Northeast Thailand and translator of the Bible into Isan. After many years translating the Bible, the New Testament was completed and published in 2016. The twenty-two million plus Isan had never had a New Testament in their language until then. He was the lone translator of the Isan New Testament, and throughout the process he knew the need for careful and detailed checking. He would translate a large portion of Scripture, then he and one or two Isan translation helpers would do a thorough and painstaking check on every word.

Lord willing, I will be leaving for Thailand very soon. While there, I will be checking the books of Hebrews, Colossians, and Philippians, which are newly translated into the Isan people's heart language, but need a final proofread to insure the highest possible accuracy and fluency ... [78] I am also networking with a missionary in Asia who is a software engineer, and hope to have a specialized computer program in the near future that will greatly speed up the initial translation process. This, however, does not alleviate the need for a personal hands-on touch and constant careful checking to insure accuracy and readability ... [79]

Checking the translation as a team of translators can be a richly rewarding activity. As explained before, this was a top characteristic of the King James translation committees. The following comments by Katherine Barnwell are helpful advice.

Some of the most helpful comments and suggestions come from other members of the translation team. If there are two translators, they will want to exchange their work for comments and suggestions. Where there is an advisor, he will also have suggestions to make. Experiment to find out which method of working is most effective for your team. Many teams find it helpful to exchange comments in writing first, and then to sit together to read the translation aloud, and to discuss points that are not yet settled. You will then make any revisions that result from this discussion, before giving the manuscript to the typist to be typed. [80]

Each member of the translation team should read it to himself several times. This will bring to light many places in the translation that can be improved. The check can be done as a group, or it can be done apart. The important thing is that the translators submit their work to other members of the team for checking. Then gather to discuss any issues. There are many ways of doing this. The team must find the best way for them.

Categories to Check in the Translation

After translating a chapter, laying it aside for a short time, and then doing a proofread and self-check, the translation should be checked by the team and others for the following things.

1. Is the format consistent? Decisions will have to be made about format when the translation is typed. The format includes things like margins, font type, font size, headers, footers, bold print, italics, underlining, spacing, verse numbering, chapter numbering, page size, etc. Each typed copy needs to be consistent in these things.

2. Is the translation accurate? Each word needs to be checked against the source text. Do the words of the translation carry the same meaning as the source words? Is any word or any meaning left out? Is anything added? Is any meaning changed? If any words have been added to make the meaning clear, make the text grammatically accurate, or include implied information, are they in italics or some other convention to show that they are not in the source text?

3. Is the translation natural? Does the translation read like the normal, usual written target language? Does it seem foreign or odd at any place? Does each chapter connect together smoothly?

4. Is the translation clear? Are there any places that are confusing or that are likely to be misunderstood? Is it easy to understand what the action is, where it took place, and who did it? Do the thoughts follow one another just as they do in the source text? How are the idioms handled? Are any idioms not understandable?

Ways to Check a Translation

Below are several ways to check a translation. These tasks always involve national speakers of the source language. The translators or selected checkers can lead in the tasks. Except for methods 1 and 2, none of these activities should be done by the translators, unless it is a translator who leads it. Instead, use as many others as you can, because it will tell you how the public may receive and understand the new translation. Develop a method to keep track of all suggested changes to the translation. As a reminder, do not wait until you finish a whole book to begin this process. Checking is easier if you do it in smaller segments. Also, doing this in segments will build anticipation on the part of the churches for the finished translation.

1. Read the translation to yourself soon after you finish translating. Lay it aside for a few days, then read it aloud to yourself. Later, all the translators should read it aloud as a group. Reading aloud may alert you to errors that you do not see from silent reading.

2. You could record the translation as you read it aloud. In preparation for this, you will read it aloud several times. Doing this accomplishes several things. Repeated reading sometimes reveals errors that you did not notice before. When others listen to the recording, they may notice mistakes. Also, the recording allows those who cannot read to help check the translation.

3. Make copies of the finished chapter and distribute them to several nationals. Ask them to read it privately and comment on anything that seems odd, unclear, unnatural, or unexpected. It is best if the comments are in writing.

4. Read the chapter or a portion of it to a group. Ask a volunteer to describe the action if the chapter is a narrative. If the chapter is a New Testament epistle, ask the volunteer to name one or two things he learns from the chapter. Usually, it will be obvious whether he understands or not. Ask about anything they do not understand. You can read the whole chapter at once or in segments. Reading it in segments is better if the chapter is from an epistle. Doing this indicates whether or not the translation is clear and understandable.

Another way to do this is to ask the volunteers to restate what you read in their own words. Use only a short passage of three or four verses for this. Is any part of the meaning left out of the restatement? Did the restatement include anything that was different than the meaning the translator intended? The reader may use some good words or expressions in his restatement that are better than those used by the translator. Write these down and consider using them.

5. Read the chapter to a group or an individual and ask specific questions about it. This is best done by reading one segment at a time. Who did the action? What did they do? What did they say? Make sure the questions you ask are specific and clear. If they are unclear, the group will not be able to answer them. Do not ask questions like, "do you understand this." Do not ask yes or no questions. Do not let the person answering look at any Bible other than the translation.

6. Ask several nationals to read the chapter while you listen. The leader uses only one copy on which to mark places that may be a problem. That way, all the reactions of the readers are on the same copy no matter how many such sessions the leader holds.

As they read, mark the places where they stop, stumble, or look confused. If several readers have reactions like these at the same places, it is a strong indication of a problem. Changes may be needed. The meaning may not be clear. The translation may be using a not well-known word or expression or an unnatural expression.

Occasionally, the reader may change a word as he reads. This may be because he is tired, or it may be because there is something unusual at that place. A reader may read the chapter is a way that the translator did not intend. He may mispronounce a word in a way that changes its meaning. This may be because the reader did not understand what he read. The translation probably needs improvement at these places.

Always tell the readers that you are testing the translation, not their ability to read.

7. Read the chapter to a group or an individual. Stop at places and ask them to fill in the missing word that you leave out. The national should be able to do this if he has understood the text up to that point.

8. Occasionally, you will be undecided between two or more alternative translations of a certain word, phrase, or verse. Present the alternatives to several people. Give them the alternatives and ask, "Which is better." This can lead to very useful discussion and help the translators to determine which alternative is best.

9. Distribute printed copies to people with Bible education, pastors, teachers, and church leaders. They write down their comments for improving the translation and send them back to the translators.

10. Use a back-translation. Back-translations are explained below.

11. After a large portion of the New Testament, such as, John and Romans, is translated to the satisfaction of the translators, print a quantity of them, marked as "First Draft" and distribute them to as many as possible. Some of them should be key people who will read through them in a final check.

11. Checking should be repeated after every major revision of a chapter or book.

Back-Translations

A back-translation is a literal or somewhat literal translation made from the target language translation back into English or another major language that the translator and the translation advisor understand. The purpose of a back-translation is to determine whether the target language translation has errors and does, in fact, communicate the meaning of the source text. It can be used in checking the translation and can be used by the translation advisor during checking sessions. A back-translation is not a proper translation, because it often shows the grammatical forms of the target language. It will not necessarily sound natural. A back translation is compared to the source text and any differences reconciled. It helps to confirm that the target language translation is accurate.

Some are concerned that doing a back translation will drastically increase the burden and work of the translators. In fact, it will do this very thing, if it is not done right. If the guidelines of this section are followed, the work of a back-translation will not increase the work of the translators or make the translation process more difficult. Rather, it will greatly increase the possibility of making a completely accurate translation.

Why Do a Back-Translation? Back translations are used by major translation ministries such as, Wycliffe Bible Translators and Trinitarian Bible Society and United Bible Societies. It is also used by professional translators. Rex Cobb, Director of the Baptist Bible Translator's Institute in Bowie, Texas, says the following.

> You need to do a back translation into English or the trade language or both ... this will show you if you have missed a word or line ... It is necessary for a consultant to check your work ... The time to send your work to a translation consultant is after the first chapter of your first book, not when you finish. If you are doing something wrong, you want to know it sooner than later! [81]

The *first* reason for a back-translation is that it is an excellent technique to check your work. It will help you notice missing words, phrases, sentences, and verses. It will also help you see the addition of any incorrect information, as well as helping you notice any confusing phrases and sentences. All the translators and all the teams can use a back translation to check the translation.

A back-translation is not only good for the current translation project but can be a help to other projects. It can be consulted by other translators in related languages for ideas about how to translate a particular verse or to solve a translation problem.

A back-translation can help the translation advisor. First, it will enable him to intelligently discuss the translation with the translators. Second, it will enable the advisor to perform an independent accuracy check on the translation. It will help him bring anything to the attention of the translators that they missed. A back translation can serve to assure the translation advisors that the translation is a true, faithful, complete, and accurate translation. This is important if the advisor is informing the churches in the USA and around the world about the translation. He can truthfully say it is a good translation if he has seen a back-translation. This is also helpful if the advisor is raising funds for printing the new translation.

Guidelines for Doing a Back-Translation

The back-translation should NOT be made by the translators or by any person who has participated in the translation work.

This is a very important, key point. A back translation will not double or increase the work of the translators *if this point is followed.* If the translators have a multiple team organization, the committee can commit one entire team to the back-translation process if it wishes to employ this strategy, but that is the only translating that team should do. In a single team setting, one person can be given this job. The translators are very familiar with the passage and all issues that have come up during the translation process. Therefore, if one of them does the back translation, it may be unintentionally prejudiced. The translator knows what he intended to say when he made the translation and, therefore, that may unconsciously influence him when making a back-translation. Also, the translator has an immense job translating the

Scriptures into the target language. To have the translator do the back-translation doubles his burden.

Making and using a back-translation is a three-step process.

1. Make a complete translation back into the source language or a mutually understood trade language.

2. Compare the back-translation with the source text. If the back-translation is made into English, then it should be compared to the King James Bible.

3. Make any corrections in the target language translation that are indicated by the comparison.

There are several more guidelines that should be followed in doing a back translation.

1. The back-translation should be made by a person who is a mother tongue speaker of the target language.

2. The back-translator must NOT look at ANY Bible text while working on the back translation. If the Back-translator looks at any translation, it will compromise his work. The back-translation should be the straightforward translation of the target language text and only that.

3. What does the back-translator do when he does not understand the meaning of the target language translation or there is more than one way to understand it? He should choose the meaning he thinks is best and put a question mark in parenthesis next to it in the back translation. He can also put a footnote showing the alternative translation(s). He should also inform the translators that he does not understand.

4. The person who makes the back-translation will need to be taught these guidelines, but the training will be short and easy.

Testing the Translation

Translation testing is different from translation proofreading and checking. Proofreading and checking are for the specific purpose of finding errors and blemishes in the translation. Translation testing looks at how people react to the translation in real situations. How does the translation communicate to ordinary people of various walks of life? The goal is to find ways to improve the translation.

After a section of the translation, perhaps several chapters, has been checked, it should be tested. This may seem to be a tedious and long process with all the proofreading, checking, and testing, but there is no short cut to making a true, faithful, trustworthy, accurate, and complete translation. Here is a short list of guidelines that can help accomplish the testing.

1. Use the translation in Bible study groups. When all members of the group are using this same translation, many things can be revealed that can help improve the translation.

2. Use the translation in family devotional times and fellowship meetings. Get feedback from spouses and children.

3. Give copies of the translation to several pastors. Ask them to pass out copies to the congregation. Use them in preaching and teaching.

4. Sunday school teachers can pass out copies to their students and use the translation to teach the classes.

5. Test as widely as you can with saved and unsaved, young and old, men and women, etc.

6. All of this should be well organized so that the translators are aware of all the efforts that are being made and the results of each.

Final Pointers

Keep a chart or a record of the passages you have checked and tested. Include which method was used and what was the result. What did you learn and what corrections were made to the translation?

It is helpful if each passage is checked and tested with multiple methods.

Some passages may need to be checked and rechecked several times. A record should be made each time.

Keep an organized record of all the comments, ideas, and corrections made on the translation. Put all of this information in a permanent file for each book of the Bible that you translate. It can be kept in writing, or it can be kept digitally. If it is digital, you must keep a backup copy of the information, including the final translation agreed on by all the translators. Multiple backup copies are best. After translation meetings, the Chinese team would make updated copies of the translation on thumb drives for each translator.

Checking and testing is an absolutely required part of translation work. It may seem like a lot of additional work, but it is necessary and unavoidable, if you want to produce a translation that is truly God's Word.

20 Printing and Distributing the Translation

Psalms 68:11 The Lord gave the word: great was the company of those that published it.

The ultimate goal of Bible translating is to print and distribute copies for the edification of believers and evangelism of the unsaved. The project is ready to print when the translating, checking, testing, editing, and formatting is done. That does not mean that every question has been answered and every error has been found. It means you and your team have translated it and thoroughly checked and tested it. More issues will likely come to light, and you may find more answers after the first printing. More corrections can be made then. It is highly doubtful that the first printing will be 100% accurate. When you have done everything you can on the translation, there may still be a few concerns about how a word or phrase here and there was translated. Keep a record of these. However, do not let them stop the first draft or first edition from being published. Make the best translation decision you can for now and print anyway.

Deciding When to Print

Sometimes, translation projects have translated the entire Bible before printing. The KJB was done this way. However, the situations I have been in are a little different. The KJB was translated by men who were church leaders in England, but many translations today are being done on mission fields around the world in the context of church planting. For many years, the books of John and Romans have been printed together for purposes of evangelism. It seems that God has honored that.

Therefore, I recommend translators begin by translating the books of John and Romans. After that, they can go on to the rest of the New Testament followed by the book of Genesis and the remainder of the Old Testament. The first printing should be a John/Romans booklet. Once John and Romans are finished, a small number may be printed for a special celebration of the completion. This should be followed by a large printing of John and Romans. In some cases, the first small printing is dispensed with in favor of a large printing. The new Togo translation was done that way. Nearly 200,000 copies were printed by Bearing Precious Seed printing ministry at First Baptist Church, Milford, Ohio. Later, the same procedure will be followed for the entire New Testament, when it is completed, and still later by the whole Bible. Of course, you may decide to print a second edition of John/Romans or of the New Testament, before the Old Testament is ready.

Finding a Printer

One of the first steps in printing is to find a printer who can do it at an economical rate. In this part, I am focusing on paper printing of a large quantity. There are other ways to print, such as voice and data. We will get to these later. For now, I want to point out two approaches that may help you identify the primary printer you want to use. In addition to that, I will show you a way to make your New Testament commercially available.

The first possibility is to choose one of the large church-based printers in the United States. I have already mentioned one of these, *Bearing Precious Seed in Milford, Ohio.* I have listed some of these below. There are many. So, I apologize to any that I have failed to mention. It was not intentional.

1. Bearing Precious Seed, Milford, Ohio, www.bpsmilford.org
2. Bearing Precious Seed Canada, www.bpscanada.org.
3. Bearing Precious Seed at Wyldewood Baptist Church, Oshkosh, Wisconsin, www.wyldewood.org/index.php/outreach/our-missionaries/bearing-precious-seed
4. Bearing Precious Seed Lansing Michigan, www.bpslansing.org.
5. Wings Bearing Precious Seed, www.wingsbps.org.
6. Bearing Precious Seed, Berean Baptist Church, Greenwood, Indiana, www.bearingpreciousseedbibles.org.
7. Victory Baptist Press, www.victorybaptistpress.com

8. Bible and Literature Missionary Foundation, www.biblelit.com
9. Bearing Precious Seed Canada, www.bpscanada.org
10. Beacon of Truth Baptist Ministries, www.btbm.org
11. BEAMS Bible Ministry, www.beamsbibles.com

The last one mentioned, BEAMS, is not specifically a Bible printing ministry. They raise funds to purchase and supply missionaries with whole hardback Bibles. If you can get one of the printing ministries to agree to print your whole Bible translation, they may wish to help get it to the field. Let them tell you in their own words what they do from their website.

> Although several ministries print tracts and New Testaments for missionaries, few ministries provide them with whole, hardback Bibles, free of charge. Therefore, this has become the primary purpose of BEAMS. We raise funds through offerings from local, independent, Bible-believing Baptist churches to purchase and supply whole, hardback Bibles for missionaries to give to those who are saved on the foreign mission fields.

Another ministry that raises funds for printing is Global Bible Translators/Bearing Precious Seed Global, www.bpsglobal.org. This organization starts Bible translation projects, trains translators, provide translation advisory services, and raises money to print John/Romans booklet, New Testaments, and whole Bibles for their projects.

There is one downside to printing at a church-based printing ministry in the USA. There is an additional cost for shipping to other countries, and that cost is large.   There may also be customs and/or port costs in the receiving country. It doesn't pay to print a small quantity. The economy is in printing 10-100,000 copies or more. Nevertheless, it is often the most economical way to print the Scriptures, and it puts the printing in the hands of the local church.

The other major way to print is to do it in the same country where the Scriptures will be used or in a nearby country. When the Bibleless Isan people of Northeast Thailand first received a New Testament in 2016, the printing was done by a Christian printer in

Bangkok. It worked out very well. A printer was sought in Nakuru, Kenya for a small run of John/Romans in Swahili. The cost was a little more than the cost of printing and shipping in the USA, but it was quicker and more convenient.

Lastly, it is possible to commercially print a New Testament through a process known as "print on demand self-publishing." Print on demand publishers receives the book through the internet and holds it in their computers. The book is printed and shipped when an order is received. It is usually advertised on Amazon.com, Amazon.uk, and www.barnesandnoble.com, and elsewhere. Orders can be placed on these web sites or the publisher's web site. It is possible to use print on demand for a John/Romans booklet or a New Testament, but not a whole Bible, because it is too large. There are a lot of print on demand publishers, but I suggest you contact the publisher of this book, The Old Paths Publications, www.theoldpathspublications.com, through their website.

Editing and Formatting the Document

Editing and formatting the document are necessary steps, otherwise the text will be, to put it simply, a tragic mess. Editing the Bible document is to prepare it for publication by correcting, revising, or adapting. It is to adapt or modify it so that it is acceptable in its appearance. The changes you have already made in the checking and testing were matters of *revising*, a process distinct from editing, but a *final edit* is an additional necessary step to make the printed document have an excellent and consistent appearance. Format, on the other hand, is the plan for the layout or arrangement of the written material. Let's look at formatting first.

Formatting

Formatting deals with how you structure the document. I encourage you to use a digital word processing app. You can get a free version of Google Docs with Gmail. Formatting deals with such technical issues as a name for the translation, page size, margins, fonts, type size, paragraph headings, spacing between sentences, styles, italics, bold, underlining, page headers and footers, page numbering, etc. These are decisions that cannot be left to the end. Formatting decisions should made at the time or before the document typing begins, and it should be maintained consistently all the way through.

Below I have suggested some specifics on a few of the formatting decisions you will have to make. These recommendations are partly based on the guidelines of Bearing Precious Seed, Milford, Ohio, USA. Other printers may have their own recommendations. So, those below may change depending on who you choose to do the printing.

1. Page size: 8" x 5.25"
2. Margins: 0.5" all around, top, bottom, sides
3. Gutter margin: none
4. Font: Serif style, such as Times New Roman
5. Font size: 10 – 12, depends on the size necessary to be easily read and to fit all the text within the number of pages required.
6. Number of pages: For single language – 64 pages. For bi-lingual - 128 pages. The number of pages must be in multiples of 32 for a web press. That means, if you have 60 pages you will have four blank pages at the end. If you also publish by the print-on-demand method, it does not matter how many pages there are, except print-on-demand publishers nay have a minimum number of pages.
7. Page numbering: bottom center.
8. Headers are helpful to readers to know the general location they are at in a book.

Editing

Editing is the final work necessary to fully prepare the Biblical manuscript for publication. It has a great deal to do with the structure of the document, but it also involves correcting any remaining problems and rechecking the formatting. Editing involves the following four steps. You should always include these steps, even if you do not perform them in the same order.

1. Content Editing.
2. Line Editing.
3. Copy Editing.

4. A final proofread

Content Editing: Content editing has to so with the flow and structure of the work. In general documents, this is rather extensive, dealing the entire structure including the organization of the content. For the New Testament, the structure of the content is pre-determined. There are some items to be noted, though.

1. The first page should be a title page. The title page should identify the book, "Gospel of John and the Book of Romans" or "The New Testament." It should also include the name of the translation, such as, "The Chinese Authorized Version." It should also identify the publisher.
2. The title page for the first printing of John/Romans booklet should make the statement "First Draft" and give the year of publication. Subsequent printing can be labeled "First Edition" with year. When the New Testament and the whole Bible is printed the title page should include the words, "First Edition" and give the year of publication.
3. The John/Romans booklet is printed to provide believers the opportunity to review the new translation and to evangelize non-Christians. It is to be given away free. The title page should also include the words, "Freely distributed, not for resell."
4. Copyright information can be included on the back of the title page.
5. Next, include a table of contents.
6. Next, add a preface to explain reasons for the new translation, source texts, and information you feel is relevant.
7. In a bilingual edition, all of the above should be in both languages.
8. Book titles and chapter headings should be displayed clearly.

Line Editing: Some equate this with copy editing, but I think separating the two here may make it clearer. Line editing is looking at the structure of sentences, phrases, and paragraphs. It looks at repetitious words and phrases that may need the use of synonyms, words that can cause confusion, sentences that need to be clearer and flow smoothly, and sentences next to one another that seem disjointed or disconnected. This and the next two steps require careful and perhaps repetitive reading.

Copy Editing: This is a close look at certain technical aspects of the text. It focuses on the specific rules of grammar, punctuation, capitalization, style, and spelling. Do verbs and nouns agree? Are the correct conjunctions and prepositions used? Are adverbs and adjectives in the proper place? Are sentences too long or complex? Are the chosen styles used consistently and habitually?

Proofread: Proofreading involves an over all detailed review of everything. It requires a careful reading of each word and each sentence. Do one more overall checking to correct typos, misspellings, grammar errors, or errors in any other things that have been previously mentioned.

One final step: There is one more thing to do after all else is finished. You will be sitting in front of a computer looking at the project in a word processing program. What do you do with it to prepare it for the printer? You will almost certainly be required to turn it into a pdf format and transmit it to the printer in an email. The printer may allow you to send it in the word processing format and he will turn it into pdf for you.

Raising Funds

Obviously, funds are necessary to print Bibles or Bible portions, such as John/romans booklets. In fact, it requires many thousands of dollars. If a bi-lingual John/Romans can be printed for 30 cents each, 100,000 copies would cost $30,000. This may seem overwhelming to the translator, but it is not overwhelming to God. "But my God shall supply all your need according to his riches in glory by Christ Jesus." (Phil. 4:19).

The first thing you will print is the John/Romans booklet, and you will need money donated from the churches. Secondly, money will need to be raised when the whole New Testament is ready. There are churches in the USA that wish to donate to projects like this. There are churches in other parts of the world that also desire to contribute. When the Isan New Testament was printed, a large part of the money came from several Chinese churches outside the USA. Since then, I have seen

Africans raising funds through Facebook. God has the money. Prayer and effort will bring it to you in God's time.

E-Book and Audio

Two additional ways to publish the Bible translation are to publish it as an *e-book* and as an *audio* Bible. If you do self-publishing with The Old Paths Publications, they can help you with e-book publishing. Also, you can do it yourself on the Amazon Kindle publishing site, https://kdp.amazon.com/en_US/. With the help articles, it is fairly self-explanatory. Publishing as an audio book is somewhat more complicated. It requires someone with a good speaking and reading voice, who is willing to read the entire Bible on a computer audio recording. This will require a large time investment. Once the e-book and audio book are ready, both can be offered on CD through the mail or as an internet download.

You can also contact e-sword about making your translation available on e-sword.

Conclusion

There are several ways to print your translation in a paper book, in large quantities on a press and one-at-a-time by publishing on demand. You can also publish in an e-book format and an audio book format. Funds can be raised by both donations and by sales. Distribution can be made free (the John/Romans booklet should be free) by churches, and you can sell Bibles for a cheap price through churches. The money collected through sales must be used to buy new copies for further resale, thereby continually spreading the word of God. The ideas I have presented in this chapter are only a beginning and a bare outline of what you can do. The details will have to be worked out for your particular situation by you, your team, the churches in your area, and your translation advisor.

21 Steps Toward a Mature Translation

Is. 55:11 So shall my word be that goeth forth out of my mouth: it shall not return unto me void, but it shall accomplish that which I please, and it shall prosper in the thing whereto I sent it.
Psalms 19:7 The law of the LORD is **perfect**, converting the soul: the testimony of the LORD is sure, making wise the simple.

Do you think God has an interest in spreading His Word? That may seem like a foolish question at this point, but it is not. Do you think God has an interest in the work of translating the Bible into the 7,000+ languages on earth? God divided the languages of the world and then told the people who speak each language, "Man shall not live by bread alone, but by every word that proceedeth out of the mouth of God" (Mat. 4:4). "All the kings of the earth shall praise thee, O LORD, when they hear the words of thy mouth" (Psalms 138:4). God does not want all people to speak the same language and God never commanded us to teach them all the same language, such as English. "And the whole earth was of one language, and of one speech … And the LORD said, Behold, the people is one, and they have all one language; and this they begin to do: and now nothing will be restrained from them, which they have imagined to do. Go to, let us go down, and there confound their language, that they may not understand one another's speech. So the LORD scattered them abroad …" (Gen 11:1, 6-8). Does it not logically follow, then, that God wants every person to have all His perfect words available in every language, so they may live by every word that proceeds out of His mouth? "And they sung a new song, saying, Thou art worthy to take the book, and to open the seals thereof: for thou wast slain, and hast redeemed us to God by thy blood out of every kindred, and **tongue**, and people, and nation" (Rev. 5:9). To fulfill Matthew 4:4, *every* language must have *all* God's Words. They must have the perfect Scriptures in a language they easily understand.

What is a "Perfect" or Mature Translation?

What is a Bible translation? In the early fifteen hundreds, Desiderius Erasmus gathered old Greek manuscripts of the New Testament and compiled them into the first printed and published Greek New Testament (1516). This NT, which is now known as the Textus Receptus or Received Text, became the standard of God's inspired words. The German Monk, Martin Luther, who rebelled against the Catholic Church in 1517, was the first to translate this Greek New Testament into German. The Greek words of God were inspired by God in the first century AD and preserved all those years and made available to Erasmus and the subsequent editors of the Received Text. Martin Luther took the Greek words of God and transferred them into German words with equivalent meaning. *That* is translating.

Are translations inspired? The Bible tells us, "All scripture is given by inspiration" (2 Tim. 3:16). That certainly refers to the Greek and Hebrew original written Scriptures. When Scripture was given, it was given by inspiration. However, translating is *not* the giving of Scripture. It is taking Scripture that has already been given and transferring it into another language. Often the claim of an inspired translation refers to the King James Bible, because the KJB was the *giving* of Scripture in English. However, if that were true, it cannot be left there. If the King James translation was inspired, then so also was the Martin Luther translation, the Rheina Valera, the Diodati, the Burmese of Adoniram Judson, and all others translated from the Received Text, because they were *given*. If these translations are inspired, then they would have no errors, because God never makes a mistake. However, having worked with Martin Luther's 1545 edition, I can say his translation has imperfections. I believe the King James Bible is completely accurate, but it is not free from error by inspiration. It is inerrant by providentially guided translating. The KJB we use today is the result of a major revision in spelling accomplished in 1769. So, the KJB we use today is the pinnacle of 245 years (1524-1611) of English Bible translating. It is a *mature* translation.

What is a *mature* Bible translation? The Bible uses the word *perfect*. By definition, a perfect translation is one that is *complete* and *accurate*. Therefore, a mature translation can be defined as *a translation that has reached a stage where it needs very little or no further correction and revision*. A Bible translation does not reach this point automatically. The first edition of a translation will almost always need improvement, and, therefore, it will need revision. In fact, it may go through several editions, being improved each time, before it can be called *mature*. There is no standard for how many times a given translation will need to be revised or for how long it will take. It seems some translations are completed, marketed, and sold to the public without any plan for further revision work. Such a translation may *never* be mature. The imperfections of the first edition will be the imperfections it retains. Our translating goal should be to do all we can to give the people the *pure* and *complete* words of God, no matter how many revisions we must do.

How the English Bible became Mature

We believe the King James Bible is a thoroughly mature translation. However, it did not become mature through the efforts of a single translation team. The maturity of the KJB was a result of continual translation effort in English over a period of about 100 years. Even then, it needed an extensive revision of spelling in 1769. If the 1769 revision had not been done, the KJB would be very difficult to read today.

The first translation into English from the newly published Textus Receptus was done by William Tyndale (1494-1536). He had to translate on the European continent because it was not safe in England. It was not much safer on the continent, but, at least, he could flee from country to country while doing his work. He published a complete New Testament in 1526. He printed revisions of the New Testament in 1534 and 1536. He published his translation of the Pentateuch in 1530 and the book of Jonah in 1531. He also translated some Old Testament books including Joshua, Judges, First and Second Samuel, First and Second Kings and First and Second Chronicles, but he did not publish them. He translated the Old Testament portions from Hebrew, but was not able to complete the Old Testament, because he was betrayed and burned at the stake in 1536.

An English preacher named Myles Coverdale (1488-1569) was exiled from England for his reformation views from 1528-1535. He went to Antwerp where William Tyndale was and probably gave him much assistance. Working from Tyndale's published translations, he completed the Old Testament books that Tyndale had left unpublished. He apparently did not use Tyndale's unpublished translations.

Coverdale's translations were done from Latin and German versions, rather than Hebrew. The complete English Bible was published in 1535 as *The Coverdale Bible*.

John Rogers (1505-1555) was another English clergyman and associate of William Tyndale. After Tyndale's martyrdom, he continued Tyndale's Old Testament translation work. He used All of Tyndale's work, including his unpublished portions of the Old Testament, and Myles Coverdale's work.

It was published in 1537 under the pseudonym Thomas Matthew, because it was not safe to be a reformer in England. He was burned at the stake for his faith in 1555 by Queen Mary Tudor. A minor revision of the Matthews Bible was edited by Richard Taverner (1505-1575) and published in 1539.

The next Bible was also published in 1539. It was a version of the Coverdale Bible and prepared by Myles Coverdale. It was called the Great Bible and Henry VIII ordered it to be read in Anglican churches.

Queen Mary I sought to restore Roman Catholicism to England and, with that effort, came great persecution. A number of English scholars fled to Geneva, Switzerland, which was a safe place for protestants. There the Geneva Version was translated and published in 1560, and it was entirely translated from Greek and Hebrew. Previously, the English Bible had been divided into chapters. The Geneva was the first to divide the text into verses. It was very popular among protestants. The English Bishops did not like it due to its anti-clergy notes. It was prepared with the influence of John Calvin and was considered too Calvinistic for the church of England, but Puritans loved it.

The Bishops Bible was translated to replace the Great Bible. The leading figure in the translation was Matthew Parker (1504-1575), Archbishop of Canterbury. It was first published in 1568. An extensive revision was done later and published in 1572. A number of Ecclesiastical terms were introduced, including "charity" in 1 Corinthians 13, and the text was brought closer to the Geneva Bible. The last edition of the whole Bishops Bible was published in 1602. The King James translators were instructed to use the 1602 edition as their base text.

Finally, the King James translation was begun in 1603 and published in 1611. It is also called the "Authorized Version." Permission to translate a new version was given by King James I, who gave fifteen guidelines for the translation. Forty-seven scholars carried the work forward, and one of the guidelines was that they could solicit the opinions of any learned clergyman of the realm. The title page of the KJB makes this statement, "Translated out of the original tongues, with the former translations diligently compared and revised." It used all the scholarship of the previous versions, along with foreign language translations. Within a few years, the KJB replaced all the previous translations.

In 1611, spelling was not consistent in English. It was not until 1755 that a dictionary was published that presented standard spelling, the Samuel Johnson Dictionary. Based on that standard spelling, the KJB was revised in 1769 to update all its spelling and correct errors in previous printings. It was an extensive and successful undertaking. The 1769 is the standard revision of the KJB that we still use today. Since 1611, all further popular English translation ceased for 278 years, until the Revised Version of 1881. God, who is Lord of all His work, clearly directed the church to cease English Bible translation efforts. The major translations being done since 1881 are based on a faulty and error ridden Greek text, since scholarship abandoned the Textus Receptus. The English Bible reached maturity in the King James Version.

Mature Bibles in Many Languages

The history of the English Bible in no way indicates that every language Bible will take a century to reach maturity, nor that the same course will be followed. It is possible to bring a new translation to maturity within a few years. There are several requirements to make a translation mature. First, it will take a willingness to listen to criticism of the translation. A translator should be eager to learn whether he has made errors and to correct them. Second, it will require diligent work to make the necessary corrections. Third, it requires persistence. The translators must not give up. The following process usually takes place.

The Initial Translation Process

As the translation is being done, a process of thoroughly checking and testing it should be implemented. Research any interpretation problems in the text and any particular translation problems that are readily apparent. Questions should be presented to the translation consultants and theological advisors. After the checking and testing have been done, the translators should make a first draft of a portion of scripture (such as, John and Romans) working closely with the translation assistants. They may print the portion, clearly marking it as "first draft" with the date. They should distribute it among as many people as possible, inviting them to make comments and criticisms. After the comments have all been collected and corrections have been made, a second draft may be made, distributed, commented on, and corrected. This process may be repeated as many times as the translators feel is necessary. Each time it is printed and distributed, it should be marked "first draft," "second draft," "third draft," and so on. Make sure they include the date of the draft. The purpose of marking it is to let all know what stage the translation was at the time.

First Edition

The checking and testing stage of translation development can go on for as long as the translators feel it should. However, the process can be drawn out too long. We have seen it happen that translators have held off printing a first edition because they think there *might* be some imperfection *somewhere*. It has also been seen that translators disagree about how to translate a specific verse or word, and the whole translation is held up because of it. Such a situation *can* make the whole effort a gigantic waste of time, because the translation never gets issued and, so, it does not benefit anyone. Sooner or later, a first edition must be published, the sooner the better. It may be imperfect in some places, but part of the reason for publishing it is that someone may find and report the imperfections. That would be a happy situation, because it gives the translators a chance to improve the translation.

The first edition should be marked as "first edition" with the date of the edition. This makes the reader aware that future editions may be issued, if improvements are made.

Future Editions

The testimony of history is that once a translation is published the review process does not end. When William Tyndale published the English New Testament, he continued to review it to find ways to improve it. He issued new revised editions in 1534 and 1536. Martin Luther did the same. The German New Testament was first published in 1522 and the whole Bible in 1534. He worked on improving the translation the rest of his life, issuing a revision in 1545, the year before his death in February 1546. Some of the future editions may come from someone other than the original translators. Future editions should always be allowed by the original translators. If one fails to allow this, he *may* find himself hindering God's plan. The Bible belongs to God, not the translator.

An important thing to note is *how* future editions are issued. After the first edition is published, it is almost certain that imperfections will be found. If several printings of the first edition are made, they should be consistent with previous printings and have no changes, even if imperfections have been found. If people buy a first edition Bible from the first printing, and others buy a first edition Bible from a second printing, it creates confusion if the two are compared and found to be different. This could undermine confidence in the translation. If imperfections in the first edition are found, they should be accumulated, and all corrections made in a second edition that is clearly marked as "second edition" and dated. This will avoid confusion and increase confidence in the translation. In the second edition, a preface should be included that explains the necessity of a second edition. This will show people that the translation is an honest one and that the translators have true accuracy as their goal.

Eventually, a revised edition will be issued and there will be no feedback that requires corrections. When that happens, the translators can rest and commit it to God as a mature translation. There may be those who complain about the translation out of rebellion or hate, but the translators can discern the difference between that and constructive helpful criticism. There may be others who complain that the translation came from the Received Greek and Hebrew texts. They may even call for revision because they hate the Received texts, but that is not a reason for a new revision. You can accept the translation as mature.

Bible translating is not a fast or easy task. Translators must not only see the job through to the first publication, but also stay with the work through subsequent editions until it reaches maturity. That task may go on beyond your lifetime. God will raise up those he needs to carry it forward.

22 Be of Good Courage

Nehemiah 2:10 When Sanballat the Horonite, and Tobiah the servant, the Ammonite, heard of it, it grieved them exceedingly that there was come a man to seek the welfare of the children of Israel.

Translating the Bible will not be easy. It is a difficult task all by itself. It takes a lot of time and there will be discouragement and frustration. There will be internal battles and disagreements. These would normally be enough difficulties, but there will also be attacks from outside. The proponents of other versions or the existing target language version will not like what you are doing, and the users of those versions may not understand you (Nehemiah 2:10). Nevertheless, you must stay faithful to the truth and steadfast in the task God has set before you.

The Book of Nehemiah tells the story of how the walls of Jerusalem were rebuilt. It reveals how God called Nehemiah to lead that task (chapter 1) and how the King of Persia approved and provided for him to do the job (chapter 2). Our heavenly King has called you to the task of translating a true, trustworthy, faithful, and accurate Bible. Our King has approved you for that job and He has provided all you need to get started. He will provide all you need all along the way. You have thoroughly reviewed the situation (Neh. 2:12-17). You have told the brethren and gained their support (Neh. 2:18). Nehemiah was called to a great task, and it took him fifty-two days to complete the wall. He stayed with it despite great opposition. You have been called to a greater task than Nehemiah and it will take you a lot longer than fifty-two days to complete it. You also will face opposition and you must continue regardless of the efforts of the devil to delay and stop the work.

One of the first things the enemies of the work may do is laugh and dismiss the effort as nothing, and they will despise you (Neh. 2:19). They may say that you are not educated, because you did not go to their schools. They may say that you are not qualified, because you are not approved by them. Remember, when they persecuted the apostles, they, "perceived that they were unlearned and ignorant men, they marvelled; and they took knowledge of them, that they had been with Jesus" (Acts 4:13). Qualification comes from being with and learning from the Lord. When they disdain you and despise you, remember: "For ye see your calling, brethren, how that not many wise men after the flesh, not many mighty, not many noble, are called: But God hath chosen the foolish things of the world to confound the wise; and God hath chosen the weak things of the world to confound the things which are mighty; And base things of the world, and things which are despised, hath God chosen, yea, and things which are not, to bring to nought things that are: That no flesh should glory in his presence" (1 Corinthians 1:26-28). When they speak this way, answer them the same way Nehemiah did: God has called us, and we trust in Him, and He will prosper us in this work. "The God of heaven, he will prosper us; therefore we his servants will arise and build: but ye have no portion, nor right, nor memorial, in Jerusalem" (Neh. 2:10).

"And next unto them the Tekoites repaired; but their nobles put not their necks to the work of their Lord"(Neh. 3:5). The above criticisms will likely come from those who are not a part of your fellowship, such as the Bible Societies. Unfortunately, there will be those in your own fellowship of churches who will not participate in the work or support it. Their opposition may be passive, and they will stand alongside watching; or they may actively oppose the work. When this happens, do not let them distract you. Keep your focus on the Lord and on the work. God will raise up enough workers to complete the task (Neh. 3:6-32).

Growing angry and indignant that the work continues, your opposition may turn to an attempt to discourage you by ridicule and lies (Neh. 4:1-3). As they realize you are not willing to quit, the ridicule and lies may be put in print, newspapers, newsletters, magazines, internet, etc. How should you respond to such attacks? First, you should take it to the Lord in prayer (Neh. 4:4-5). Next, don't be discouraged, but keep on with the work (Neh. 4:6). "Blessed are ye, when men shall revile you, and persecute you, and shall say all manner of evil against you falsely, for my sake" (Mat. 5:11).

In Nehemiah's day, the enemies of the Lord even threatened violence against those involved in the work (Neh. 4:7-14). This had the effect of turning the Jew's attention to defense rather than building and caused some hinderance (Neh. 4:15-23). This possibility cannot be discounted, but we have not seen this so far and pray that you will not face it. It is, perhaps, more likely that the devil will cause trouble between the members of the translation team or between some of them and other believers in the church (See Neh. 5:1-13). These kinds of problems can be the worst of all. You can withstand all the attacks from outside and be defeated by the smallest relationship difficulties and disagreements with those on the inside. They can be so severe that they can knock translators completely out of the work. Much prayer and Biblical wisdom is required for these difficulties (See Nehemiah's example in Neh. 5:7-19).

In another attempt to stop the final completion of the wall, four times the Jews' enemies proposed meetings to discuss the work (Neh. 6:1-4). Nehemiah refused the meetings. They may be nothing, but a waste of time, at best. It is an attempt to distract you from the work. Keep your focus on one thing only: finishing the translation well.

Next, there may be slander, lying gossip, and the threat of legal action. The threat will likely come in written form. Nehemiah was accused of planning to make himself into a king. The Jew's enemies threatened to report that to the King of Persia (Neh. 6:5-7). You could possibly face the threat of a lawsuit over copyright. This kind of threat requires a response (Neh. 6:8), and it may have to be a legal response. We believe that there will easily be enough differences between the new translation and the existing versions to make copyright problems a non-issue. Nevertheless, you should be well aware of the copyright laws of your country. However, as in Nehemiah's time, the threat will be meant to make you afraid and cause you to stop the work (Neh. 6:9). Pray for strength and courage to continue.

A man named Shemiah tried to trick Nehemiah into hiding in the temple to save his life (Neh. 6:10-13). He did this so the Jew's enemies could turn it into an evil report (Neh. 6:13). We live in a day when our enemies try to turn public statements into something we did not mean. Your opposition may try to trick the translators or anyone associated with the translation to make statements or do things they can twist their way. Be careful. It would be wise to stay away from anyone who is opposed to the translation work.

Bible translating is a work near to the heart of God and the devil hates it. Therefore, he will oppose it. But, if you are strong and continue until the work is done, there will be many who will recognize that it was led by God, and it will be to His glory (Neh. 6:15-16). So, our encouragement to you is to be strong, of a good courage, and do not let anything distract, discourage, or stop you from this work and from continuing on to translate other languages.

Have not I commanded thee? Be strong and of a good courage; be not afraid, neither be thou dismayed: for the LORD thy God is with thee whithersoever thou goest. (Josh. 1:9)

About the Author

Dr. Steve Combs is an ordained minister. He spent his early years in Kentucky, Virginia, and finally Ohio. He was not raised in a Christian home. He had some Christian influence from his grandmother, but that had little effect on him. Due to discussions with a Baptist preacher and a Sunday School teacher, who visited his home, he began to read the Bible. The Word of God had its effect. He came under strong conviction of his sins. A friend invited him to a nearby church during revival meetings. As a result, he received Christ as his Savior.

Since then, there have been major transformations to his life. God called him to preach and enabled a backward shy individual suffering from an inferiority complex to stand before crowds and confidently proclaim the Word of God. God gave him a business background as a CPA. God put him in several ministry positions. He has served as a Bible Institute teacher and Dean, a youth pastor, assistant pastor, and a senior pastor. He holds a Doctor of Theology from Covington Theological Seminary.

Currently Steve Combs is Assistant Director and a Global Translation Advisor for Global Bible Translators/ Bearing Precious Seed Global, www.bpsglobal.com, a ministry of Plantation Baptist Church in Plantation, Florida. Global Bible Translators starts and assists Bible translation projects around the world.

He is married and has four married children.

Acknowledgments and Bibliography

Individuals:

This translation guide contains principles gleaned from the writings and comments of and discussions with the individuals below. My thanks to them.

Dr. David Brown, Pastor, First Baptist Church of Oak Creek Wisconsin; President, King James Bible Research Council
Dr. Rex Cobb, Director, Baptist Bible Translators Institute, Bowie, Texas
Ron Meyers, Missionary and Translator for the Isan in NE Thailand
Daniel Olachea, Translator, Translation Consultant, World View Ministries
Yura Popchenko, Missionary and Translator in Ukraine
Dr. Phil Stringer, Vice President of Church Relations, Day Spring Bible College and Seminary
Dr. Jim Taylor, Missionary to Korea, Armed Forces Baptist Mission; Translation Advisor for GBT; Korean Bible Translator, Author
Dr. H. D. Williams, M.D., Ph.D., President, The Old Paths Publications
Dr. Stephen Zeinner, General Director, Global Bible Translators/Bearing Precious Seed Global

Books:

In addition to the above individuals, the following books and writings were consulted.

Abbot-Smith, George. *A Manual Greek Lexicon of the New Testament.* (Charles Scribner's Sons: New York. 1936)

Barnwell, Katherine. *Bible Translation an Introductory Course in Translation Principles.* (Dallas, Tx: International Academic Bookstore, 2002).

Beekman, John and Callow, John. *Translating the Word of God.* (Grand Rapids: Zondervan Publishing House, 1974).

Brown, David. *Providential Preservation: the Doctrine that Virtually Disappeared.*

Cobb, Rex. Bible Translation Notes, 2015, Classroom notes, Baptist Bible Translators Institute.

Combs, Steve. *A Practical Theology of Bible Translating.* (The Old Paths Publications: www.theoldpathspublications.com, 2019).

Phillips, Dan. *God's Wisdom in Proverbs.* (Woodlands, TX: Kress Biblical Resources. 2011)

Hills, Edward F. *The King James Version Defended.* (Des Moines, Iowa: Christian research Press. 1973).

Patton, Robert D. *Issues in Missiology, Volume III, Translation Issues.* The Old Paths Publications, Inc: Cleveland, GA. 2012.

Richardson, Don. *Eternity in Their Hearts.* Regal Books: Ventura, Ca. 1981.

Scott, Paul W. *English for Bible Readers.* Morris Publishing: Kearney, NE, 2008.

Turner, Charles V. *Biblical Bible Translating.* (Sovereign Grace Publishers: Layfayette, In. 2001)

Williams. H.D. *The Miracle of Biblical Inspiration.* (The Old Paths Publications: Cleveland, GA) 2009. PDF download. Jan. 2019.

Zodhiates, Spiros. The Complete Word Study Dictionary. E-Sword. Rick Meyers. Version 10.2.1. Franklin, Tn.: 2013. Downloaded computer software.

Web Sites and articles:

A Defense of the Bible. https://www.adefenceofthebible.com/ 2021/01/14/ common-expressions-that-originated-from-the-bible.

College Essays. https://www.collegeessayguy.com/blog/college-essay-format.

David L. Brown. *Early Witnesses to the Received Text.* Logos resource pages.org.

Enago. https://www.enago.com/author-hub/what-are-the-steps-in-editing-document.

Lawrence, Nathan. *Is Yeshua "the only begotten" or "the one of kind, unique" Son of Elohim?* https://hoshanarabbah.org. 9/9/2017.

Luther, Martin. An Open Letter on Translating, 1530. http://sermons.martinluther.us/Letter_on_translation_ml.pdf. Translated from "Ein sendbrief D. M. Luthers. Von Dolmetzschen und Fürbit der heiligenn" in Dr. Martin Luthers Werke, (Weimar: Hermann Boehlaus Nachfolger, 1909), Band 30, Teil II, pp. 632-646. Revised and annotated by Michael D. Marlowe, June 2003.

Misty Davidson. Borrowed Words–How English Borrows from Other Languages. https://commongroundinternational.com. Common Ground International, Impacting Communities Through Language. 2018.

Owlcation. https://owlcation.com/humanities/FourStepsofEditing

Oxford English Dictionary. *Grammar in Early Modern English*. Oxford University Press: 2022. https://public.oed.com/blog/grammar-in-early-modern-english/#pronouns-and-determiners. Web.

Purdue Online Writing Lab. Verb Tense Concistency. https://owl.purdue.edu/ owl/general_writing/ grammar/verb_tenses/ verb_tense_consistency.html. 10/28/2020. Web.

The 1689 Baptist Confession of Faith. https://www.the1689 confession.com/1689

The Free Dictionary. https://www.thefreedictionary.com

Wagenmaker and oberly, LLC. *A Nonprofit's Guide to Copyright Law for Derivative Works*. Wagenmakerlaw.com. April 27, 2015.

Watts, M. H. *Subscriptions to the Epistles.* Trinitarian Bible Society's Quarterly Record No. 587, April-June 2009, pages 13-14, which is available online at www.trinitarianbiblesociety.org/ site/qr.

Wilbur Pickering. *In Defense of the Objective Authority of the Sacred Text.* Walkinhiscommandments.com. 2009.

Beyond this, we have learned some valuable lessons over the past fifteen years by working with translation projects in Mandarin Chinese, Korean, Isan (Thailand), Telugu (India), Ewe (Togo, West Africa), Swahili (Kenya, East Africa), Bukusu (Kenya, East Africa), Cebuano (Philippines), Guarani (Paraguay), Malayalam (India), and German. Peripherally, we have had some smaller experience with the following languages: Burmese, French, Sorani, Amharic, Twi, and others.

Index

NOTES

¹ The 1689 Baptist Confession of Faith. https://www.the1689
confession.com/1689/chapter-1. Jan. 19, 2019.

² Steve Combs. *A Practical Theology of Bible Translating.* The Old Paths
Publications: 2019. Print. Pg. 33. (A considerable amount of the
information in *A Practical Theology of Bible Translating* is repeated in
this chapter. This is important, because some may start with the
current volume without reading the theology.)

³H.D. Williams. *The Miracle of Biblical Inspiration*. (The Old Paths
Publications: Cleveland, GA) 2009. PDF download. Jan. 2019.

⁴Merriam-Webster Dictionary online. Merriam-webster.com. Web. 5-
2019

⁵Gary La More. *Thou Shalt Keep Them: A Biblical Theology of the
Perfect Preservation of Scripture*. Cited. David Brown. *Providential
Preservation: the Doctrine that Virtually Disappeared*. Print. Jan. 23,
2019.

⁶ Dan Phillips. *God's Wisdom in Proverbs*. Woodlands, TX: Kress Biblical
Resources. 2011. Pg. 188.

⁷ Global Bible Translators, www.bpsglobal.org

⁸ Dr. Jim Taylor, *In Defense of the Textus Receptus*.
theoldpathspublications. com. 2016. Nook Edition.

⁹ Dr. David L. Brown. *Early Witnesses to the Received Text*. Logos
resource pages.org. Web. 4-2019.

¹⁰ Dr. Wilbur Pickering. *In Defense of the Objective Authority of the
Sacred Text*. Walkinhiscommandments.com. 2009. Web. 4-2019.

¹¹ Dr. Edward F. Hills, The King James Version Defended. (Des Moines,
Iowa: Christian research Press. 1973). Print.

¹² Jim Taylor. Unpublished study notes. 3-2019.

¹³ *Oxford English Dictionary*. Web. https://public.oed.com/blog/early-
modern-english-an-overview. Accessed June 2022.

¹⁴ Oxford English Dictionary. Grammar in Early Modern English. Oxford
University Press: 2022. https://public.oed.com/blog/grammar-in-early-
modern-english/#pronouns-and-determiners. Web. Accessed June
2022.

Notes

---

[15] Paul W. Scott. *English for Bible Readers.* Morris Publishing: Kearney, NE, 2008.

[16] *American Heritage® Dictionary of the English Language, Fifth Edition.* © 2016 by Houghton Mifflin Harcourt Publishing Company. Cited www. thefreedictionary. com

[17] List 1-6 from: Charles V. Turner. *Biblical Bible Translating.* (Sovereign Grace Publishers: Layfayette, In. 2001) Print. P. 59-61.

[18] Robert D. Patton, *Issues in Missiology, Volume III, Translation Issues.* The Old Paths Publications, Inc: Cleveland, GA. 2012. Print. P. 128.

[19] Noah Wester. Webster's Dictionary, 1828 Edition. Included in E-sword.net free Bible software download, copyright 2000-2019. Web.

[20] Martin Luther. An Open Letter on Translating, 1530. http://sermons. martinluther.us/Letter_on_translation_ml.pdf.   Translated from "Ein sendbrief D. M. Luthers. Von Dolmetzschen und Fürbit der heiligenn" in Dr. Martin Luthers Werke, (Weimar: Hermann Boehlaus Nachfolger, 1909), Band 30, Teil II, pp. 632-646. Revised and annotated by Michael D. Marlowe, June 2003.Accessed 8/2022.

[21] Martin Luther. An Open Letter on Translating.

[22] Baptist bible Translator's Institute. https://baptisttranslators.com/

[23] Misty Davidson. Borrowed Words–How English Borrows from Other Languages. https://commongroundinternational.com. Common Ground International, Impacting Communities Through Language. 2018.

[24] Turner

[25] As I am indebted to many authors for most of the information and concepts in this book, I will mention two, to whom I referred for most of the information in this section on Figures of speech: 1) Dr. Charles Turner and his book, *Biblical Bible Translating*, and 2) my friend, editor, and publisher, Dr. H. D. Williams, *Word-for-Word Translating of the Received Texts*.

[26] The first two examples are from Dr. Charles Turner, P 146.

[27] John Beekman and John Callow. *Translating the Word of God.* (Zondervan Publishing House: Grand Rapids. 1974). Print. P. 206.

[28] Beekman and Callow. P. 206.

[29] American Heritage® Dictionary

[30] American Heritage Dictionary

[31] American Heritage Dictionary

[32] American Heritage Dictionary

[33] American Heritage Dictionary

[34] Collins English Dictionary – Complete and Unabridged, 12th Edition 2014 © HarperCollins Publishers 1991, 1994, 1998, 2000, 2003, 2006, 2007, 2009, 2011, 2014. Cite The Free dictionary. https://www.thefreedictionary.com.

[35] Charles V. Turner.

[36] Charles V. Turner. P. 139.

[37] Beekman and Callow. P. 161.

[38] Charles V. Turner. P. 139.

[39] American Heritage Dictionary.

[40] Dictionary of Unfamiliar Words by Diagram Group Copyright © 2008 by Diagram Visual Information Limited. Cite. The Free dictionary. https://www.thefreedictionary.com.

[41] Beekman and Callow. P. 229.

[42] Charles V. Turner. P. 110-114/Barnwell, P. 165-167.

[43] Dr. Jim Taylor. Email to the author 11/16/2022.

[44] A Defense of the Bible. https://www.adefenceofthebible.com/ 2021/01/14/ common-expressions-that-originated-from-the-bible. Accessed 10/2022.

[45] *Collins English Dictionary. Complete and Unabridged, 12th Edition*. (H arper Collins Publishers. 2014.) Cited, The Free Dictionary. 2003-2020. Web. 11/2/2020.

[46] Beekman and Callow

[47] Dr. Jim Taylor. Comment to the Author.

[48] Natanael Steinbart. Email to the author, July 21, 2022.

[49] The Complete Word Study Dictionary. *E-Sword*. Rick Meyers. Version 10.2.1. Franklin, Tn.: 2013. Downloaded computer software.

[50] Dr. Charles Turner, P 140.

[51] Purdue Online Writing Lab. *Verb Tense Concistency.* https://owl.purdue.edu /owl/general_writing/grammar/verb_tenses/verb_tense_consistency.html. 10/28/2020. Web.

[52] M. H. Watts. Subscriptions to the Epistles. Trinitarian Bible Society's Quarterly Record No. 587, April-June 2009, pages 13-14, which is available online at www.trinitarianbiblesociety.org/ site/qr.

[53] Beekman, John and Callow, John. Pg 221.

[54] H. E. Dana and Julius R. Mantey.

[55] Webster

[56] Word Study

[57] Webster, 1828.

---

[58] Lawrence, Nathan. *Is Yeshua "the only begotten" or "the one of kind, unique" Son of Elohim?* https://hoshanarabbah.org. 9/9/2017. Web.

[59] G. Abbot-Smith, *A Manual Greek Lexicon of the New Testament.* (Charles Scribner's Sons: New York. 1936)

[60] Word Study

[61] Steve Combs, The Translator's Concise Lexicon of the Textus Receptus.

[62] Email to the author.

[63] Don Richardson. Eternity in Their Hearts. Regal Books: Ventura, Ca. 1981. Print. pp. 9-20.

[64] Richardson, pp 41-47

[65] Richardson, pp. 54-56

[66] Richardson, pp. 56-59

[67] Wikipedia

[68] Wikipedia and The English Kikuyu Bible found on Google Play. Homegrown Devs. 2022

[69] This information comes partly from Wikipedia and partly from David Misiko, a member of the Busuku tribe.

[70] Denis Okoth. *Communicating Christ Among Folk Religionists, Kingdom Ministry in Satan's Nest/ Luo Animistic Beliefs and Religious Practitioners and How to Reconcile Them to Christ.* Missology.org. Web. 2022.

[71] Webster 1828

[72] Charles Turner

[73] Charles Turner

[74] Truth in Reality. https://truthinreality.com/2012/10/12/the-254-versions-of-the-english-bible-since-1881

[75] Wagenmaker and oberly, LLC. A Nonprofit's Guide to Copyright Law for Derivative Works. Wagenmakerlaw.com. April 27, 2015. Web. Accessed June 2022.

[76] Charles V. Turner. P 36.

[77] Dr. Robert Patton.

[78] Ron Meyers, AAsian Bible Translation News Communique Update,@ Isan Bible Translation Project. http://www.isanbible.net. Web. 24 Dec. 2004.

[79] Ron Meyers, e-mail to the author, 3 December 2003.

[80] Katharine Barnwell. *Bible Translation An Introductory Course in Translation Principles.* SIL International, Third Edition. 1986. P. 178.

[81] Bible Translation Notes 2015 by Rex Cobb, Director Baptist Bible Translators Institute. Bowie, Texas.